Eminem

Recent Titles in
Hip Hop in America

The Wu-Tang Clan and RZA: A Trip through Hip Hop's 36 Chambers
Alvin Blanco

Free Stylin': How Hip Hop Changed the Fashion Industry
Elena Romero

Eminem

THE REAL SLIM SHADY

Marcia Alesan Dawkins

Hip Hop in America
Juleyka Lantigua-Williams, Series Editor

 **PRAEGER**

AN IMPRINT OF ABC-CLIO, LLC
Santa Barbara, California • Denver, Colorado • Oxford, England

Library of Congress Cataloging-in-Publication Data

Dawkins, Marcia Alesan.
  Eminem : the real Slim Shady / Marcia Alesan Dawkins.
    pages cm. — (Hip hop in America)
  Includes bibliographical references and index.
  ISBN 978-0-313-39893-3 (hardcopy : alk. paper) —
ISBN 978-0-313-39894-0 (ebook) 1. Eminem, 1972—Criticism and interpretation.
2. Rap (Music)—History and criticism. I. Title.
  ML420.E56D38 2013
  782.421649092—dc23   2013012390

ISBN: 978-0-313-39893-3
EISBN: 978-0-313-39894-0

17 16 15 14 13   2 3 4 5

This book is also available on the World Wide Web as an eBook.
Visit www.abc-clio.com for details.

Praeger
An Imprint of ABC-CLIO, LLC

ABC-CLIO, LLC
130 Cremona Drive, P.O. Box 1911
Santa Barbara, California 93116-1911

This book is printed on acid-free paper ∞

Manufactured in the United States of America

To the Real Slim Shady in All of Us . . .

Contents

Acknowledgments

This book was born in Queens, New York. And this book, of course, is not my work alone. I discussed earlier versions of these thoughts and arguments in lectures or workshops at Harvard University, Brown University, the University of Arkansas, Fayetteville, Vanderbilt University Law School, Belmont University, Lipscomb University, Villanova University, Simmons College, Emerson College, the University of Southern California, and the University of California, Los Angeles. I also made presentations based on the research for this book to the annual meetings of the National Communication Association and the American Studies Association. And, as always, I had the benefit of many meals and coffees with my colleagues over the years at Brown University and USC Annenberg, including Larry Gross, Ernest J. Wilson III, Randall A. Lake, Stacy L. Smith, Chris Smith, Bob Scheer, Duncan Williams, Marcus Shepard, T. J. McDonald, Omar Bahgat, Ryan Houston, Ulli Ryder, Evelyn Hu-Dehart, Janet Cooper-Nelson, Tyler Rogers, Alex Agloro, and Patricia Balsofiore. I have also benefitted from close and careful readings of the draft by Ebony A. Utley, Sadiqua Hamdan, and Ric Whitney. My utmost gratitude goes out to Daniel J. Sharfstein, for giving me access to his brilliant legal mind as well as the archives at Vanderbilt University Law School; to Sybril Bennett, for her admonitions that disruption did not start and cannot end with Eminem or hip hop; to Joe Lopez (aka DJ Bazooka Joe), for tuning my ear to the frequency of Eminem's sonic artistry; to Rafael Matos Sr., for opening my eyes to Eminem's prophetic rhetoric; to Jeff Hall, who made me feel it was okay to admit that "Kill You" is my real favorite Eminem song; to Lisa Rueckert, who gave me a vision for this project, literally; to Ramon Fuertes and Zana Bru, for their entrepreneurial encouragement; to Jennifer Stoever-Ackerman and Craig E. Carroll, for their intellectual contributions via personal interview; to Lisa Corrigan, for her firm admonitions that feminist women love Eminem; to

David Hino, for his meditations on love and hate; to J. Z. Matthews, for her gentle reminder to look for a bigger definition of justice; to Shoshana Sara and Maysa Gayyusi, who listened to and talked about Eminem with me in Jerusalem and Ramallah, respectively; and, to the amazing Marshall Bruce Mathers III himself, who, despite not knowing that I exist, will always be my muse.

Finally, and most important, I give thanks to my family and friends for their willingness to listen to Eminem's music with me religiously and to deal with the potty mouth I developed as a result. I thank my closest friends, Jason S. Woodson, Ivette Lora, Shinina Butler-Nance, and Zainah Alfi Mir for telling me I could do it. I thank my sister, Lindsay, for reminding me that there's a little Slim Shady in everybody. I thank my parents, John and Olga, for instilling in me a love for music and art of all kinds. I thank my cousin, Kate Breen, for her spirited conversation. I thank Harry Guillermo Mendoza, not only for the gifts of time and space to embark upon this project, but for helping me see the relationships among the material, social, and spiritual aspects of myself. And, most of all, to my readers, thank you for your interest in my take on the real Slim Shady.

Prelude

My fascination with Eminem was solidified when *The Slim Shady LP* hit record stores on February 23, 1999. However, *The Slim Shady LP* and its lead single "My Name Is" weren't my first exposure to the controversial artist or his work. Eminem caught my ear a year earlier when I was at New York University (NYU) writing my master's thesis on the rhetoric of underground hip hop. While I dissected lyrics written and delivered by the likes of Company Flow, Natural Resource, BlackStar, J-Live, and Shabaam Sahdeeq, I came across a single released by Rawkus Records called "5 Star Generals" (1998) on which Eminem made a guest appearance. I would later learn that this was an old track the rapper recorded for cash and then forgot about while he was unsigned. Nevertheless, Em's first lines about sinning boldly by shooting nuns in Bible class and damning hell itself hit me like a ton of bricks. But, in an effort to be fair, I suspended my critical impulse and resisted the temptation to take offense from a literal interpretation of his words. After all, my research taught me to attend to what rappers shouted as much as to what they whispered. To me, Eminem's lines sounded like a raised middle finger, a declaration that expressed a defiant and angry identity. And I knew that lines like his, which were sure to engage and enrage his listeners, would make him famous and infamous.

To my surprise, my 89-year-old Cuban American grandfather, Rafael Matos Sr., a poet and a reverend, heard something exciting in Eminem too. I stopped by my grandfather's house in Hollis, Queens, on my way home from NYU around the time the video for "My Name Is" was in heavy rotation on MTV. I could hear the song blaring from his television. This struck me as strange for two reasons. First, my grandfather wasn't fluent in English, so he was more inclined to watch Spanish-language channels like Univision. Second, he'd never expressed much interest in rap music other than commenting that he noticed kids rapping in the parks near his house every now and then. Of course, I knew that many of those boom-box-toting kids were now superstars like Run-DMC and LL Cool J.[1] Because my grandfather didn't know that, I was surprised to catch him watching English-language rap videos. When I entered the living room my grandfather sat transfixed. After the video ended, I asked him if he knew what he was watching. Sitting up in his blue La-Z-Boy recliner he said, "I'm watching some guy who calls himself Eminem. I can tell he's probably a heathen and I don't care. I love what he's doing with his words." I was shocked. My grandfather went on to tell me that despite the obvious language and experiential barriers that stood between him and Eminem, he was in awe of the way the rapper was using his voice and his words as instruments. And what really got me was when my grandfather said that Eminem's unapologetic tone reminded him of many preachers' fiery delivery over the years. I could not believe it. Grandpa's encounter with Eminem was spiritual.

My grandfather's intense reaction to Eminem sealed the deal. I was determined to learn more about this guy who calls himself Eminem, and Slim Shady, and Marshall Mathers. I asked a friend of mine who was immersed in New York City's underground hip hop scene, DJ Bazooka Joe, what else of Eminem's was already out there. After telling me about how Eminem's performances in competitive rap battles like the Rap Olympics had impressed many hip hop aficionados, Joe suggested I track down Eminem's first albums *Infinite* (1996) and *The Slim Shady EP* (1997). I followed orders and was shocked to find little of the shock rap I expected on *Infinite*. In fact, the album reminded me of the style of rap I was used to hearing as a kid from Queens, New York—a style that rappers like Nas, AZ, Lord Finesse, and Jay-Z had perfected in mid-1990s on classics like *Illmatic* (1994), *Doe or Die* (1995), *The Awakening* (1996), and *In My Lifetime, Vol. 1* (1997).

Some songs on *Infinite* were downright uplifting, like "It's Ok," in which Eminem outlines his plan for commercial success and sets his goal of properly providing for his family and being a good Christian man. Other songs didn't really make much sense to me, like the title track in which he employed words like "entity," "lamination," and "cerebral" just because he could and not in ways that were ironic or imaginative. One song, "Backstabber," Eminem's very first professionally recorded single, echoed an embryonic Slim Shady's fascination with revenge fantasies and misogyny but still managed to end on a positive note about his love for women. Overall, the album showed definite signs of talent and portrayed Eminem as an authentic hip hop fan. But its amateurish production value and derivative style revealed a need for mentoring and developing a unique identity within the larger rap culture if Eminem was to avoid becoming the next Vanilla Ice. Years later, Eminem would seem to agree with my assessment of his professional identity crisis when he said, *"Infinite* was me trying to figure out how I wanted my rap style to be, how I wanted to sound on the mic and present myself. It was a growing stage."[2] Perhaps hip hop culture's expectation of a fully formed and authentic image with at least one flamboyant alter ego, reflected in the successes of artists like the Wu-Tang Clan and Ice Cube, is why only 1,000 copies of *Infinite* were pressed and the album was largely ignored by radio stations, music retailers, critics, and talent scouts outside of Detroit.

The Slim Shady EP was another matter. Although it didn't display the finely tuned production and lyrical polish for which Eminem's later work would receive acclaim, the album brought the caricature of Slim Shady to life. In the process, it also reshaped Eminem's image for public consumption as a sarcastic, aggressive, politically incorrect, and decidedly different kind of white guy. For starters, in the song "Low, Down Dirty," Eminem labeled himself "Rated R" and diagnosed himself with multiple personality disorder. "Just the Two of Us" was a rough draft of the soon-to-be-scandalous "'97 Bonnie & Clyde." And, introducing a meme that would come back to haunt him in rap's and religion's gossip circles, in "Murder, Murder" he sold his soul in exchange for commercial and financial success. Eminem described the album as his clarion call to the recording industry and a means of attacking all those who criticized his efforts on *Infinite*. The material on this album was closer to what I had come to expect after hearing Eminem's Scribble Jam and Rap Olympic battle raps and guest appearance on "5 Star Generals." Despite some ongoing production defects, Eminem's delivery on *The Slim Shady EP* was flawless. His ability to layer multisyllabic rhymes on top of and inside rhyme patterns was virtuosic. He had definitely studied Big Daddy Kane and, though his flow wasn't slow, I could tell he'd studied Biggie too. I understood the potential Dr. Dre heard in this album, and I agreed with legendary rapper Rakim's appraisal that "you can't take nothing away from Em's thoughts and his pen."[3] Eminem was born to write rhymes and to rap and, maybe more important, to show us what it sounds like to break the rules with which we were taught to make sense out of life.

I was no longer sure what to make of Eminem or Slim Shady as "My Name Is" launched him into global popular culture and, surprisingly, into my own saintly grandfather's good graces. Promotional materials including endorsements from Dr. Dre, Missy "Misedemeanor" Elliott, and LL Cool J piqued my interest and left me wondering. Was he rap's racial outsider who would understand my experience as one of the genre's gender outsiders? Based on much of what I'd heard thus far the answer was going to be no. Was he testing the limits of the first amendment? Maybe, but not in ways that were qualitatively different from many other gangsta rappers and hardcore rock and heavy metal singers. Was he a thugged-out mental patient who'd escaped from the ward to rap about the mental condition and demographic changes of young white America? Probably, based on some of his interviews and antics. Was he a spiritual commentator? Possibly, if for no other reason than to describe confrontations with sins and sinners. Was he a brand strategy that could actually gain traction in popular culture? Definitely. Eminem's timing was perfect. With the violent murders of Tupac Amaru Shakur (aka 2Pac) in 1996 and Notorious B.I.G. (born Christopher Wallace) in 1997, two of the culture's most talented and (in) famous performers, hip hop was ripe for a new flawed character from a new flawed place somewhere in the middle like Detroit to confuse and bemuse its audiences. Enter Eminem. Who was this guy—Eminem, Slim Shady, Marshall Mathers—really? And who would he turn out to be? This book will examine these and similar questions and answers, and the questions and answers they raise.

Eminem: The Real Slim Shady is the sum of 15 years of trying to describe, interpret, and evaluate Eminem's willingness to "clean out his closet" and take us along for the ride. Not a traditional biography, this book is about how Eminem became a hip hop icon by unveiling the events of his life right before our eyes. (Or, at least how he became popular for his remarkable ability to make us think that's what he is doing.) In short, this book is less about who Eminem is and more about what Eminem means. As a consequence, the book explores how Eminem practices identity through the prism of *persona*—a mask worn that becomes a character played by an actor and eventually refers to an individual human being—and how that practice made him a formidable presence in global popular culture. I will examine how Eminem's personas work as a fused performance team, reciprocally dependent and familiar with each other and the audience. It will explore why and how Slim Shady, Marshall Mathers, and Eminem share different moods and different sounds, provide unique slants to lyrics, and, ironically, create a sense of individuality for Eminem as an artist. In "Renegade," a duet with Jay-Z on *Blueprint* (2001), Eminem admits as much by saying that depending on which persona is rapping, his music could be considered hate-mongering gangsta speech, spiritual nourishment, or sublime political and social commentary. Over and over again he proves that he really can be whoever we say he is. For that reason it seems to me that the best way to understand Eminem's identity practice—and ongoing cultural significance—is to unpack the multiple personas developed in his work. And, if Eminem has anything to say about it, we will see just how plural, complicated, and loud those personas can get.

Eminem's use of personas proves that there is always more than one side to any person. In fact, the three personas he presents can be considered "material," "social," and "spiritual" dimensions of self.[4] Sociologists say the material self is made up of all the tangible things we own. We reveal our material selves through what we wear and buy—our bodies, body art, clothes, cars, homes, and businesses—and also by what we do not wear or buy. Eminem uses his alter ego Slim Shady as material self. Slim Shady has nothing and at the same time is so valuable that he is a hot commodity as we see him represented in Shady Records, Shade 45 satellite radio station, and Shady Limited clothing line. Slim Shady has made Marshall Bruce Mathers III rich by giving voice to everything that's impolite and offensive, especially violence against himself and others. Slim Shady also represents Eminem's troubled childhood and everything it lacked.

In contrast, Marshall Mathers, the spiritual self, raps about how Slim Shady is just a mask. Marshall Mathers is who Eminem says he is on the inside, representing his attitudes, beliefs, values, and overall spiritual journey. Mathers is the one that has to deal with the stress created by Eminem's fame, Slim's evilness, and his own search for redemption. And Mathers's lyrics suggest that our confusion over which self is acting at any particular moment reflects the experience of being pulled in many directions in everyday life. The uncertainty created by expressing these unique selves and points of view is appealing to many audiences who are looking for a spirituality that embraces rather than rejects the fears and delights of everyday experience.

Unlike the fixed moods of Slim Shady or Marshall Mathers, the persona we call Eminem is someone under constant construction. Eminem is a social commentator who gives the rapper a license to be different in each situation he encounters or controversy he creates. As a result, the lyrics that emerge from Eminem's lips are more elaborate and institutionally oriented than Slim's or Mathers's. Making sense of these selves is Eminem's job and the reason audiences keep coming back for more. Eminem is a social critic who reveals his power as he interacts with fans and collaborates with other artists in unique hip hop cyphers and situations. And Eminem's status as social critic is reflected in the controversies he sparks and the power he wields, most easily seen through his dominant media presence, followers on sites such as Facebook, YouTube, and Twitter, his continued accumulation of fan-based awards like the People's Choice and MTV, and collaborations with performance artists ranging from superstars like Elton John, Pink, and Rihanna to relative unknowns like Kendrick Lamar, Bukari, and Shabaam Sahdeeq.

In the first part of this book, chapters 1-3, I give in to the urge to understand Eminem's popularity from its beginnings. I look at the rapper's experiences and influences as an impoverished youth with dreams of hip hop grandeur. His mother, Debbie Nelson, loomed large during this part of his life; in his lyrics and especially in his poignant "Cleanin' Out My Closet" (2002), she was blamed for her drug use, abandonment, and domestic instability. I explore the public and private effects of Debbie's upbringing on the rapper, giving voice to both sides of the story. Next, I turn to the man cast as Eminem's adoptive father, Andre Romelle Young, also known by his stage name, Dr. Dre. I explore the credibility, authenticity, and stability Dre provided as bona fide gangsta rapper turned mentor. In the process I compare the rapper's real and imagined racial identities. Lastly, I turn to "the real Slim Shady" as a product of Debbie's and Dre's biracial parenting, examining how he writes a new definition of family in his lyrics through his relationship with daughter Hailie. In the process I probe Slim's remarkable ability to engage and enrage audiences by dealing with the perils of his family's life and expressing the bitter and controversial identity politics that mirrored the nation's shifting demographics and race relations at the turn of the 21st century.

In the second part of the book, chapters 4-6, I consider Eminem as one of hip hop's foremost spiritual rappers. Marshall Mathers is proof that every person can be a walking, talking house of horrors but still find a way to relate to the divine, supernatural, and otherworldly. I begin by exploring the rapper's relationship with his professed higher powers, showing how they are both spiritual manifestations of justice and reflections of hip hop's greatest sins, especially its homophobia, genderphobia, and enactments of hegemonic masculinity. Then, I explore how Mathers deals with guilt and redemption in his art. Specifically,

I look at how Mathers's spirituality takes shape as he breaks society's rules and challenges traditional notions of justice. Ultimately, I isolate and examine love–hate themes that are expressed in his work. To do this "spiritual" work I conduct the first extended analysis of his catalog, looking at 200 of his most popular tracks over a 20-year period.

The third part of the book, chapters 7-9, surveys Eminem's career as a social critic. Here I argue that society is like a building whose foundation is cracked, that Eminem dives into the crack to make it bigger, undermining the norms by which society is organized, and that in doing so he incurs ire and disgust. I start by looking at Eminem's sex, sexuality, and gender controversies through the lens of public conflicts ("beefs") with GLAAD and Lynne Cheney as well as recording artists including Tori Amos, Pet Shop Boys, and Mariah Carey. I continue by looking at Eminem's race and class conflicts through the lens of his beefs with *The Source*'s Benzino and cultural commentators who interpret his white trash identity as a guise for racial passing and minstrelsy. I also examine Eminem's responses to each of these critiques using "realness" despite his reliance on personas and performance, and his attempts to provide a backstage pass and an explanation for his expressions in his lyrics when they are criticized. Finally, I explore Eminem's battle with corporate America by way of a lawsuit for what I am calling "digital reparations," which could entitle all artists to a 50–50 split with recording companies for recordings licensed to digital distributors such as iTunes.

In the conclusion, "Coda: Shady 2.0," I discuss Eminem's legacy in terms of the diverse rappers to whom he's given a home on Shady Records and the others he's worked with and inspired. I give special attention here to Eminem's effect on Los Angeles collective Odd Future Wolf Gang Kill Them All and collaboration with Nicki Minaj in "Roman Revenge" (2010), where Minaj goes into character and introduces her own personas using Slim Shady as a role model. I then look briefly at the careers of Eminem's protégés—D12, 50 Cent, Yelawolf, Slaughterhouse, and Bad Meets Evil—and their relationship to his three personas. I end with a discussion of a new generation of "real Slim Shadys" who are standing up even though they are not signed to Shady Records' current roster, including Odd Future, Asher Roth, Bizzy Crook, Machine Gun Kelly, Mac Miller, Young Sinatra, Ca$his, Hopsin, Iggy Azalea, Azealia Banks, Angel Haze, and White Girl Mob (aka Kreayshawn, V-Nasty, and Lil' Debbie). In so doing, I reveal "The Real Slim Shady" as a reflection of the individuals who see themselves in any and all of his personas and a world that requires us all to put on faces and hide behind masks every day.

So whether you are like me (a cultural critic, communication professor, and hip hop fan from Queens), my grandfather (an 89-year-old Spanish-speaking poet and reverend), or an ordinary high school or college student today, this book is for you. Why? Because it does more than list biographical facts, it provides a picture of this artist's mind by interpreting his own words in lyrics and interviews. It explains how and why Eminem exposes his weakness and failures—be they biological, legal, spiritual, economic, or personal—and explains how exposing these failures has made him one of the best-selling music artists of all time.

CHAPTER I
"I'm Sorry Mama"

Parent–child relationships can contribute to the best and worst parts of anyone's emotional development. No one reflects this truth more than Eminem, whose relationship with his mother, Debbie Nelson, is as dedicated as it is tumultuous. In an interview for BET, taped to promote the *Relapse* album in 2009, Eminem speaks empathetically of his mother: "One of the things . . . I realized is at the end of the day, she's my mother and I love her because she's my mother . . . Even though we don't really speak. You know what I mean? She is my mother, and I do love her, and I think I got a better understanding of what she is going through or what she may be going through. You know what I mean? Now . . . when I see myself and how I actually became . . . There's a little compassion factor that goes with that."[1] These remarks stand in sharp contrast to the way Eminem depicted his mother earlier in his career. In a 1999 interview with *Consumable Online,* he was especially crude: "I talk to her every now and again, but as little as I can . . . I really don't have much reason to talk to my mother. My mother's done so much fucked up shit to me that it's like, now that I don't have to talk to her, I ain't gonna."[2] In order to account for his apparent change of heart, we must understand what kind of woman raised a son who could show her such public contempt only to later show her compassion. Perhaps more importantly, we must understand why this mother–son connection proved to be the fuel for so much of Eminem's artistic will.

Mother–son relationships are a common theme in popular culture. Recording artists from nearly all genres have recorded odes to mothers. These songs usually hit the airwaves in heavy rotation around Mother's Day, a time to remember and celebrate the critical and multifaceted roles mothers play in their children's lives. And in the 1970s, when Eminem was a child, mother adoration was in full bloom. Paul Simon's "Mother and Son Reunion" (1972), The Intruders' "I'll

Always Love My Mama" (1973), The Spinners' "Sadie" (1974), Pink Floyd's "Mother" (1979), and Sir Elton John's "Mama Can't Buy You Love" (1979) are among the popular mother-themed songs. Mothers were also the topic of conversation in "the dozens," a game by which every rapper has been influenced even if he or she has never played it. According to Elijah Wald in *The Dozens: A History of Rap's Mama,* the dozens is a cruel, humorous, creative game of insults that has profoundly influenced rap music. In its most simple forms, the dozens is cultivated wit in the form of "yo' mama" jokes. In its more advanced forms, it is a modern cultural tradition that can be traced back to African rituals. Whether interpreted as street poetry, nonsensical insults, or an occasion to praise and blame mothers for their children's successes and failures, the dozens has proved to be a cornerstone of hip hop communication and culture.

Thanks to the dozens, mother–son relationships are such a prominent theme in rap music that *GQ Magazine* compiled a list of "The 10 Gushiest Mother's Day Rap Songs."[3] Entries include Kid Cudi's "Soundtrack 2 My Life" (2009), Jay-Z's "Blueprint (Mama Loves Me)" (2001), Brand Nubian's "Momma" (2004), and "Dear Mama" (1995) by 2Pac. Each one tells a story about the hardships caused and overcome by single mothers' life choices. The fact that these songs deify and demonize mothers is neither strange nor uncommon. According to Michael Eric Dyson in *Holler If You Hear Me,* "the sharp juxtaposition of maternal acknowledgment and disparagement is a characteristic symptom of rap music's artists."[4] Eminem is no exception. Like 2Pac, Eminem reminds us that poor single mothers are often stereotyped as dysfunctional women who push all men, including their sons, out of their lives. And both 2Pac's and Eminem's relationships with their mothers are as much about togetherness as they are about separation. But unlike the case of 2Pac, or any of the other rappers listed by *GQ,* Eminem's mother is not African American. As a result, she poses a challenge to her son's authenticity as a rap artist. While her class background and lifestyle choices positioned her son within hip hop's grasp, her racial background presented an obstacle her son would have to overcome since hip hop is considered an African American musical genre. Eminem developed a unique strategy to ensure that he would be taken seriously. He would live out his lyrics by depicting his mother as a menacing character in his work. Translation: If Eminem's mother could not be racially black, then she could function symbolically as the shady force that created the life he would live and describe. A closer look at the turbulent mother–son relationship reveals how it would later make Eminem legitimate within hip hop's cultural frame.

"MY MOM"

Debbie Nelson (aka Debbie Mathers; aka Debbie Mathers-Briggs) may not have been a particularly horrendous parent before her son became famous. She was, however, a poor mom, a single mom, an addicted mom, a demanding mom, and sometimes a hurtful mom. Debbie definitely had difficulty providing a stable family life for her son and by all accounts this is one source of his animosity toward her. Here's how Eminem remembers his life with Debbie in a 1999 interview for *Rolling Stone.*

> My mother had a different boyfriend every day of the week . . . Hardly anything we ever had in the house was ours, ever. My mother never had a job. The only one I can remember her having was at some candy store when I was a little boy. And she was a nursing assistant for a week and a half. She said it hurt her fucking back too much. My mother was lawsuit-happy . . . She did whatever she could to get money that way without fucking working. My mother never had a job, that's why we was always on welfare, ever since I can fucking remember . . . That's why I dropped out of school. As soon as I turned fifteen, my mother was like, "If you don't get a fucking job and help me out with these bills, your ass is out . . ." I worked at Gearse Machinery . . . I swept floors and made $140 a week working full-time. My mother would keep the hundred and give me the forty. Then she would fucking kick me out . . . I stayed with my mom until I was eighteen, but I kept getting kicked out . . . My mother did a lot of . . . dope and shit, so she had mood swings. She took a lot of pills . . . [and] naps. She'd go to sleep cool and wake up and start yelling.[5]

In keeping with this vivid description audiences first meet Debbie in "My Name Is" (1999). She is Slim Shady's lazy, substance-abusing, television-watching mother. We learn that she does not even have the proper anatomy to breastfeed him, meaning that she is physically incapable of nurturing him. In "Brain Damage" (1999), she beats him over the head with a remote control. In "Our House" (1999), she discourages his pursuit of becoming a rapper and tells him to stop talking black. In "I'm Back" (2000), she reveals her own sadistic tendencies when she understands why her son mutilated a kitten. And in "Evil Deeds" (2004), she has sex with Satan and bears his son, Slim Shady, who cannot help doing bad things because he is a bad seed. In other songs Debbie fails to provide emotional or financial support. In "My Dad's Gone Crazy" (2002), she nags her son incessantly, trades insults with him, and goes off to get high. In "Cleanin' Out My Closet" (2002), she wishes him dead. In "Lose Yourself" (2002), the poverty in which she lives is too much for him to bear. In "Marshall Mathers" (2000), she sues him for $10 million for defamation of character. In "Without Me" (2002), she is cursed for suing her son once the lawsuit is settled. Later, Debbie is also to blame for the absence of a supportive father figure in Eminem's life. In "Insane" (2009), she fails to protect him from his stepfather's sexual abuse. Ultimately, Debbie becomes a version of Slim Shady. In "Bagpipes from Baghdad" (2009), Slim says that he reminds himself of his mother. In "Never Enough" (2004), her dysfunctional parenting is the reason for her son's success. In "My Mom" (2009), she is a drug addict whose son is just like her. And in "The Apple" (2011), she is a "sick . . . bitch" who is the matriarch of a sick family.

Although each of these mother attacks is bitterer than the one before, two stand out as especially revealing: "Cleanin' Out My Closet" and "My Mom." "Cleanin' Out My Closet" appeared on the album *The Eminem Show,* which was the best-selling album across all genres of 2002. The album is now officially certified diamond, having sold more than 10 million copies worldwide, according to the Recording Industry Association of America (RIAA).[6] The song's official video has been viewed nearly 25 million times and boasts a 90-to-1 "like" to "dislike" ratio on Eminem's Vevo YouTube channel at the time of this writing. In *Eminem: The Stories Behind Every Song,* music critic David Stubbs describes the song as follows: It is easy to see "the homicidal, tear-streaked, inter-familial rage here, the sense of the most basic human link, between mother and child, being horribly, publicly violated."[7] The song begins with a call from Eminem to his producer Dr. Dre (who represents the song's actual producer Jeff Bass) for a louder snare drum sound in his headphones. This request indicates that the testimony Eminem is about to deliver is for public consumption. What is more, he wants it to sound perfect so that the message will be received as intended.

The door to the closet is opening as we hear the song's first verse. It begins with an appeal to the piece of Slim Shady in all nonwhite, female, LGBTI, and perhaps even non-Christian fans who may have experienced some form of institutional or personal discrimination in their lives. This verse is also directed at critics whose literal interpretations of his words are not only upsetting but proof that they are simply not smart enough to understand him. He then turns his attention to his most vocal critic, his mother, whom he portrays as completely ridiculous in the rest of the song. The chorus, printed by a young Marshall Mathers and delivered to his mother inside a Mother's Day card, is essentially an apology for the public delivery of the message and an explanation that it can be no other way.

The second verse goes back in time to 1973, when Eminem was less than one year old and living with both parents. We learn that he and his mother were victims of his alcoholic father who physically abused them and eventually left mother and son to fend for themselves. Eminem takes us back to the beginning to help us understand how and why this mother–son relationship is unraveling in his adult life. It seems the real grief Eminem is expressing in "Cleanin' Out My Closet" is over the fact that his mother stayed rather than that his father left. As a consequence, the song tries to paint a new picture of fatherhood and masculinity. From this perspective, it makes sense that we would see Eminem's face throughout the video as infant, child, adolescent, and adult, while we never see Debbie's face. We only see her messy blonde mane, her housecoat, and slippers. This confirms that Eminem is not interested in empathizing with his mother or in expressing her humanity. Rather, he turns her into a ghost, a presence he cannot escape no matter how hard he tries.

The verse then travels forward in time to 2002, when Eminem cannot imagine being a deadbeat dad. He prominently displays the tattoo of his daughter Hailie as he thinks about her, and how he would do anything in his power to provide for her and her difficult mother, Kim Scott (whose image is tattooed across his chest). These images tell us that even though his upbringing made conflict the primary means of communication with the people closest to him, it did not stop him from finding healthier outlets for his emotions as an adult (like rap music). He then admits that he has made some mistakes, had some brushes with the law, and will make sure not to engage in this kind of rash and irresponsible behavior again. An underlying theme is, of course, that he grew up without a dad and without a proper mother. He uses parental abandonment in two ways here. First, he explains that he had no idea how a man interacts with other men or with a woman whom he really loves without violence. Second, he explains why his music is filled with so much angry, violent imagery, and why his home life is depicted so depressingly. He then closes the verse by equating his life with his art, referring to both as "The Eminem Show." One reason for this equation is that his mother's brother, Todd Nelson, sold the family's home in Warren, Michigan, and the new buyers, lawyer Sebastian Lucida and real estate developer Roland Fraschetti, put it up for auction on eBay as item 1788349972 in 2002. This auction confirms that, at the time these lines were penned, the rapper feels no clear sense of personal boundaries or real sense of safety in the world. Home is gone forever and only the stage remains. Perhaps the only place he may one day find safety is in his grave, which he is digging throughout the song.

The third verse is again addressed to fans and critics, who are advised to listen carefully so that they do not interpret this song as complete disrespect. The audience is asked to step into his shoes and imagine him as a young man watching his mother take pills, make paranoid accusations, and rely on welfare and public housing. At least one other source corroborates Slim's claims. In an interview with *Salon.Com* in 2000, Don DeMarc, one of Debbie's former live-in boyfriends, stated that she often used "pain pills" to self-medicate conditions ranging from toothaches and headaches to backaches resulting from injuries sustained in a car accident.[8]

After establishing his mother's identity as an addict, Eminem accuses her of abuse by way of Munchausen's Syndrome by Proxy (MSBP). MSBP occurs when a child has an illness fabricated by a parent, usually a mother who is seeking attention from doctors. In an eloquent turn of phrase, Eminem turns MSBP around on his mother, asking her if his notoriety and media attention are now making her sick. He also vows to keep his daughter Hailie and brother Nathan away from her dysfunctional behavior by any means necessary. He then issues his response to a song his mother recorded called "Dear Marshall" (2000) by taking on the role of dutiful son. He reminds her that she wished him dead after his uncle Ronnie committed suicide in 1991. Slim has a tattoo that reads "Ronnie R.I.P" on his upper left arm, which commemorates Ronnie for introducing the rapper to hip hop several years earlier. Slim touches his tattoo when he grants Debbie her wish in "Cleanin' Out My Closet," and says that he considers himself "dead . . . as can be" when it comes to his mother. To bring the point home, he delivers the refrains while digging his and his mother's graves. The end of the song represents closure, as the closet door swings shut.

The closet door bursts open when Debbie takes a starring role in "My Mom" (2009). "My Mom" appears on the 2009 album *Relapse,* which

Eminem claims is not his best work even though it earned platinum status in a little over one year. In a May 6, 2011, post for *MTV Hive,* blogger Kenneth Partridge describes the song as follows: "'My Mom' is hardly the most entertaining Debbie Mathers dis track in Em's catalog, but coming at a time when he was still in the grips of prescription-drug addiction, it might be the most real—a Mother's Day card with a bill for rehab attached."[9] As in "Cleanin' Out My Closet," the song begins with a nod to Dr. Dre and the fact that it is being recorded. After a quick microphone check and an outline for how the song will proceed, the actual chorus begins. The chorus is one part proclamation and one part lamentation. First, Eminem declares that Debbie loved Valium and lots of drugs more than she loved her son. Then he admits that he is a drug addict because he has become his mother.

The first verse addresses fans and critics in an attempt to negate any problems they may have with yet another hate-filled mama missive. Then, it travels back in time to when Eminem was a child who developed a substance abuse problem. Debbie allegedly laced all of his food and drink with Valium. He claims that his own mother made him a drug addict. He elaborates in a 1999 interview given to *Rolling Stone* by explaining that he once had to go to court to testify against his mother where he had to explain that Debbie lied to him when she said that he suffered from abnormal hyperactivity and needed to take Ritalin. Being high and addicted is then presented as the root cause of his underachievement in school, which he explains in "Brain Damage" (1999), when he writes that he dropped out after repeating the ninth grade three times. But in "My Mom," when Debbie is confronted with her son's problems, she tries to make him take a drug test. He refuses, stating that he no longer wishes to be under adult supervision. He just wants to be left alone.

In the second verse, he accuses Debbie of trying to feed him paint thinner and painkillers. When he refuses to eat, she says she will "throw [him] in the basement again." The verbal abuse continues when she threatens him by committing to a future in which she will continue to poison him, even on Thanksgiving. When he tries to change the subject and asks why she is suing K-Mart and his own estranged father, Debbie tells him it is because she needs money. This money, we are left to assume, is going to feed her habit and not her family.

Because of Debbie's example and neglect, her son has become a party animal that needs more and more Valium to get even the slightest buzz. Although he wishes he could get over it, he finds himself returning to the drug in the same way he finds himself continuing to write songs about his mother. Again, the dysfunctions she displayed when he was a child have become the source of his problems as an adult. He is still living his lyrics. To prove this, he continues by offering up a litany of accusations against his mother: for instance, she killed the family dog by making it overdose on prescription drugs, and she forced her son to take drugs when he was demanding too much of her attention. In fact, he even recounts a time when he stumbled into bed high off prescription pills his mother insisted he take as a young man. The song winds down as he repeats his main point: he is his mother, and he is an addict because his mother was an addict. It closes when he addresses Dr. Dre again, telling him how difficult it was to get all of this off his chest.

Although "My Mom" and "Cleanin' Out My Closet" rely on sexist blame-the-woman logic, they do support the thesis that, even if he is exaggerating them, Eminem is living out the situations his lyrics bring to life as a way to help him overcome the obstacles he faces in the rap game. But before we can confirm the ultimate success of this strategy, we must pay attention to Debbie's account of her triumphs, trials, and tribulations with her son to shed light on the conflicting personas and perspectives expressed in his work.

SETTING THE RECORD STRAIGHT

Debbie Nelson gave birth to Marshall Bruce Mathers III on Tuesday, October 17, 1972, in Saint Joseph, Kansas, a small town in northwest Missouri with a population of 75,000. Marshall was finally born after 72 hours of labor. He weighed 5 pounds 2 ounces. He was not just her son but also her chance at a new start in life. She was 15-years-old at the time and married to the first of four husbands, Marshall Bruce Mathers Jr. (whom she called Bruce). According to Debbie's autobiography, *My Son Marshall, My Son Eminem: Setting the Record Straight on My Life as Eminem's Mother,* Bruce was her knight in shining armor. When he proposed to her, she just could not say no, in spite of the fact that she was only 15-years-old. In retrospect, Debbie says this was partly because he was several years older than she and filled a void left by her father when her parents divorced.

Bruce and Debbie met when she was 14 and living with her mother and stepfather. Debbie's home life was tumultuous, and she was looking for a way out. Her parents were alcoholics, and her stepfather attempted to sexually abuse her at age 12. When, in a drunken stupor, he tried again a few years later, Bruce intervened. Debbie was grateful, and soon her gratefulness turned into love. But love would eventually turn into hate, as Debbie found herself repeating her family's cycle of abusive relationships. Not long after they were married Bruce began beating Debbie and drinking heavily. The situation deteriorated after Marshall was born. And when Marshall was a little over one year old, Bruce hit Debbie's head repeatedly and with such force that she was knocked unconscious. Once she awoke, she disobeyed doctors' orders, grabbed Marshall, and left North Dakota for her family's home in St. Joseph, Missouri. This would be the first of at least 20 moves the mother and son would make over a 25-year period.

Sadly, Bruce was not the last abusive relationship from which Debbie would escape. In addition to her next three marriages, one of which resulted in the birth of her second son Nathan, there were several men who entered and exited her life. By all accounts, she did not hide this part of her life from her children. Despite her victimhood and lack of parental guidance, Debbie paints herself as a loving and devoted mother. To prove it, she takes on her son's accusations one by one.

Debbie begins by challenging the date of birth her son presented to the public, which shaved a few years off in an attempt to make him appear younger, cooler, and smarter. She provides a copy of his birth certificate as proof. Then she rejects the "white trash" label her son has used to describe them. Her denial hinges on the fact that she, her son, and his father are not purely white. They are all mixed race. Specifically, she, Bruce and their son Marshall are part white and part Native American.

After dropping that bombshell, she denies she has a substance abuse problem. She says that she was against drinking and drug use because of her dysfunctional upbringing. Various men in her life did try to sway her by getting her to try whisky, marijuana, and lysergic acid diethylamide (LSD). However, these experiences made her so sick and paranoid that they solidified her straightedge stance. Although she does admit to smoking cigarettes off and on, she claims to have made her home a drug-free zone. She also says she is a member of Mothers Against Drunk Driving (MADD). In an attempt to further explain herself, she provides her definition of drugs: "To me drugs are illegal substances, like cocaine and heroin, not something the doctor prescribes."[10] She admits to taking prescription drugs only twice: once after the divorce from her second husband, Fred, and once after injuries she sustained from a car accident became too painful to bear. And she never hid pills

under her mattress as was alleged in "My Name Is" (1999). She concludes by saying that she has read that her son has a problem with
Stilnoct (a type of sleeping pill). The obvious irony here is that she
denies everything the press has said about her while she takes reports
of her son's alleged addiction as fact.

Debbie continues by painting herself as a proud and loving mother.
She documents with pictures her attendance at Marshall's first rap performance as M&M with his group called Bassmint Productions. And
later, she says that she loved his first album *Infinite* even though few
others did. When the *Slim Shady LP* and its videos first hit the airwaves
in February 1999, she says his words about her did not bother her too
much. She knew it was his way of playing to audiences as Slim Shady,
whom she would describe as "a comic antihero who inflicted violence
on all the people who'd annoyed Marshall in the past. This, he told
me, included school bullies, Kim, and the people who'd sneered at his
Infinite album. 'It's a big joke, Mom,' he assured me. 'The songs are
funny. They aren't meant to be taken seriously.'"[11] But the songs were
taken seriously. And Debbie's resentment set in as people harassed and
assaulted her when she left her home because her son turned her into
"the most hated mother in America."[12]

Surprisingly, some biographers have supported some of Debbie's
claims. For instance, in *The Dark Story of Eminem,* Nick Hasted writes
that Debbie really did nurse her son back from a life-changing brain injury in 1982. Debbie found her son lying in a bloody mess on the floor
of the bathroom at Dort Elementary School. She later found out that
her son had been bullied and beaten by D'Angelo Bailey, as he would
later recount in "Brain Damage" (1999). After waking from 10 days in
a coma, doctors said her son would have to be institutionalized. Debbie
rejected the notion and took her son home to care for him. It was a slow
and painful recovery, but eventually he learned how to walk, write,
talk, eat, and tie his shoes again.

Nevertheless, Debbie maintains that she was neither lazy nor abusive. In fact, as she tells it, she was overprotective and too loving. She
felt so badly about Bruce not showing interest in their son that she
worked multiple jobs to give her son whatever he wanted. In addition, contrary to what *Rolling Stone* printed in 1999, she did not steal
her son's paychecks. She did not need to because she was working
to provide for her family. Debbie claims that she was also nurturing.
That is why, for instance, the "My Name Is" lyrics were so disturbing
and hurtful. As Debbie tells it, she desperately wanted to breastfeed

her son but could not because she came down with "toxicoma" poisoning after his birth, which she says prevented her from doing so. She also denies Marshall's allegations of MSBP and other forms of abuse. She admits that her younger son Nathan was removed from her custody in 1996 by the state of Michigan for MSBP, but denies the truth of these charges. Using the Indian Child Welfare Act (ICWA), a federal law designed to keep Native American children with Native American families, Debbie's attorneys argued persuasively that the state violated the ICWA's guidelines during custody proceedings. Attorneys even cited Marshall's court testimony supposedly saying that Debbie was a good mother. In her memoir Debbie says her son's choice not to claim his own Native American background was a way to make it easier for him in hip hop. She says he thought that audiences wouldn't be able to relate to him as a person of color because he looked white and wasn't (even part) black. She also says that her son's choice to identify as white-only was another way to put personal distance between them.

The distance between mother and son definitely increased when Debbie "accidentally" sued her son for defamation of character in the amount of $10 million. Debbie writes that the whole thing was based on miscommunication with her ex-lawyer. She says that executives from Aftermath Records actually encouraged her to keep the suit going because the controversy was great for Marshall's record sales, even though she earnestly wanted to drop it. She says that Marshall begged her to settle, saying he would be happy to give her $25,000 to make things better. After the settlement check came through, and after Debbie received a mere $1,600, Marshall barely spoke more than a word to her. At one of Hailie's birthday parties, the mother and son had a brief conversation, after which he gave her a Mother's Day card containing $500. Debbie drove home crying and described herself as heartbroken.

Notwithstanding their complicated mother–son relationship, Debbie says that Kim, Marshall's long-term girlfriend, ex-wife, and baby's mama, was the real problem. Debbie admits that she welcomed Kim and her sister into her home as teenaged foster children in hopes of nourishing and nurturing them. But as soon as Kim and Marshall started dating, things got ugly. Debbie paints Kim as a demonic force out to control her son's mind and money. She confirms Marshall's allegations that Kim refused to put his last name on their daughter's birth certificate and that Kim used their daughter as a weapon for emotional blackmail. She also says that Kim used to terrorize Marshall with verbal and physical abuse as described in "Bad Influence" (1999). Debbie concludes that Marshall took his frustrations with Kim out on her, even attacking her physically around the time of his 20th birthday. While she attempts to move on with a spirit of forgiveness, her son takes a different path, which leads to a more public form of confrontation for all involved.

Debbie is not the only one with things to say about Kim. Byron "Big-Naz" Williams, former bodyguard and author of *Shady Bizzness: Life as Eminem's Bodyguard in an Industry of Paper Gangsters,* says that Kim was Debbie reincarnated. Williams believes that the rapper's intense attraction to Kim is based on the fact that she displays all the negative characteristics of his mother. Also, the will to see their relationship through to the end is really a function of Slim's desire to go back in time to when he was a child and fix the relationship he had with his mother. It is now public knowledge that his many attempts at reconciling with Kim were unsuccessful. As songs like "Kim" (2000) and "Love You More" (2004) express, it seems the greater the passion he felt for Kim, the more she let him down.

Returning to the rapper's relationship with his mother, one of the few things Debbie admits to is the heated exchange recounted by her son in "Cleanin' Out My Closet," while asserting that it was really Kim's fault. According to Debbie, Kim had all of the living room furniture removed from the family's home on the day of Debbie's brother Ronnie's funeral in December 1991 without providing any explanation for her actions. Marshall called Debbie to tell her about it, and they got into a fight. "'Fuck you, bitch!' he shouted . . . He swore occasionally, but he had never addressed me like that before . . . I couldn't believe what was happening. 'I hate to say this, but I'm sick of you,' I screamed. 'I wish this was you instead of Ronnie.'"[13] She regretted the comment immediately and apologized. And she has apologized many times in the years since. But her son kept his word. He will never forgive her. Debbie says that he chose Kim over her.

In hopes of extending an olive branch, Debbie recorded a song with a hip hop group called Identity Unknown (aka ID-X) entitled "Dear Marshall" (2000). She begins the song by referring to herself as her son's "only mother," clearly emphasizing that many other women may come into his life as lovers, wives, or daughters, but she cannot be replaced. Debbie describes the rest of the two-minute and twenty-five second song as follows:

I started the poem by saying I still love him, but we had a problem; something had gone wrong between us . . . I explain[ed] how I'd tried to be mom and dad to him, giving him everything he ever wanted because he was perfect in my eyes . . . I finished it with a plea that he'd stop his attacks, rewriting his lyrics.[14]

The song also expresses her sincere joy over his success in the recording industry and her unwavering support. She says that she will always support Marshall because he was her first "true love." She admits that as a mother, she did not always know best. By spoiling her son, she inadvertently taught him that anger was the best way to get what he wanted. The song closes when Debbie asks "the real Marshall Mathers" to rise and take responsibility for his part in their failed relationship.

From a distance, we can see that the song says a lot more than this simple description lets on, and for that reason, we can read it in at least three ways. First, we can read the song as a rejection of the idea that parents are all-knowing and infallible, so, in a strange way, Debbie's parental missteps helped her son to mature and make decisions that resulted in his success. Second, we can read the song as a declaration of love, as Debbie's way of saying that her son will always be a part of her and, perhaps, the best part. Lastly, we can read the song as a rejection of society's disappointment with mothers who do not behave as society says they should. To understand which of these readings is most accurate, and to understand the complex nature of this mother–son relationship, we must turn to the place where it finally fell apart and the film that made that place famous: 8 Mile Road, Detroit, Michigan, USA.

8 MILE

Just like Slim's and Debbie's story, the story of Detroit is two-sided, maybe even more than two-sided. For the purpose of shedding light on Slim's life and times, we will pick up the story of Detroit in the mid-20th century. This Detroit was a bustling metropolis. Known as "Motor City," it was home to the big three American car companies—Ford, Chrysler, and General Motors—whose high-paying salaries attracted many people to the area. The video for "Beautiful" (2009) confirms this when its opening credits describe the city as follows: "In 1950, Michigan was one of eight states that contributed 36% of the world's GNP [gross national product]. Detroit was the greatest manufacturing city in the world." The video reminds us that Detroit was also known for its music. In 1959, Berry Gordy Jr. purchased a two-family home at 2648 West Grand Boulevard and called it "Hits-ville USA." From this location, Berry transformed Motown Records from a small startup business into the world's largest independent record company by the mid-1970s, when the headquarters was moved to Los Angeles, California.

Motown Records and the Big Three automakers built their businesses on the principles of the assembly line. Just as cars began as simple metal frames and emerged as finely tuned machines, talented unknowns could come to Motown and emerge as polished and professional superstars. Many talented artists got their first big breaks at Motown, including Diana Ross and the Supremes, Smokey Robinson and the Miracles, Martha and the Vandellas, Stevie Wonder, Rare Earth, The Four Tops, The Temptations, The Countours, The Funk Brothers, and The Jackson 5. Each of these acts also helped lay the foundation for and create the musical tradition that would soon produce the real Slim Shady.

But another city was lurking beneath all of this cultural and economic success built on the factory model. As 1960s civil rights legislation outlawed segregation in more and more aspects of day-to-day life, many Detroit dwellers fled to the suburbs, and so, a "segregated, devastated wasteland called 'Amityville' by Eminem"[15] was born. Amityville was a world unto itself, comprised of the area between the city of Detroit and its northern suburbs. Amityville was a place plagued by police brutality, racial profiling, unaffordable housing, economic inequality, growing militancy, and rapid demographic change. Everything in Amityville revolved around 8 Mile Road. This racial and economic border zone is also a geographical border, separating the city from the suburbs. As such, one side of 8 Mile was predominantly black, poor, and underemployed. The other side was predominantly white, middle- to upper-class, and reported few of the social issues plaguing the black side. These sides were separate, unequal, and antagonistic social worlds that clashed in 1967's race riots.

The Detroit Riot of 1967 began when police raided an after-hours drinking establishment in a predominantly black area. When the officers tried to arrest everyone there, a crowd gathered in protest. Once the police left the scene, a small group of men vandalized an adjacent business. The vandalism spread like wildfire, including looting and arson. After five days, 43 people were killed, 29 of them by police. Over 1,000 people were injured and more than 7,000 people were arrested.[16] Although the rioting lasted less than a week, it left an indelible mark on the city. To this day, downtown Detroit is a shadow of its former self, awaiting requiem and revival.

Enter Debbie and Eminem. In the late 1970s, the mother and son lived right in the middle of this socioeconomic devastation, as the city became the murder capital of the United States. In his autobiography, *The Way I Am,* Eminem describes this area as "a shithole on Fairport Street off 7 Mile."[17] It is here that he met his D12 (aka Dirty Dozen) friends and future wife Kim and made his first appearance at the Hip Hop Shop (which later moved to a new location). All of these experiences are brought to life in the fictional biopic *8 Mile* (2002).

8 Mile is the hip hop *Rocky.* Like *Rocky,* it tells the story of a working-class underdog forced to do battle with his deepest fears and most bitter rivals. However, in *8 Mile,* the hero uses his words instead of his fists as triumphant weapons. Along the way, he breaks up with his girlfriend and moves into his alcoholic mother's trailer so that he can save enough money for a demo tape. In freestyle raps, he makes fun of his own dead-end factory job and the economic conditions that put him there. However, when it really counts, he chokes. He stands mute in front of an audience of underground hip hop heads because he is overwhelmed by the fact that he is white and they are not. Things soon get better and worse. His new love interest encourages his dreams and proves unfaithful. His mother demands financial assistance and discourages the career path that could be the end of all their worries and he takes his licks when he is badly beaten by his neighborhood enemies and rap rivals, an all-black group named The Free World.

But, as with all two-sided stories, there is more going on than meets the eye. According to cultural critic Eric King Watts in "Border Patrolling and 'Passing' in Eminem's *8 Mile,*" the film's more subtle and significant stories are about the rapper's relationship with his mother and his racial identity. To ensure his status as a credible and bankable hip hop icon, the film portrays its protagonist, Jimmy "B-Rabbit" Smith Jr., as a kind of racial minority. Even though he looks white, because of his mother's life choices he has many of the stereotypical trappings of nonwhite characters in film. To begin, he was actually outnumbered by a population of hostile people from a different racial background, making him a true racial minority. Add to that being poor, undereducated, into rap music, and the product of a broken home, horribly led by a young, single mother. If we think of Jimmy Smith (B-Rabbit) in this way, as a *white-looking person of color,* then he is no different from the many mixed-race film protagonists who were passing—presenting

themselves as other than how society defines them—to succeed or
survive in mainstream Hollywood cinema.[18] In fact, although it is not
stated, Rabbit's father could be black since he is named after one of
hip hop's greatest emcees, LL Cool J (aka James Todd Smith). But in
8 Mile, what we do not know about Rabbit is as important as what we
do know. And, as is always the case, when it comes to our protagonist
life imitates art. The key to his success in the film and in real life turns
out to be surviving his mother and how his relationship with her gets
played out. He must adhere to the rigid class politics in which she
raised him, politics that brought him into contact with rap music. But
he must also overcome the bitter black-and-white racial politics and
grapple with the complicated racial identity she passed on to him by
emphasizing her shadier attributes.

Much like the way audiences are introduced to Debbie in the video
for "Cleanin' Out My Closet," when we meet Stephanie Smith (Kim
Basinger), we do not see her face. We see only her long blond hair and
naked back. We get this view because she is straddling her young lover,
Greg, as they have sex on the family's living room sofa. Rabbit walks
in on them and is repulsed. Stephanie tries to explain, telling her son
that everything is okay because she is expecting Greg to take care of
her when his big insurance check comes in. The sex is her insurance
against Greg's abandonment. When Greg does not come through, she
lashes out at her son, the only consistent male presence in her life, putting her darkness and weakness on display. Eric King Watts explains
the scene thus:

> Lying on the bed in a fetal position and sobbing helplessly, [Stephanie] needs
> Rabbit's strength and heroism. Although she screams at him . . . she does not
> wish to be alone. Her darkness explains Rabbit's angst . . . [and] warrants
> Eminem's ugly put-downs of his mother on his CDs and elsewhere. Her
> weakness, her miscarriage as a "good mother," provokes in Rabbit both an
> awful fear that he may end up like her and a desperate quest to succeed.[19]

Deciding that he just cannot take it anymore, he screams at his mother
and asks her what is wrong with her. He cannot understand why she
treats her children this way. As in "Cleanin' Out My Closet," a mother's
inability or unwillingness to assume her parental responsibilities will
cause her eldest son to become the parent he never had.

If Stephanie is a shady (or menacing) woman, then Rabbit's new
girlfriend, Alex, is even shadier. Sound familiar? As mentioned previously, Rabbit is drawn to women who are just like his mother but who

might be able to give him what he never had: a family he can lead. Although audiences do not know if Rabbit and Alex have a family, the possibility is introduced. On their second meeting, outside the factory where Rabbit works, Alex watches approvingly as Rabbit defends a gay coworker with a freestyle rap. She shows her approval by taking him to an empty part of the factory and initiating unprotected sex. After sex, she encourages him to continue rapping because she believes he can succeed. For a moment, Rabbit thinks that Alex might be different, that she could give him more than motivation. But he soon learns he is wrong. Alex turns out to be just like his mother. Alex is out for hers and will offer sex to any man who might be able to provide for her financially. What dawned on him when he found his mother straddling Greg is now confirmed: women operate most efficiently as sexual vessels for men but are incapable of being real partners or leaders. He finally realizes that the only surefire way to become a man is by relying on himself, putting his life on display in his lyrics. This proved to be an effective strategy on- and offscreen, turning the real Slim Shady into one of the world's most popular musicians of all time.

8 Mile ultimately played a starring role in the rapper's career by setting an entertainment industry record in November 2002 with the No. 1 movie, single and soundtrack. The film also showcased his talents as an actor and put his rough relationship with his mother on display for the world to see. In the process the film complicated his reputation in mainstream popular culture. Before the film's release and success Eminem the rapper was a poor, bad, white guy who hated his mother. After *8 Mile* he was a savvy businessman with a sensitive side, who, incidentally, may not be white, and whose menacing mother may have hated him first.

FINALE

The real Slim Shady has been transformed by overcoming the obstacles put in his path by his mother, as his 2009 BET interview concerning their relationship demonstrates. In addition, it is telling that he is the only one who is capable of this kind of change. By leaving everyone behind, especially his shady mother, he becomes master of his own destiny. His ultimate change in perspective is represented as he now talks about her with a degree of compassion. He can empathize with his mother because he has survived her. He has transcended everything she represents: poverty, brokenness, instability, addiction, and a complicated racial identity. And he can speak to her, through the media, a space in which he retains ultimate spin control.

As it turns out, Slim has survived himself, too. He has turned his personal tragedies into gold through music, books, and film. He has learned how to prioritize his work to provide for his family. He has harnessed his anger to defy social convention. He has become authentic and marketable. And he did it all by living out the mother–son drama presented in his lyrics. As long as Debbie personifies his insecurities and liabilities, he is able to identify (at least stereotypically) with non-white audiences, and Debbie's presentation of her family's racial identity suggests that her son might not actually be just white, either. The rapper proves that he is not merely a cultural appropriator, like the many fake white rappers who preceded him. He is someone altogether different: a mash-up of Eminem, Marshall Mathers, Jimmy Smith Jr., and B-Rabbit that is known to the world as "The Real Slim Shady."

But it has yet to be determined whether Slim will survive the changing demographics of his audience. In 2006, the *New York Times* reported that racial minorities would likely be the U.S. majority by 2042. This prediction has been confirmed by the results and analysis of the 2010 U.S. Census.[20] Since the United States will soon be a nation with no majority race, three possibilities for Slim's ongoing relevance emerge. First, he can continue to capitalize on the resentment fueled by his mother–son relationship, a resentment that many white males are vocalizing as part of a growing conservative backlash that relies on the same old blame-the-woman logic. (Think Newt Gingrich, who refused to answer questions about his infidelity raised by his former wife in the 2012 GOP debates. Or Rush Limbaugh, who referred to Georgetown law student Sandra Fluke as a "slut" and "prostitute" after she testified about the utility of birth control before Congress in February 2012. Or Don Imus, who referred to the entire women's basketball team from Rutgers University as "some hard-core . . . nappy-headed hoes" after they won an important game in April 2007.)

If option one is no longer satisfying, Slim can choose to market himself as a post-racial poster child whose acceptance as one of rap's greatest artists indicates that old racial paradigms are falling away. If this is true, then the fact that he chooses to identify differently than his mother, and sometimes chooses to defy racial labels all together, begins to make more sense. And we can take his current roster of white, black, Latino, and multiracial protégés as signs that new and progressive racial coalitions are being made among young men who have the potential to reach beyond popular culture and into mainstream politics. As an example of this post-racial harmony, take BET's 2011 *Shady 2.0 Cypher*, a segment in which each new racially and ethnically diverse member of the Shady Records family freestyled over a beat, which was ranked best by a racially diverse and multinational audience.

Or, he can do something much more shady. He can identify as white on the outside and as something else on the inside, redistributing notions of traditional power along the way. To do so, he must continue referring to his mother as his antagonist but lighten up a bit by showing a little empathy because she is no longer in his way. And he must begin referring to Dr. Dre as more than a professional colleague and friend. In fact, Dr. Dre must become his father, and the real Slim Shady must become a loyal son. As Dre's and Debbie's son Slim can also address the growing number of people in the United States and abroad who identify themselves as something other than either black or white. In addition, perhaps most significantly, he can speak loudly into the headphones of an increasingly fatherless generation from a new place of authenticity, understanding, and marketability.

CHAPTER 2
Daddy Dearest

If having an unstable mother is tragic, then having an absent father is downright dreadful. Such is the case with Eminem who, in the voice of Slim Shady in "My Name Is" (1999), says that if we ever see his biological father we should "tell him that [Shady] slit his [father's] throat in this dream [he] had." This lyric is the first of many that speak to Eminem's father issues. Perhaps the most poignant among them is "Cleanin' Out My Closet" (2002), where Eminem describes the emotional aftershocks of his father's abandonment. He raps, "I wonder if he even kissed me goodbye," then quickly denies the thought and spews a venomous death wish directed at his dad. It seems like Marshall Mathers III needed to admit that he was hurt while Slim Shady was just too numb to care. Dad left? So what? Slim Shady did not need him. Slim made it without him.

The rapper went on the record with *Rolling Stone* to explain what he knew about his father. He said, "My mother tells me I was six months old when my father left. He lives in Los Angeles now. He tried to get in touch with me when I first blew up. I told my mother to tell him to go fuck himself. Fuck that motherfucker, man, not one letter. Not one, all these years. Nothing . . . I saw one picture of him. He was about nineteen but I couldn't really tell if I look like him or not. The picture was kinda cracked and fucked up."[1] This public display of emotional ambivalence and confusion is, at least partially, a response to the open letter to the rapper written by his father in 2001 and published in the now defunct London tabloid *News of the World*. Highlights from the letter, addressed to Eminem, include the following:

> HELLO, son. You think I dumped you . . . and never came looking for you. You're convinced I'm a drunk who never answered any of your letters . . . I want you to read this . . . [to] hear the truth . . .
>
> . . . [O]ne day . . . I came home from work and everything was missing . . . To read now that it was me who walked out makes me choke with tears of rage.

> . . . I didn't receive even one letter from you . . . [T]hat made [your mum's] version of me being uncaring sound like the truth.
> . . . [T]here hasn't been a day when I haven't thought about you. Love, Dad.[2]

Beneath its touching veneer, this note from father to son is ultimately manipulative, as Dad (aka Bruce) attempts to show loyalty to and bond with his namesake by blaming everything on mother Debbie. Dad's blame-the-woman logic proves unpersuasive, indicating at least some degree of his son's belief in or respect for Debbie's side of the story. If Debbie's story carries at least a kernel of truth, it is easy to understand why Slim never got in touch with his biological father. After all, what the rapper knows is that his many adolescent attempts to reach his father were rebuffed. And there is no record that father and son have ever spoken. Eminem's maternal grandmother, Betty Kresin, confirms this lack of father–son communication in an interview with BBC Radio One's Briggy Smale on February 9, 2001.[3] But in lyrics, writing as though his father is listening, Slim Shady becomes the messed-up answer to his father's scheming words and deadbeat deeds.

Slim Shady is a persona suspended in adolescence because he never learned life lessons about authority, relationships, and leadership from his father. Instead, Slim learned how to keep people at bay by making them as angry as he was at his father. That is why he can give everybody the middle finger, and he says that he does not have to care or respond. Slim is that hate-filled and hateful person living inside Eminem and Marshall Mathers who, despite all evidence to the contrary in terms of rap skill, is operating out of inferiority and neediness. Here is the rapper's description of Slim Shady: "The more I started writing and the more I slipped into this Slim Shady character, the more it just started becoming me . . . My true feelings were coming out, and I just needed an outlet to dump them in. I needed some type of persona. I needed an excuse to let go of all this rage."[4]

Take the song "Evil Deeds" (2004) as an example. From the beginning he inquires about his father, "Where's my Dad?" In "The Way I Am" (2000), Slim just cannot be bothered to attend to the needs of those who love and, more poignantly, need him. And in "So Bad" (2010), he is the product of his father's rejection: "I musta got my pimpin' genes from him, the way he left my mama." As evidenced by these songs, it is clear that Slim Shady received the messages of insecurity and inferiority his father (perhaps inadvertently) passed down. Slim simply was not good enough to make his father stick around. And, as he expresses so vividly, he is anything but happy about it. Slim is also the part of Eminem whose raison d'être was solidified after his first public performance because he got booed so badly. Public rejection reminded Slim of his father's rejection. Describing Slim in his autobiography *The Way I Am,* the rapper writes, "It wasn't that I just wanted to shock people; there was part of me coming out too, like me being pissed off at the world."[5]

Slim Shady invests his energy in lashing out at the world rather than admitting that he wanted to be loved by his father and was not. Consequently, Slim offered a whole new way of being for Eminem and Marshall Mathers: He "wasn't just a new type of lyrics, it was also that I delivered them in this high-pitched style. As Slim, I had a whole different voice, and that's how I knew that this was going to be a whole new persona for me."[6] That high-pitched style is a marker of Slim's adolescent perspective and insecurity. In form and function the Slim Shady persona allows Eminem to express insecurity based on lack of fathering.

PARENTAL GUIDANCE

As it happens, Slim's biological parents are not the only ones who had a hand in raising him. In "Revelation" (2001), he explains that hip hop "overwhelmed" his life and moved him to "a whole 'nother realm" where he could express his aspirations unapologetically. A decade later he added, "I certainly feel like if it wasn't for rap, obviously, I wouldn't be here, but it gave me my voice, it gave me my outlook, it gave me strength, you know what I came back from, overdose and a whole load of shit—without rap I wouldn't be able to do a fucking thing."[7] Slim Shady loved hip hop, and perhaps most important, hip hop's rappers loved him back. In interviews, he explained this relationship as the first love of his life, where he talked about the seminal role hip hop pioneers like LL Cool J, Doug E. Fresh, MC Shan, Ice-T, NWA, and The Beastie Boys played in his development. For instance, in a statement to MTV News regarding the death of The Beastie Boys' MCA (aka Adam Yauch) in May 2012, the rapper said, "I think it's obvious to anyone how big of an influence the Beastie Boys were on me."[8] He describes all of these old school rappers as a refuge, saying that he spent many hours playing their songs over and over to learn the words and master the moves.

In an interview with author and urban marketing guru Steve Stoute, the rapper explains his introduction to hip hop through the music of Ice-T, LL Cool J, and Doug E. Fresh and the Get Fresh Crew:

> Ice-T was one of the first rappers that I ever really heard, when I was ten or eleven. My uncle [Ronnie] brought me over cassettes of Ice-T and the *Breakin'* soundtrack had "Reckless" on there. That's when I started to get into it. And then, I got turned on to Run-DMC, and got put up on the Fat Boys and then the Beastie Boys came out. And the Beastie Boys kind of got my thought process going that maybe it could be possible. Then LL probably made me actually want to do this . . . that's who really made me start dabbling and made me really think, Wow, I can put some words together . . . But as I started to get just a little bit older, around fifteen, as far as storytelling, I remember taking a beat from Doug E. Fresh from "Play This Only at Night" (1986).[9]

Slim's words here are confirmed by biographer Nick Hasted in *The Dark Story of Eminem,* who describes the young rapper as an avid hip hop student and aspiring performer who was able to "abstract . . . himself from the futile, bored adolescent life he could have had . . . [because] rap had shown him a route out."[10] Slim obviously chose to take that route out and once he made it he was able to interact with many of the hip hop father figures who inspired him along the way. For instance, original gangsta rapper Ice-T, who interviewed Slim about his rhymes for the documentary film, *Something From Nothing: The Art of Rap* (2012), told MTV that Slim's style was precise and technical, stating that listening to him "was like . . . listening to a scientist."[11] This is not the first time Ice-T spoke positively of Slim. In a rare 2004 interview with British television to promote the album *Ice-T Presents the Westside,* Ice-T expressed his admiration for the younger rapper.

> I love [him]. I think he's like . . . the bastard son of a million gangsta rappers. He's like our embryo. A trick baby. We planted that embryo way back with Ice T and NWA, and he's a young white kid listening to the music, and this is what happens, and this is what you get. You get [Slim Shady], and I'm proud of my son. I love him. You know . . . [Slim Shady] is very respectful to the music and . . . rhyme-for-rhyme, if you put him up against any of the rappers today, he's just as good if not better than them. So, you know, one thing hip-hop has never been is racist . . . If you're a white kid and you can rap, we'll give you that mic and let you do your thing.[12]

According to Ice-T's description, Slim is a science-fiction experiment like Dr. Frankenstein's monster. Slim is the monstrous persona, the "trick baby," who was abandoned by his father and felt confused, angry, needy, and afraid. Intelligent and articulate, Slim's lyrics describe his encounters with people and about how he learned to observe and distance himself from them over time. Through observing the parents, peers, rappers, and politicians around him from a distance, Slim became educated and self-aware. He goes so far as to describe himself as "a monster, because nobody wants to see Marshall no more. They want Shady."[13] And like Dr. Frankenstein's monster, Slim learned how to stand out to people from many different walks of life. In his loneliness, Slim eventually sought to befriend other rappers in Detroit's underground hip hop scene. As recounted in "Yellow Brick Road" (2004), he presented himself first to Proof, an aspiring black rapper, who paid little attention to his white skin and received him with kindness and hospitality. Although not everyone Slim met took him as seriously as best friend Proof did, he eventually experienced similar warm reactions throughout his commercial career from rappers including T.I., Redman, The Game, Akon, Missy "Misdemeanor" Elliott, Nicki Minaj, and LL Cool J.

These kinds of earnest reactions are what Steve Stoute refers to in *The Tanning of America: How Hip-Hop Culture Wrote the Rules of the New Economy* as hip hop's contribution to global society, a polyethnic sense of identity and identification. Quoting sociologists, Stoute describes polyethnic as "tan," an ethnic identity that is distinct from white and black racial identities in general, and from an individual's cultural or racial roots in particular.[14] Stoute touts Shady as one of the 21st century's most prominent polyethnic "tan" personas. And, based on his many artistic, cultural, and economic successes, hip hop's polyethnic audiences agree. In "Evil Deeds," Slim asserts his polyethnicity unashamedly. "Predominantly white, predominantly black. Well . . . I guess that I'm between predominantly both of 'em." In "The Way I Am" (2000), he contradicts stereotypes held about white people who love hip hop when he says that he is tired of "cocky Caucasians" who think that he is just "trying to be black." With lines like this, Slim not only acknowledged his million gangsta rapper fathers, but he did so in a way that kept hip hop's cultural frame intact even as the music reached a broader and more diverse demographic in terms of race, ethnicity, nationality, and age. In this way, Slim distinguished himself from the troubled history of crossover artists like Elvis Presley, whose success opened the gates for white rock-n-roll artists to take over the stage at the expense of their black counterparts. Instead of ignoring hip hop's history and reproducing the old racial politics that privileged whites, Slim embraced his polyethnicity.[15]

Slim's polyethnic success was ensured by two factors. The first was numbers. On February 8, 1999, only five days before the *Slim Shady LP* was released, *TIME* Magazine ran a cover feature called "Hip-Hop Nation: After 20 Years—How It's Changed America." The article created a media frenzy when it reported that rap replaced country music as the nation's top-selling musical genre; that rap's purchasing audience was now 70 percent white; and that hip hop culture was creating a more socially progressive and increasingly multiracial generation.[16] Slim Shady was a member of that young and gifted generation whose brains were bathed in beats and rhymes.

The second factor that ensured Slim's initial success was the nature of his relationship with hip hop legend Dr. Dre (born Andre Romelle Young). Dre became his friend, mentor, and father figure. Time and time again, Dre has not only seen Shady's vision but used his clout, credibility, and connections to bring that vision to life. As a member of NWA (Niggas With Attitude), Dre knew all about the power of rap to expose hypocrisy and yell back at personifications of authority, like the police. Dre also knew how to get to the heart of hip hop's most powerful and profitable fan base, suburban white males, while staying grounded in black musical and social traditions. To take hip hop to a different level, Dre had to give suburban white males a face with which they could identify, which was rooted concretely and authentically within hip hop culture. Dre knew that Shady's brazen posture would first appeal to gangsta rap fans and eventually to mainstream music audiences who would find him physically attractive and safe in a polyethnic pop culture environment.

Shady would figure prominently in Dre's polyethnic vision for taking hip hop to new heights, which Dre explains in an interview with VH1.Com:

> I didn't even know he was white when I heard the demo. Jimmy Iovine told me a little later. Then my wheels started turning. I thought he would be able to get away with saying a lot more than I would get away with saying. If a black guy said that stuff, people would turn the radio off. That's reality . . . Eminem is over the top. He pays attention to what he's doing in the studio, and he makes sure his records are coming out right. He . . . has a strong career ahead of him.[17]

Dre was right. Slim rapidly gained mass appeal precisely because of his anger and hostility, which are the same qualities that usually turn black rappers into scary gangstas. Confirmations of Dre's perspective came pouring in. For example, *New York Times* best-selling author and pop culture expert Neil Strauss wrote, "characters like Eminem, who buck the conventions of society to follow their own path, are not the villains but the heroes."[18] However, it must be noted that not everyone saw the Slim Shady persona in this light. Dre biographer Ronin Ro explains:

> At Aftermath, Dre auditioned the songs for black employees. Some said, "Yo, that shit is dope," he claimed. He thought so too, until most asked, "What are you doing?" "Yo, Dre is fuckin' buggin' out," said another employee. Even the general manager questioned his judgments. "Look, this guy is blonde with blue eyes. What the fuck? What are you doing?"[19]

These naysayers within the recording industry were not alone, as many politicians, cultural critics, and academics would agree that Dre made a mistake in bringing Shady to the world.[20]

Dre ignored the negativity, saying that he did not care what anyone else thought. He had confidence in his protégé and felt that Shady could be bigger and better than Elvis, who many described as a white man with a black voice. Dre would make sure that Shady would not be at all like Vanilla Ice either, who became infamous as an inauthentic imitator. Instead, Shady would be presented as someone with a different edge, the kind of entertainer who had a way of reworking rather than transcending the color line. Shady would not be so much a white rapper as he would be a polyethnic tan rapper who needed a formal introduction to the world. Audiences would be willing to take things from Shady that black rappers would never get away with. But they would also be wary because he was not black. Enter "My Name Is" (1999).

Musicologists and sociologists have studied "My Name Is" extensively in the many years since its release. From its beats to its lyrical flow and rhyme schemes, the song is considered part of the 21st century's polyethnic turn, an attempt to redefine what race means in America. One thing was for sure, the hip hop ethic of polyethnic inclusion meant that whiteness could not be considered the norm or normal anymore. In an increasingly "tan" America, whiteness equaled difference and distance. And a tanning America also required audiences to perceive hip hop as being open to all, including whites, rather than as black-owned, which is exactly what Dre and Eminem proved through satire. In some ways, the creative crew followed Dre's well-developed formula for successfully launching rap careers by way of introductory jingle singles (think Snoop Doggy Dogg's 1994 hit "What's My Name?"). However, "My Name Is" had to also rise to the challenge of turning racial naysayers and critics into polyethnic fans. The best way to ensure this transformation was for Slim to make fun of normal and clean-cut images of whiteness—politicians, rockers, pop stars, suburban family men, talk-show hosts—and distinguish himself as much as possible from those images. These images of Slim are interspersed with images of the real Slim Shady as an exception to the stereotypical norms of whiteness—a malnourished mental patient under Dr. Dre's care who never knew his father, drives drunk, chases teachers around classrooms, is thrown out of strip clubs for being too obscene, does drugs, and has hairy palms. By the way, in case audiences missed it in the lyrics, Slim has a white trash side that walks around in boxer shorts and lives with his mom in a trailer park. Obviously satirical, an important point is being made here about stark racial disparities and perceptions.

And here it is. Shady and Dre are subtly implying that white people use alcohol and drugs at remarkably similar rates as people of other racial backgrounds. What is more, by emphasizing Shady's white side, the pair is also highlighting the vulnerability and neediness of all lower-class white people, a group that works hard to make sure that they are not perceived as being on the bottom rung of the social ladder in an increasingly racially and ethnically diverse nation. Slim does something shady to climb the social ladder. He appeals to racial capital rather than financial capital and introduces himself as a polyethnic persona (whose ethnicity is different from his racialized appearance), sent by "Dre to take the world on" by rapping in an unapologetic style. At key moments in the song, Slim makes costume changes into hip hop jump-suits and baggy jeans, sways to the beat, lowers his voice, and bends down to meet the offstage audience to reinforce this tanner side. These audiovisual images are Shady's and Dre's ways of anticipating and battling any insults and criticisms that would be sure to come their way on the bases of race and racism. More than that, "My Name Is" grapples with the sad social truth that people are likely to criticize Shady's and Dre's continued collaboration as celebrities because regular people in the United States are as racially segregated as ever. As Rich Benjamin argues in his book, *Searching for Whitopia,* white people have fled from the urban center and even the increasingly diverse suburban periphery to exurbs known as "whitopias." The result is that people of all racial and ethnic backgrounds continue to live in increasingly homogeneous spaces while racial and ethnic stereotypes continue to thrive.

Taken as a whole, the song's true genius comes from its use of a polyethnic persona to challenge ideas about whitopias and racial stereotyping in popular culture. In "My Name Is," Shady uses a polyethnic persona to criticize biases that paint people of color as criminals because something is inherently wrong with them or because they just do not respect society. Shady also satirizes biases that blame white people's criminal acts on something that is wrong with society at large, like political malfeasance, family drama, or economic recession. By marrying these two biases together within the "My Name Is" song, Shady becomes a walking contradiction that shows audiences just how inauthentic we can be when we define social deviants and social deviance in racial terms. And, at the same time, Shady shows audiences his own authenticity and his disgust for culture swiping appropriators who may enjoy the music as fantasy while living out their daily lives in whitopias. He lives his lyrics as much as any other rapper does even though they are set in the trailer park rather than the ghetto.

Dre's vision and experience also came to bear on finding just the right image to pair with Shady's raging rhymes in "My Name Is." When Eminem walked into the studio after bleaching his hair with peroxide, Dre knew he had struck gold. He declared, "That's it! We found your image! . . . This is the identity we've been looking for the whole time."[21] Dre has sharpened Shady's edge and referred to the rapper as brave and unique, and their collaboration revived both of their careers over the years. But the pair shares more than creative synergy and similar aesthetic sensibilities. Time has revealed that they share a sense of grief over lost father-and-son connections that bound them together as a polyethnic father–son unit for hip hop audiences everywhere. It is to this imagined family relationship that we now turn.

FATHER–SON CONNECTIONS

Slim learned as much about family ties in the absence of a real father Bruce as he did from the very real presence of Dre in his life. He learned about loyalty, about risk-taking, about family business, and about the business of producing rap records. Ro elaborates:

> With each song, [Shady] went from not knowing how to work a drum machine to learning more about hooks ("This is easy") to absorbing

how Dre did things. Finally, during a session, he programmed a drum beat, and sang . . . From here, Em insisted on creating his own drums and melody for a song called, "Still Don't Give a Fuck." As he hummed a tune to Dre's players, Dre told him, "You don't even realize it, but you're producing."[22]

Over the years, the duo expressed their affection for each other in much the same way that family would—through heated arguments interrupted with bouts of defending each other. For example, throughout the single and video for "Guilty Conscience" (1999), they played the good cop, bad cop routine. They bumped heads, Dre almost strangling Slim, and then they reconciled. But Slim recently revealed that the goal of his career has really been to get a response out of Dre in the same way that many sons seek to get reactions from their fathers. We know that Dre always understood Slim, saw his vision early on, nurtured him, and encouraged him to be as daring as possible. But what we may not know is that Dre shares some of the same issues that plague Slim like domestic violence, lost friends, and a severed father–son relationship. Dre did not live with his biological father either and became a father at a young age.

Slim has never been shy about exploring or expressing his father love for Dre. In single after single, he promised that he would be there for Dre whenever he was needed. Some prominent examples are "If I Get Locked Up" (1999), "What's the Difference" (2001), and "Forget About Dre" (2001), in which Shady confesses his love for Dre and promises his loyalty and support. In 2010, the pair collaborated on the Grammy nominated track "I Need a Doctor" to give audiences some added perspective on the depth of their connection. The video for the single was released on February 24, 2011.[23] Almost eight minutes long, it features a more mature Slim helping Dre recover from a coma caused by a near-fatal car crash. Moments before the accident, Dre is sitting by the water, breathing deeply, and reflecting upon his life. The date is February 18, 2001, his 36th birthday, and Dre is replaying his life like a home movie. Then, speeding along the California coast in a black Ferrari 360, he begins remembering the best moments of his life, like getting married, having a family, working as a deejay in the late 1970s and early 1980s, and making music with legendary rappers like 2Pac, Shady, Snoop Dogg, Xzibit, Ice Cube, MC Ren, Slim, and Eazy E. He also remembers what it was like to lose some of those family members and colleagues including Eazy E, TuPac, and his own son Andre Young Jr. The last thing heard as the spectacular car crash unfolds is his daughter's farewell, "Good night Daddy."

Fast-forward 10 years to February 2011. The scene shifts from the crash site to an underground medical facility in Marin County, California, filled with spirits, scientists, and computers. Slim walks past the many puzzled doctors and warily enters the room where Dre is suspended in repose. The accident and coma are visual representations of the creative roadblocks that have delayed Dre's long-awaited final solo album, called *Detox*. The chorus begins to set the mood as the feminized spirit of hip hop delivers a diagnosis and prescription. Hip hop "need[s] a doctor" to be brought "back to life." Hip hop cannot let Dre go yet. Slim hears hip hop's words, which only increase his insecurity and neediness. He is scared, impatient, and unstable without Dre in his life. Slim hears the sound of a heart monitor beating change to a flat line. This soundscape suggests that even the most advanced science and life support cannot bring Dre back. Only his love for hip hop, articulated by his most loyal protégé and polyethnic son Slim Shady, can resuscitate him and the music that brought them together.

Clips of Dre's family, music, and tour videos flash in the background as Slim begins the first verse. These images symbolize that it is not just Slim who needs Dre to move forward but hip hop itself. Slim begins by reminding Dre that he is keeping his promise of public acknowledgement for Dre's impact on his life. Slim is desperate to save Dre's life now the same way Dre saved his in 1998 by believing in him and in his musical capabilities. Slim is grateful to return the favor by contributing to Dre's legacy by way of his final studio album *Detox*.

Slim then jogs Dre's memory of their shared vision. Slim is desperate to understand why Dre does not respond. He cannot understand why Dre does not want to move forward. Shady then remembers why. Dre is now a father without his eldest son and namesake because his son died in 2008 of a drug overdose. Dre cannot get over the fact that his son chose drugs over his father's love. Shady understands Dre's deep sense of grief. Shady is Dre's mirror image because he is an eldest son and namesake (allegedly) rejected by his own biological father because of alcoholism. Slim, a former drug addict and present-day father, was able to break the cycle of addiction and rejection in his own life because of the loyalty that fatherhood created (i.e., the love he has for his own biological and adopted children). In the same way, Slim now plays the role of loyal son to break the cycle of loss and despair for his own adoptive father Dre. "I don't think you realize what you mean to me," screams Slim as images from one of Dre's biggest videos, NWA's "Express Yourself" (1989), play in the background. The message is clear. Hip hop needs Dre to express himself once again.

When the second verse begins, we find Slim standing next to Dre, as Dre is suspended in an isolation tank filled with life-giving amniotic-like fluid. Dre is still asleep, so Shady becomes even more sincere and intense. Slim is in pain because Dre cannot see his own creative power. In this way, he is highlighting his adopted father's own wounds and signifying that this coma is a means of coping with those wounds. Shady can see things plainly and has confidence in Dre, yet Shady does not know what to do in this situation because he is not used to playing the fatherly role in this relationship. He reminds Dre how their relationship works: Dre is the mentor, and Shady is the follower. Then Shady begins to list the many reasons why. First, Dre believed in Shady when no one else would or could. Second, Dre risked his status and career for Shady, a fact that brings Shady to tears even as he recounts it over a decade later. Third, Dre saved Slim's life. Slim Shady came from and had nothing before Dre entered his life. Fourth, Slim is currently dying without Dre since Dre is the only one who can fill the void that fatherlessness opened in Slim's persona. Slim begs Dre to come back because he is not sure whether he can make it without Dre. Remember, Slim is always and only a son who cannot take another father's rejection. At these words, Dre's fingers begin to move. Slim's pain and passion create a quaking within Dre, and he responds. Dre's reaction suggests that he understands the father hunger Shady knows all too well. The significance of their father–son relationship is solidified, and the men emerge with a bond reinforced from the experience of relying on each other for survival.

The third verse opens with a change of soundscape and perspective. The flat line representing Dre's near-death state turns into a heartbeat, and Dre wakes up from his coma. Dre has to relearn how to walk, talk, and rap. Again, Slim relates to this experience because he underwent the same type of rehabilitation at age 10 when he spent 10 days in a coma after being beaten by a school bully. Slim looks on as Dre opens his eyes, takes his first steps and, perhaps more importantly, recites his first new rhymes. Dre responds to Slim's verses line-by-line, beginning by stating that he will never forget the first time they met. He even remembers what Slim was wearing: "a yellow jump suit." He remembers how impressed he was with Slim's talent and vision from the very beginning, so much so that it cost him many friends from Death Row

Records who were unwilling to go along for the ride. And now, in the end, when he needs his friends the most, he finds no one there. No one but Slim that is. And that is where Dre's role as Shady's father is solidified: in that moment between Shady being among the last people Dre thought about before the crash and the first person there and the first voice he hears to stimulate his recovery. In this way, Shady represents Dre's legacy, his "Aftermath," the force hip hop fans will continue to reckon with even after Dre makes this one last record. Dre affirms that Slim is indeed his polyethnic hip hop son. "I Need A Doctor" reveals that to understand Slim Shady (the polyethnic adolescent) and Eminem (the tan man he is becoming), we must understand Dre as the primary father figure in his life.

FAMILY VALUES

There are three major lessons to be learned from Dre's and Slim's very public polyethnic father–son relationship. The first lesson is about rebuilding a family in which one can love and be loved and protected. Dre's flashbacks to his NWA days suggest that an alternative is needed to gangsta rap personas and the thug lifestyles such personas reflect as a notion of family. For his part, Slim too provides an alternative to taking the route that 2Pac and Eazy chose, which is a literal dead end. Here Dre and Slim have followed their formula of putting their pasts and their dysfunctions on display to reach out to audiences, who may be struggling with similar issues. In this way, the pair continues to prove their naysayers wrong because they have learned from their own and others' mistakes and they have learned to rely on each other. In fact, this reliance has taught each man how to meet more mature needs and heal old wounds. Importantly, healing is dramatized through father–son communication. This is why we see Slim tell Dre exactly how he feels about him, that he will not accept any attempt by Dre (even an unconscious one) to dissolve the family unit. Slim will always need his father as his compass. Because of the room to grow provided by their relationship, father and son can begin to let go of the pain of the past while honoring its value.

The second lesson to be learned from Slim's and Dre's polyethnic father–son relationship is about change. In "I Need a Doctor," we can see how the texture of personal experience and open heart-to-heart communication can bring about change within an individual. In addition, we can see how that change can lead to social transformation through music. What becomes clear is that change hinges on the intentionality of our encounters. Fathers must be intentional in mentoring their sons and sons must be intentional in expressing love and admiration for their fathers. Dre and Shady have been nothing but intentional in the development of their relationship with each other and with their fans. Their intentionality provides them with a reason to keep inspiring one another and the millions of youth who listen to them. Both artists understand the power of hip hop to influence young people's personal lives (who they emulate and identify with) and political decisions (who they choose to love and support). Thus, the father–son duo is saying that society's racism, fatherlessness, and stereotypes are issues that they have taken personally, and through their changes of heart they have been able to enact a model for personal and collective change. The message is clear: promoting caring family relationships is a powerful way to change society at large.

The third lesson to be learned from this unique father–son relationship is about empowerment. The personal change and familial developments that have occurred in "I Need a Doctor" allow Dre and Slim to overcome many of society's limitations. For instance, the pair has overcome impoverished and dysfunctional family backgrounds. They have transcended the boundaries of gangsta rapper personas by boldly expressing their emotions and their reliance on one another. Now, neither Dre nor Shady has to walk alone or look back at the past with dread. Stepping through and echoing the words of Martin Luther King's "I Have A Dream" speech, as displayed through and sampled by the flashbacks to NWA's "Express Yourself " in "I Need A Doctor," they are able to march forward into a new and empowered way of thinking and living by remembering and sampling from the past, indicating that what hurts us can heal us too.

Larger-scaled social empowerment is achieved in a context where race and racial politics are acknowledged and where people of different racial backgrounds see each other as and function as a family. Throughout their relationship Slim and Dre are inviting audiences to free themselves of conventional limits that define family. For Slim and Dre, family does not necessarily include those to whom they are biologically related or racially resembled. So, Slim's hunger for a father is not just the story of one white guy and one black guy or even of two talented rappers. Instead, it is the story of a polyethnic son from an empowered (even if imagined) interracial family who speaks and acts without the disabilities of shame and colorblindness.

CHAPTER 3
The Shady Bunch

Slim's lyrics prove that children cannot raise themselves. Without caring parents or mentors it is exceedingly difficult for children to grow into healthy, well-adjusted adults. So far, we have seen how Slim and his mother Debbie Nelson have battled in life, in lyrics, and in court. We have seen how Slim and his biological father Marshall Mathers II have responded remotely to one another through the press even while they have never spoken. And we have also seen how Slim's real parental guidance, which came from hip hop, was solidified when he became part of Dr. Dre's polyethnic hip hop family as an adopted son. Now, we will see how Slim has extended that family through his own resilience and how he has given voice to that resilience in his music. He is open about his attempts to forge a new family by twice marrying and divorcing Kimberly Ann Scott (aka Kim) and adopting Alaina (the biological daughter of Kim's twin sister), Nathan (his younger half-brother), and Whitney (Kim's second child by another man). We will pay special attention to Slim's relationship with his biological daughter Hailie Jade Scott (Mathers).

Hailie was born on December 25, 1995. She joins her father in the hook for "My Dad's Gone Crazy" (2002) and for a few lines on "Hailie's Revenge" (2003). She also features prominently in a number of other songs, most notably "Just the Two of Us" (1997) on *The Slim Shady EP,* which was later renamed "'97 Bonnie and Clyde" (1999) on *The Slim Shady LP.* The song "Hailie's Song" (2002) on *The Eminem Show,* "Mockingbird" (2004) on the album *Encore,* the single "When I'm Gone" (2005), and the song "Going Through Changes" (2010) on the *Recovery* album are dedicated to Hailie.

Throughout each of these songs, Hailie is more than a daughter. She is a symbol that forces her father to confront the interconnections of his troubled childhood, his relationship with ex-wife Kim, and the physical and social displacements he experienced from them as a result of his celebrity. Slim uses his lyrics as a way to bring the past into the present, and his lyrics dedicated to Hailie are presented as acts of remembrance, resilience, and reproduction. As a child who grew up in a troubled family, Slim bears the scars of suffering, devastation, and loss. As an adult who is in the process of healing, he transforms these childhood scars into badges of honor by appealing to images of his own daughter in songs like "'97 Bonnie and Clyde," "Kim," "Hailie's Song," and "Mockingbird." In the process, he creates the intimacy and security of the past he never had, adapting the images of parent and child for his own purposes in pursuit of a new definition of family. This fatherly sensibility must be why the real Slim Shady beat out Barack Obama on a celebrity Dad survey compiled by social network aggregator Starcount in June 2012.

SHADY'S BABY

"Hailie's Song" and "Mockingbird" are first and foremost lullabies. And like any lullaby, these are important parenting tools. Lullabies are songs of rest, of bonding, and of love. As noted by Gail De Vos, Merle Harris, and Celia Barker Lottridge in *Telling Tales: Storytelling in the Family,* parents from many cultures sing these soothing songs to their children. The beauty of the lullaby is that "the rhythm and repetitiveness . . . allows your voice, even if you don't have perfect pitch, tone, or rhythm, to sound beautiful to babies and toddlers because [it is] sung by the people they love."[1] Lullabies play on the fact that no other instrument is as intimate or nuanced as the human voice.

As is to be expected, in Slim's hands, the lullaby is a darker experience as the form, content, and delivery are altered to reflect the sadness his family life evokes. In a recent study of Slim's lullabies, cultural critic Steen Kaagaard Nielsen found that

> the melodrama in these songs, whether small or grand, tragic or comical, results from the fact that the dysfunctional family unit portrayed fails to live out the dream of the stereotypical patriarchal, nuclear family held by the traditional head of family through the eyes of whom all songs are seen and told. To the narrator the basic conflict is one between family protector (the first person narrator) and home wrecker (his adulterous wife) with their offspring (a baby daughter) in need of protection.[2]

To emphasize his family's emotional rollercoaster, Slim's lullabies go back and forth between minor and major keys. The major keys represent

Hailie's presence while the minor keys represent her absence. What is more, a father rather than a mother sings these lullabies to underscore the absence of maternal forces from Slim's family. The father sings because, in "'97 Bonnie and Clyde," he murdered the mother and disposed of her body at the bottom of a lake. In many ways, therefore, Slim is singing these lullabies both to his own daughter and to himself by taking on the role of the parent neither has known.

Slim's first and perhaps most famous lullaby is "'97 Bonnie and Clyde." It is also one of his most extreme songs, which was adapted from the *Slim Shady EP*'s "Just The Two of Us." The song's title paints the father–daughter duo as outlaws in the aftermath of the mother's murder. The song's loving chorus, "just the two of us," is sampled from Grover Washington Jr.'s 1980 ballad as an expression of daddy–daughter affection. The song also serves as inspiration for the cover of *The Slim Shady LP*. A white woman's legs and bare feet protrude from the trunk of a car in the foreground. Father and daughter stand together on a pier from which the woman's body is about to be dumped in the middle ground. A full moon reflecting onto a large lake appears in the background.

"'97 Bonnie and Clyde" is delivered in song, speech, and rap. Slim plays the part of the father, Hailie plays the part of the daughter (with gurgling samples), and a lifeless Kim plays the role of the dead mother. With the scene and characters in place, the song begins with the sound of dragging something heavy and dumping it into the trunk of a car. Slim begins with a message to Hailie, telling his daughter that he always wants to be in her life and that no one, not even her mother, will keep them apart. He then straps her into her car seat and begins driving. Like any young child, Hailie is curious about her surroundings. When she picks up his bloody knife, he says it is a toy. When she does not quite believe him, he comforts her and asks her to help him play in the sand. When she starts looking around for her mother, he says, "Mom wants to show us how far she can float." When Hailie wants to know what is on her mother's throat, he tells her it is just a painless scratch and that what Hailie thinks is blood is just ketchup. He promises Hailie that her mother will wash it off in the water while father and daughter wait for her. Just the two of them.

Then Slim tells Hailie about life and afterlife and that "Dada" is probably going to be punished for what he has done and therefore will not be going to heaven. You see, Hailie's mother Kim is pregnant with another man's child. Slim explains in simple terms what has happened, that Kim has betrayed their family, and Hailie tries to climb up and out of the car seat. He comforts her and puts her to sleep. He wakes her up when they get to the water with baby talk. He tells Hailie not to cry. Mommy is just asleep; she is not dead. Then, he asks Hailie to play a game with him. Part of the game is getting Hailie to tie a rope around a rock and dump Kim's body in the lake on the count of three. "Wee!" They shout as Kim's body makes a big splash and gets submerged. Now their problems are over: no more stepdad, no new brother, no more restraining orders, and no more unhappiness. Slim and Hailie get two more things out of the trunk, the lifeless bodies of Mommy's new boyfriend and his young son, and dump them along with Kim. Finally, the father–daughter duo is free and safe. The themes of freedom and safety mark this song as a lullaby in spite of its dark overtones. In addition, the predictable and repetitive melody lends anchors the harrowing situation described by the lyrics. By the end of the song the music has soothed the child and she is calm. Hailie can rest assured that her father will always be present in her life and he will stop at nothing to keep them together. Hailie has also learned that if she wants to survive in this world she should not follow her mother's example.

"Kim" is the prequel to "'97 Bonnie and Clyde." In it, Slim plays the roles of himself and Kim. "Kim" is definitely not easy listening though it does open with a cute vignette between Shady and Hailie where he addresses her lovingly with baby talk. Suddenly, the mood shifts, and we realize that Shady has caught Kim cheating and is about to kill her, her lover, and his young son. Throughout the entire song, Slim tortures Kim by telling her exactly how he is going to carry out the murders and cover them up. He plans to make it look like Kim killed her lover and his son in a fit of violent rage and then killed herself. He describes this in a chilling fashion: crying, whining, rapping, pleading, talking, and singing. The song ends where "'97 Bonnie and Clyde" picks up, with the same sounds of dragging Kim's body and putting it in the car's trunk. Then, we realize Hailie was there the whole time. Hailie saw everything. And Shady hopes she has learned the not-so-subtle lesson he is continually teaching her: under no circumstances is she to be like Kim, the cheating wife and mother. Instead, she is to stay with her father as his innocent baby girl, a nonsexual and therefore nondangerous female, to whom Shady can confess undying love in the same breath as he narrates a chilling murder.

For his part, Slim sings about his love for his daughter very tenderly in "Hailie's Song" (2002), and, as music critic David Stubbs notes in *Eminem: The Stories Behind Every Song,* "it's fair to say that he takes to singing like a cat out of water—not well."[3] To make up for the rapper's inability to carry a tune, and to express the sadness and happiness that are intertwined in this moment, the song goes back and forth from major to minor keys. Despite his lack of talent as a singer, his singing voice does get the point across. He is completely overwhelmed by love for his child when he sings in major keys, and at the same time, he cannot let go of the bitterness he feels toward Hailie's mother Kim when he sings in minor keys. This theme is not new, as it inspired the two controversial songs we have just discussed, "'97 Bonnie and Clyde" (1999) and "Kim" (2000). These songs were written after Kim left Slim and took Hailie with her.

> According to Eminem, Kim had developed . . . contempt for Em's inability to provide for the family. Em knew it was true. "It was like, fuck, I can't afford to buy my daughter diapers," he told *Rolling Stone.* Yet, even though they reunited . . . he never forgot or forgave this act of betrayal.[4]

Slim imagined Kim's murder as an act of revenge in "'97 Bonnie and Clyde" and took that murder to repugnant heights in "Kim." In each of these songs, he coos at his daughter and addresses her lovingly with baby talk while at the same time addressing Kim chillingly as he kills her with his words and his hands. Naturally, songs like these put further distance between Slim and Kim, even causing her to attempt suicide after a performance in which the rapper kicked a doll version of her across the stage while on tour. According to *People Magazine,* Shady physically assaulted "Kim," represented by an inflatable sex doll, then turned her over to the audience for more of the same.

> [A]t a concert in Portland, Oregon, Eminem told the crowd, "I know a lot of you might have heard or seen something about me and my wife having marital problems. But that shit is not true. All is good between me and my wife. In fact, she's here tonight. Where's Kim?" He then pulled out an inflatable sex doll, simulated an act of oral sex and tossed it to the crowd, which batted "Kim" around like a beach ball.[5]

After the couple divorced for the second time, Kim was interviewed by *20/20 In Touch,* during which she described Slim as a less than perfect husband but "an excellent father" who is an active presence in Hailie's life.[6] That fatherly side makes its appearance in "Hailie's Song," where the violence to which Hailie has borne witness is replaced by a more mature attitude of reflection and resilience.

As "Hailie's Song" begins, Slim has just been awarded custody of Hailie. He begins by singing about needing to find a reason to live and about how Hailie has given him that reason. He wonders why he is plagued by feelings of insecurity and doubt and asks whether he is insane. She is the antidote to his craziness and neediness. He has realized that even though life can bring a string of traumas and disappointments, there will always be a solution and a reason to go on. For Slim, the only solution and reason is Hailie. He continues by describing what it feels like to have the pressure of "everyone" in his family looking to him for support and guidance. And just when he thinks that things cannot get worse, he thinks about his daughter—and she returns.

The next verse opens as Slim marvels at the way Hailie is growing up. He goes on to address criticisms from those who misunderstand him and his lyrics. They drive him insane and that insanity, coupled with his own insecurities, makes him hopeless. He does not think he will survive. However, all of that changes when he regains custody of his daughter. The world makes sense when he connects with her, and order is restored to his world. Part of restoring order requires him to set the record straight about the real Slim Shady. He is rapping and not singing this time. And he is not an absentee father like Marshall Mathers II. He is a man from a troubled family and not a criminal. He is a proud and loving father trapped in an unhappy marriage. He recounts all that he endured at Kim's hands including lies and jail time, physical and emotional abuse. And though he wishes he could have done things differently, perhaps even chosen another mother for his child, he eventually stops. He returns to reality and realizes that it is this crazy path that has brought him his beloved daughter. Then he feels the weight of pressure lift because he has stayed the course. He reminds himself that everything has changed because Hailie is back in his life. The fact that he and Hailie are reunited is proof of his resilience, and by the end of the song, Hailie knows Dad is "a soldier." His daughter understands his resilience and that the pair will never be separated again because her father will always fight for her. As the song ends, Slim sings again. He blows his daughter a kiss and sends her this message: "Daddy's here and I ain't goin' nowhere, baby. I love you."

"Mockingbird" picks up right where "Hailie's Song" leaves off. Only now, two more years have passed. Slim and Kim have reconciled and split up again, after she accused the rapper of putting their daughter in danger because he included her voice on an underground track called "Hailie's Revenge" (2003), which fueled the industry beef between Ja-Rule and 50 Cent. Slim's inability to consider the consequences for such actions have left him alone again, and he composes "Mockingbird" to document the experience.

The video for "Mockingbird" starts as a home movie reel with Hailie dressed up as a clown for Halloween. These introductory images are paired with the dark room in which Slim watches the reel with a sad look on his face. Then the music starts. The tones of this lullaby tell us that the song is about innocence lost, separation, and caring. The quick montage that follows reflects the change in Slim and his family before and after fame (dark hair, shots of him with Kim and baby Hailie, versus peroxide blonde hair, no Kim, and an older Hailie). As he watches the reels, he provides Hailie with some fatherly advice: "What Daddy always tell you? Straighten up little soldier. Stiffen up that upper lip. What you crying about? You got me."

This introduction brings up the image of a soldier to make three primary points about resilience. First, Slim accepts that his troubled family has left its mark and that the scars may heal even if they do not disappear. Second, it signals Slim's desire to break the cycle of his family's troubles and put the past in its place. Finally, it tells his daughter Hailie that she is part of a new family that will eventually live well because her father takes responsibility for his role in their lives. Singing this sad song to an empty room reminds the viewers and listeners that Slim's relationship to his family is strong, complex, and distanced. And as the lyrics come pouring out in rap and in song, they reflect his attempts to come to terms with his conflicting desires for an unbroken home life (i.e., reunions with his parents and ex-wife) even as he remains aware of that life's destructive potential. Slim turns to the image of his parent–child relationship with Hailie as a way to negotiate the destabilized relationship to reality that came first through his own experiences with his troubled youth and then through the demands of fame.

The song's first verse is about Kim's and Slim's tumultuous relationship and how their struggles have affected their daughter. Slim recognizes and can see through Hailie's resilient exterior. He can see that she wants to cry, and he knows why. She is seeing everything he saw as a child—broken homes, parents fighting and leaving—everything he never wanted her to see. Here, Slim mourns another broken home that repeats the cycle of troubled family relationships in which he was raised. He tells her to stay strong even though he and Kim are away. He and Kim are only available through media. Slim is away because his job is so demanding, and she sees him mostly on television. Meanwhile, Kim has become headline news. She is in and out of trouble with the law due to charges of drug possession and maintaining a drug house after a party she threw at a Warren, Michigan Candlewood Suites hotel in September 2003. In November, Slim was granted custody of Hailie, and Kim ran away instead of going to court. In February 2004, she violated probation by failing a urine test. Rather than lashing out against his estranged wife as in previous songs, in "Mockingbird," Slim turns their family's misfortune into a positive sign of growth. He tells Hailie that even though her parents can never be together again, they both love her and will be a part of her life.

The second verse tells the history of this family's life. Slim tells Hailie how drastically their life went from rags to riches, from being unhappy because they were unable to buy Christmas presents or live in a decent neighborhood to being unhappy because even though they could now have anything they wanted, they just could not manage to be together. He tells her how he and Kim tried to cope in their own ways through infidelity and substance abuse and how they just lost control over their situations. Slim was arrested for allegedly attacking a man he caught kissing Kim and for brandishing a gun to intimidate Douglas Dail of Insane Clown Posse. He apologizes because he could not shield his daughter from any of this. He realizes that this failure is exactly why he is sitting alone in an empty house with only these memories to keep him company. Then, when he looks at the photo album titled "Daddy's Little Angels," he realizes how much time has passed and how things have changed. He comforts Hailie and himself by saying that Daddy will always be present in their lives and that Mama is only absent temporarily.

The song closes with the chorus from "Hush Little Baby." While the original lullaby's lyrics promise many rewards to the baby if she will be quiet, in "Mockingbird," Slim promises Hailie that she and her mother will be all right if they can exercise some resilience and just make it through the confusion that has engulfed their lives. Later, Slim promises Hailie that he will take revenge on mockingbirds that will not sing and diamond merchants who do not deliver the goods. This way, she and all the other children who identify with Slim will know that he is a serious father figure, a protective force with which to be reckoned. The message is clear: for some people, the mockingbird will never sing and the diamond ring will never shine, but a loyal parent can step up to the plate to provide emotional and financial support. Slim will now fill that role for his daughter and adopted children (niece Alaina, brother Nathan, and Kim's daughter from an affair Whitney) and just as his own million gangsta rapper fathers did for him when he was a troubled youth, Slim will always be there: Slim's babies are loved.

SHADY'S LITTLE LADY

As Hailie grows older, she takes on an even more significant role in Slim's lyrics. She is always his muse. As an infant, she represents all the potentials and possibilities that passed her parents by. As a child, she represents a reason for her father to succeed and survive. As a teen, she becomes her father's conscience and, in some ways, the reason he can finally be himself. We see this transformation in "When I'm Gone" (2005).

The song is one part lullaby and one part last will and testament. The video opens in a meeting of what appears to be Narcotics Anonymous. We watch as a former addict who has been clean for six years declares how happy he and his family are now that he is "not . . . that person anymore." This resonates with Slim who takes the podium next and introduces himself to the group as Marshall. This introduction is significant because it is a serious rejoinder to the sarcastic lyric delivered in "Just Don't Give A Fuck" (1999), where the rapper mimics the introduction he might give at a future meeting of Alcoholics Anonymous and talks about a strange unnamed disease he carries. In "When I'm Gone," things are definitely different. The platinum blonde fire-breathing monster Slim is nowhere to be found, except in Hailie's memories. In his place stands Marshall Mathers, who has questions, ranging from the experience of unconditional love to the experiences of spitefulness and resentment, which need to be answered.

He asks the audience how love could turn into resentment without him even noticing. He then answers the questions by saying that he was too busy being Slim and attending to his own wounds from childhood to invest the time and energy it took to be a true father. He always thought of himself as his daughter's protector, but he never thought he would have to protect her from himself or Slim. Slim was so obsessed with providing material goods for his family that he did not realize his family really needed emotional support more. He questions the real good Slim has done him outside of the material realm when he realizes that Slim gave Marshall Mathers an excuse to verbally and physically abuse Kim, who looks exactly like Hailie. How could he love the younger version, Hailie, so much and hate the original, Kim? The answer is Slim. Slim is a crazy hypocrite who causes his daughter pain because he would not attend to her needs. From now on, he will only write songs about how much he loves her.

Marshall pays tribute to Slim as the one who "made" him and admits that he is now intent on putting Slim to rest with a lullaby "rock-a-bye-baby." At the end of this song, Slim, Marshall's needy adolescent self, will fall cradle and all. The chorus gives Hailie instructions for how to proceed when Slim is gone. She is not to mourn but to smile. She is to know that Slim passed on and did not feel any pain. Slim Shady is gone. Marshall and Eminem no longer have the desire to be Slim because that persona is not who they really are.

The second verse describes a bad dream in which Hailie cries and screams as Slim pushes her on a swing. She does not want her father to perform anymore. She is foreshadowing Kim's suicide attempt after one of his performances. When he tries to console her and tell her that he will stop performing and stay with her, she tells him that she no longer believes him. He has been singing this same song for too long now. Hailie tries to keep him from leaving. She even barricades the door. But when she realizes that she cannot stop Slim, she gives him a locket with her picture inside that she says will protect him from the stage. When he looks up, Hailie is gone, and he is about to break his promise again by performing. He tells himself that this will be his final performance and that he needs everything to go perfectly so the crowd will know he loves them. He leaves his bedroom, walks out onto the stage, finds a microphone in his hand, and begins to perform.

As the next verse starts, Slim is still performing before a crowd of 60,000 in Stockholm, Sweden. He is rapping in his signature *Eminem Show* blue suit with red tie and white shirt. The crowd is eating it up. But there is something different going on here. Marshall and Slim are disconnecting. Slim is giving a flawless performance, but Marshall is peeking out and is not happy with what he sees. While scanning the crowd, a young girl catches Marshall's eye. She looks exactly like Hailie. Wait. She is Hailie. Hailie has managed to follow him halfway around the world to get Slim's attention and tell him that Kim's suicide attempt is real. She tells her father that she was right not to believe him because he is a liar. They exchange words but Slim or Marshall can only speak to her through a microphone, suggesting an inability to detach from his role as performer Hailie screams and Slim or Marshall is silenced. She tells him that she still loves him and wants to give him a token of her esteem, a gold coin that reads "Number One Dad." This is obviously intended as irony and as a cruel joke. After handing over the coin, she announces her departure from her father's life. She tells him to keep performing because he obviously loves the crowd more than he loves his own family. She also tells him that he should just swallow another pill if he is ridden by guilt and cannot sleep. These biting words refer to the rapper's stay at rehab for his dependency on sleeping pills. Not only does Hailie say that his addiction put him out of his misery, but she also sarcastically reminds him that taking pills will also help him keep up with Slim's reputation for substance abuse and living out his lyrics. With those cutting words, Hailie disappears.

Slim finds himself backstage now. The curtain has closed and he is disoriented. He thinks he sees Kim and Hailie, but he cannot be sure. All he can see clearly is a loaded gun. He picks up the gun and sees Slim's reflection in the mirror. Then he puts the gun to his head and pulls the trigger while screaming, "Die Slim!" The mirror breaks into a million pieces and everything goes quiet. Slim is gone. His life flashes before Marshall's eyes. The plane Slim was going to take home crashes and burns. Slim is at peace. Next, Marshall hears his alarm clock go off. When he awakens, he hears birds singing, sees Hailie playing, and finds Kim to give her a kiss. This is the first time in the song that he makes use of all his senses at the same time, suggesting that he is finally truly awake and alive. When he finally greets his daughter, she looks at him knowingly, blows him a kiss, smiles, and winks at her half-sister Whitney. These gestures suggest that these events were not just a dream. Hailie knows Slim is gone, and she is following his orders. She will not grieve but smile. But the audience knows Slim is not really gone. He is still alive under Marshall's covered head. His presence is still felt because the curtain closes and the crowd continues to applaud.

"When I'm Gone" stands in sharp contrast to "Hailie's Song" and "Mockingbird" because Hailie is talking back. She is no longer a passive receptacle for her father's love. Her words and actions indicate that she thinks and feels for herself. And, she thinks and speaks to remind the adults around her that parents earn their children's love and respect when they keep their promises. As Hailie gets older, her father realizes that his time with her is precious and fleeting. He realizes that only he (Marshall Mathers) has the power to make sure he does not lose his wife and children to Slim and the entertainment industry he has conquered. He realizes that it is time for the real Slim Shady to lie down and the real Marshall Mathers to stand up, for it is only when Slim is silenced that Mathers and his family can grow up.

WILL THE REAL HAILIE JADE PLEASE STAND UP?

At the time of this writing, Hailie is 17-years-old, and she is now allegedly talking back to people other than her father. Hailie might actually be talking to the world, and she might be doing it through the microblogging site Twitter. Twitter allows "tweeps" (aka Twitter users) to post quick 140-character updates, or "tweets," to a network of followers. Twitter asks participants to tell followers what they are doing—and Hailie is responding. Her answers take the form of a "feed," a frequently updated stream of messages about everyday life, breaking news, photos, interesting links, haiku poetry, and commentary on life. Like all tweets, Hailie's can be posted and read from the web, SMS, or third-party clients for desktop computers, smartphones, and other devices. Being so accessible to the public has put Hailie squarely within her father's sacred territory: sparking controversy.

In March 2011, a Twitter account authored by Hailie appeared. It was taken down shortly thereafter due to pressure from Slim's management team. Announcing her return to the microblogging website later that year, @Angry_Blonde declares herself: "I am back to twitter!! The REAL Hailie Mathers I have NO myspace! only Facebook and twitter."[7] @Angry_Blonde retweets support for her father, talks of him as being "the best," and generally appears to interact positively with her 94,000-plus followers. She seems to be normal, at least on the surface, as a scan of her Tweets reveals only one inflammatory outburst when she referred to Taylor Swift as a "whore" for dating a singer from the pop group One Direction. Mostly, the content is about what a wonderful father she has. It appears to be very important to @Angry_Blonde that her followers know that she is a regular girl whose father is really just a regular guy. What is more, she defends her father from critics and is open about not betraying his trust by taking on an online persona. In doing so, she creates a new expectation of intimacy between herself, her father, and his fans. @Angry_Blonde is doing the emotional work of maintaining her ever-expanding network of followers, most of whom are also her father's fans, and making them want to know more about her and—less about her father—as an individual. @Angry_Blonde's followers should be following her because they want to know about her and not about her famous father.

@Angry_Blonde is quick to announce that she has a private life with access to her father and that her thousands of followers do not have access to her private life or her father. Protective tweets like these reinforce the boundaries of @Angry_Blonde's status as loyal daughter, normal teenage girl, and budding celebrity. As a result, @Angry_ Blonde is showing us that any regular person can become a celebrity in her own right if she knows the right people and is a savvy user of today's social media.

Here's the thing: @Angry_Blonde is not Hailie. A publicist for the real Slim Shady confirmed to *The Huffington Post UK* that the Twitter account was a fraud and that Hailie is not on Twitter at all.[8] Within minutes, Paul Rosenberg (Eminem's manager) declared the account "100% fake" via Twitter. The @Angry_Blonde profile was promptly deleted, again. But it is now back online and as gushing as ever. In fact, after being duped by and creating a frenzy over @Angry_Blonde's account, *E!*'s editor had to admit that something interesting is going on here: "Hats off to @Angry_Blonde, the keeper of the most elaborate imposter account we've seen yet."[9] @Angry_Blonde is successful because she mastered some of the Twitterverse's top techniques. She uses public acknowledgment, in the form of @replies, to connect with followers. When followers receive @replies back, they are publicized within the fan community. And when @replies include Slim's @Eminem handle, they get even more exposure. In keeping with a celebrity persona, @Angry_Blonde's public acknowledgment of friends, peers, and celebrities is almost never critical. Instead, she mentions fans to show her connection and availability, give back to loyal followers, and manage her popularity. She follows musicians like Rihanna, Kesha, Adele, Nicki Minaj, and Royce Da 5'9". She follows tech gurus such as Noah Everett, the founder of TwitPic. And she follows magazines like the Spain-based *Pacha* and young pop stars like Justin Bieber and Odd Future's Earl Sweatshirt and Tyler, the Creator, which appeal to her demographic and carry the whiff of product placement.

Here's the other thing: @Angry_Blonde (or @Angry-Blonde1) is not the only not-Hailie on Twitter: meet @hailiejade_x. In May 2012, *Buzzfeed* published photos from what was reportedly the now-17-year-old's Twitter feed. The photos posted to this account of Hailie do bear a resemblance to the famous rapper, and they also appear to be linked to two Facebook fan pages dedicated to Hailie Jade Scott Mathers.

Throughout these pages, @hailiejade_x mimics Slim's trademark angry stare and has mastered the female version of his hip hop swag. She even posted pictures of herself drinking Smirnoff Ice with some friends. Once these pictures surfaced, Paul Rosenberg (Eminem's manager) promptly responded by tweeting that Hailie does not have a Twitter account. For his part, Nathan Kane Mathers (Eminem's brother) went even further by refusing to answer any questions tweeps asked about his famous brother and niece via Twitter.

Despite denials and evasions by those close to the family, which I have playfully dubbed the Shady Bunch, questions remain. Who is the real Hailie Jade Scott Mathers? What if the tweeter known as "@hailiejade_x" or "@Angry_Blonde" really is Eminem's daughter? Could it be that the media coverage attracted by her tweets made the original Angry Blonde stand up? Or could he be angry that several of the pictures depict his underage daughter drinking illegally? Is the rapper just horrified that she tweeted about teen idols that would indeed make Slim puke?

But there are other, more serious, questions about the emergence and popularity of Twitter's not-Hailies that need answering. Who are these fake-Hailies? Could they be friends of the real Hailie or could they be people she has hired? After all, it is common practice for celebrities to hire ghost tweeters or have others manage their accounts. It could be that the real Hailie lacks the time or interest to maintain an account but views it as a good marketing tool for future entertainment endeavors. Another possibility is that the real Hailie may have hired a fake-Hailie to avoid her own father's supervision. Clearly her father and his management discourage direct access to fans, and they may have even expressly forbid her candid tweeting. The fake-Hailies could be a way for the real Hailie to assert some autonomy without disobeying her father's orders.

Another question begging to be answered is this: If "@hailiejade_x" and "@Angry_Blonde" are indeed fake Hailies, and if they have not been hired by the real Hailie, then what are they after? On one hand, they could be after fame and celebrity for themselves. If this is the case, then we can understand their Twitter accounts as a way to imitate Slim by using these Twitter handles as personas. It can also be argued that "@hailiejade_x" and "@Angry_Blonde" see their followers as a fan base and maintain popularity by presenting themselves carefully so that their images can be easily consumed by the masses. On the other hand, the fake Hailies could be after a more personal connection. Specifically, they could be after the kind of father–daughter bond and unconditional love from the real Slim Shady that the real Hailie gets.

Take this doting tweet from a follower: "@Angry_Blonde your dad is awesome and you must be for being his daughter."[10] Messages like these ensure that the real Hailie becomes the face for everything fake-Hailies do not have. If the fake-Hailies do not have dedicated parental love and guidance in real lives, they will settle for the admiration of followers that comes from being a cultural phenomenon, just like the real Slim Shady. This kind of thinking is exactly what motivated Marshall Mathers to take on the Slim Shady persona in the first place. If the fake-Hailies are also victims of parenting and if they have not been nurtured at home, then they could be using these Twitter accounts and the followers they get for validation. And the fake-Hailies' statuses— not full-blown celebrity, but not fan—is made clear through the tweets. The fake-Hailies might simply want to be part of something bigger or greater than they believe they are in real life.

The fake-Hailies also force us to consider the impact of gender and misogyny on identity formation. As Hailie is the only woman who has fared well in the rapper's songbook, these young women might be looking to identify with the rapper's only positive representation of femininity. It should not be surprising that these young women do not want to identify with Slim's mother, lovers, or ex-wife after he has trashed them so brazenly over the years. Because of their ages, the female demographic that @Angry_Blonde and @hailiejade_x represent has not lived in a world in which the real Slim Shady is unknown. Therefore, it could be that this demographic is eager to identify with and as Hailie precisely because our culture finds it so difficult to address its taste for Slim's deep contempt for and violent rage against other women in his life.

A defense of Slim's mad masculinity is most clearly seen in the Twitter feeds of the fake-Hailies and in media coverage of the rapper's career. This stance indicates that society is unwilling to grapple with the scarier aspects of the rapper's lyrics because misogyny and violence against women continue to be popular with a certain audience. In a 2009 *New York Times* article, Jon Pareles explains why:

> Both Eminem and Dr. Dre . . . concluded the world wanted more Slim Shady. "I talked to my son about it," said Dr. Dre, "and he was like: 'The kids want to hear him act the fool. We want to hear him be crazy, we want to hear him be Slim Shady and nothing else.'"[11]

Slim resonates with this demographic precisely because he is working out parental issues in public, in horrific and often exaggerated ways that relate to gender and society. On one level, Slim is challenging deep norms about attachment parenting, a philosophy that says children form strong emotional bonds with their parents in ways that have lifelong consequences, and doing vicious things with it. By acknowledging how messed up his (and to a lesser degree his daughter's) upbringing was, he is beating the idea of attachment parenting to a pulp. He is saying that some children do not need their parents even if they are around and engaged and that other children will turn out exactly like their parents did even if they are estranged. In doing so, Slim argues that parents contribute to the moral lapses of their children, which is why children should rebel. Like father, like daughter, or so it goes.

On another level, however, it seems that Slim's rebellious message is received differently on the basis of gender. While young males want more of Slim, young females want to be Hailie as a way to shield themselves from the ongoing epidemic of men's violence against women in lyrics (especially violence against women men know). If nothing else, Slim is Hailie's unwavering protector, and presenting oneself as his daughter is one way of protecting oneself from misogynistic lyrics aimed at other women. These young women get behind Slim's fatherly image to show us how young self-respecting women can listen to and enjoy his music. And with tweets like "he's there for me no matter what and I will always be there for him:),"[12] fake-Hailies are carving out a space to listen to the music and still feel good about themselves.

Fake-Hailies are also answering important questions: How do you listen to Slim's music as a self? As a woman? Where do young women fit in here? The answers to these questions take the form of resistance and submission. On one hand, young women are using Hailie's voice as a way to fight off the vicious misogyny found in so many of her father's lyrics. In this sense they can be considered activists who are empowering the daughter by giving her a voice and invading the rapper's private space. Since men are not generally used to having their spaces invaded, particularly in public, this kind of behavior tends to anger them and so we get the heated reaction from Slim and his all-male management team. On the other hand, these fake-Hailies are submitting to Slim when they defend him and claim to be part of his legacy as normal American teenage girls. They have learned the lessons he's taught the real Hailie throughout his songbook: that the only way to stay in his good graces is to be a nonsexual, adolescent female.

But there are other explanations. First, some tabloids suggest that the fake-Hailies may not be able to have online identities under their own names due to parental oversight or bullying. Either of these reasons would make identifying with Slim and his daughter a no-brainer. If the fake-Hailies are looking to escape their parental supervision, then they have much support in Slim's youth-oriented and parent-phobic lyrics. But if they are looking for a refuge from bullying, online or otherwise, then being known as Slim's (fake) daughter could also be fruitful. We know from "Brain Damage" (1999), "As The World Turns" (1999), "Bully" (2003), and "No Love" (2010) as well as the rapper's autobiographies and interviews that he was bullied as a child. In fact, in 2010 the official court transcript was released from the case his mother Debbie Nelson brought against the School District of the City of Roseville, Macomb County, Michigan, for failing to protect her son from bully D'Angelo Bailey when he was 10-years-old. Since then, the rapper has spoken out against bullying and expressed his zero-tolerance policy when Anderson Cooper interviewed him on *60 Minutes* in 2010. He went on to say that his music was his way of fighting back somewhat nonviolently against childhood and industry bullies. We also know from songs like "Hailie's Song," "Mockingbird," and "When I'm Gone" that Slim considers his primary parental role to be that of a resilient soldier who will wage war on anyone who attempts to mess with his family; therefore, everyone who messes with the fake-Hailies puts themselves within the real Slim Shady's crosshairs. Slim prides himself on doing what he says most parents do not: protecting his children.

POSTSCRIPT

Despite the complex family dramas and social commentary Slim's lullabies and the fake-Hailies's tweets bring to life, they still leave open the question of what the rapper's fans, along with @Angry_Blonde's and @hailiejade_x's followers, are after. One answer could be to have their curiosity satisfied. For instance, many overzealous fans called the rapper when his phone number was posted on the website of a hacker group calling itself "illmob" that broke into Paris Hilton's T-Mobile USA cell-phone address book in 2005. Today, followers might want to go backstage and see what life as a member of the Shady Bunch might be like. What does Hailie look like? Is she as troubled as her famous father appears? Is her dad really as dysfunctional as the Slim Shady persona suggests? This curiosity-oriented hypothesis holds some weight in light of the long-standing fascination popular culture audiences have with celebrities' children, especially in the wake of Whitney Houston's death and the many reports of her daughter's substance abuse and mental breakdown. And we cannot forget about the frenzy that continues to surround Michael Jackson's children since their father's death in 2009. Remember, Slim's fans know that he has been (mostly) killed off, especially after "When I'm Gone," and they might want to know how Slim's legacy influenced Hailie over the years since his demise.

Clearly fans are interested in how the fake-Hailies are playing with their own surroundings and life experiences. By creating fan fiction, the fake-Hailies are able to simulate dynamic and real experiences through their tweets, so real that they have fooled even the most adept tabloid journalists. The fact that they have duped so many proves that the fake-Hailies have mastered the art of gaining credibility and collective intelligence within popular culture by remixing samples from the Shady Bunch's real life with contemporary media content to produce messages that resonate with today's audiences. What appears to be a shameless Twitter hoax might be better described as a challenge that leaves audiences unsure of how to read this truly unreliable persona (Slim), his daughter (Hailie Jade), and their autobiographical fiction.

CHAPTER 4
Marshall Mathers:
The Everyman's Man

Marshall Bruce Mathers III is no longer simply a birth name. It is a household name. Marshall Mathers is Eminem's true, intimate, ultimate, and permanent self. In Eminem's music, we come to know Mathers as Eminem's spiritual self, the one who explains good and bad behavior and communicates attitudes and morals. Mathers also handles the stresses created by Eminem's fame and Shady's controversies as well as his own personal demons.

Mathers takes center stage on the *Marshall Mathers LP* (2000), although traces of him can be found on previous and later recordings, especially *Recovery* (2010). Touted as one of the 500 greatest albums of all time, *Rolling Stone* declared, "Before his second album, Eminem was a shock rapper with a sense of humor; after *Marshall Mathers,* he was the voice of a generation."[1] The *Marshall Mathers LP*'s earnings—1.7 million copies sold in the first week of its U.S. release and 21 million copies sold worldwide to date—certainly attest to the fact that Mathers articulates thoughts and feelings that resonate strongly with audiences.[2] Furthermore, the success of *Recovery* as the world's first album to sell over 1 million copies via download reflects the fact that Mathers's coming to fame during the digital music era led to faster consumption of his work. The rapid consumption of Mathers's messages suggests a need to consider the rapper's personas, music, and lyrics seriously.[3]

As more and more audiences bear witness to his art and life, it is hard to ignore that, for some, Mathers has taken on the role of spiritual self or "Everyman" in popular culture—a persona that represents humankind and its spiritual encounters in ways that ring true to shared experiences.[4] In communicating these encounters, Mathers defines spirituality as a natural aspect of everyday life; a personal struggle that is best observed when rules are broken and guilt is induced. To prove the point Mathers's brand of spirituality is brutally honest, expressing motives that justify guilt-inducing behavior and can apply to society at large. To begin with, Mathers explains why Slim Shady can kill you, provide you with drugs, steal from you, physically abuse you, and emotionally torment you. Then he explains why he, Marshall Mathers, actually adores you and can even save you from the menace to society Slim Shady and all those like him have become. And he convinces you that you cannot do anything about any of it. You certainly cannot place any blame on Slim Shady, Eminem, or Marshall Mathers. After all, Slim Shady is an accident of birth "born with a dick in [the] brain, yeah, fucked in the head" as he mentions in "Insane" (2009) and Eminem "don't even exist" as revealed in "Brain Damage" (1999). In autobiographies, *Angry Blonde* (2000) and *The Way I Am* (2008), however, Mathers presents himself as the most real embodiment of damaged goods. He tells "the story of a . . . kid who had a pretty shitty life,"[5] growing up along the color line in lower working-class Detroit with his single mother.

If we believe Mathers's words, then we must also believe that nature and nurture have left no options for him (or Slim Shady or Eminem) other than to break with society's rules and norms in an attempt to create spiritual encounters on his own. By narrating and embellishing autobiographical experiences, Marshall Mathers becomes Eminem's and Slim Shady's moral compass. He embroils young audiences in spiritual dramas that speak to the helplessness they experience and the obstacles they may face on the journey to adulthood. Along the way he emerges as a spiritual wanderer who seeks to eliminate his feelings of guilt because he has forsaken the straight and narrow. As a result, he shows audiences difficult situations, asks them to question right and wrong, presents ways to deal with feelings of guilt for asking such questions, and creates possibilities for being redeemed by changing the rules for everyone. For this reason Mathers takes the stage and dedicates his performances "to anybody . . . who's been through personal struggles."[6]

THE DRAMA OF GUILT AND REDEMPTION

As a formula for making sense out of life's most difficult moments Mathers's musical structure confirms the ongoing relevance of Kenneth Burke's *dramatistic* perspective, which was explained in his 1962 work, titled *A Grammar of Motives*. Burke claimed that people, like actors, make sense of the world through dramas. As with any dramatic actor, Mathers's success and survival depend on the quality of the dramas he constructs and his ability to make audiences identify with the actors, actions, and motives he provides. Without these identifications, audiences would be unable to navigate the world he depicts and find coherent purpose for his actions. Mathers carefully chooses his language to create compelling dramas that emphasize a particular view of the world. His best and most popular dramas ask audiences to think about doing evil deeds and consider what consequences and condemnations, if any, will follow. These dramas about good and evil in everyday life become spiritual claims that emerge from a solitary scene and can justify guilt-inducing behavior in ways that can apply to society at large.

Spiritual dualities of good and evil have long been dramatized in terms of guilt (feeling uncomfortable over having broken some rule) and redemption (being saved from error or punishment). The impulse to affect and potentially redeem society at large can be explained by the fact that guilt plays a starring role in the drama of human experience. Guilt is a problem that needs to be solved. Every person grapples with feelings of guilt, discomfort, or pain, and language is the primary means of taking on the struggle. Burke's dramatistic perspective says that because we make sense out of life's dramas through language, our language creates hierarchies and rules that will be challenged and broken which in turn lead to feelings of guilt. Finally, according to Burke, guilt is about where we belong, what we should do, and how we appear to others. For these reasons guilt is inevitable and sets off the guilt-purification-redemption cycle. In this cycle, our language creates hierarchies that cannot be sustained because humans by nature will disrupt their own social structures. When disruption happens, individuals feel guilt or a sense of discomfort that they attempt to purify through some form of punishment that will reestablish the social structures that were initially disrupted and will inevitably be challenged again. Guilt creates the need for redemption. Purification is the only way redemption is attained. However, because guilt is a consistent part of human existence, purification strategies that lead to redemption will always be temporary.

The first way Mathers seeks to redeem and purify himself in his lyrics is through transcendence, or following a higher calling. Examples of transcendence occur when Mathers blames his behavior on societal and cultural traditions (like political correctness or class distinctions that transcend his desire to make others comfortable), natural forces (like biology or nature that transcend his need to change), or spiritual forces (like God or Satan that transcend his desire for doing the right thing). The second way Mathers seeks purification is mortification, or taking blame and punishing himself. Mortification is commonly practiced as part of any Twelve Step Program, which requires its members to make a list of all persons they have harmed and make amends. Mathers had to take this step in order to overcome his addictions according to the album *Recovery* (2010). For example, in "Talkin' 2 Myself" (2010), Mathers apologizes to fellow rapper Lil' Wayne for a jealousy-fueled lyrical attack. The third and most popular purification strategy is victimage or scapegoating, the blaming (and often sacrifice) of others for one's actions. Most often, Mathers blames his mother for his skewed perspectives and ghastly behavior, as in "My Name Is" (1999), "Our House" (1999), "Criminal" (2000), and "Cleanin' Out My Closet" (2002). However, victimage also requires us to understand Mathers as someone who just cannot help himself and is absolved because of other people's faults. But we can only understand Mathers in this way some of the time. Other times Mathers is a persona that asks us to blame society, science, or supernatural powers for his actions. Less often, Mathers admits guilt and seeks purification by accepting punishment. Mathers enacts guilt and seeks purification using the redemptive strategies of transcendence (social–scientific–spiritual condemnation), victimage (other condemnation), and mortification (self-condemnation) in Eminem's dramas. We will now examine the song/video "Space Bound" (2010) to find out how he uses all three.

PERFORMING GUILT AND REDEMPTION

To be blunt, the scene in "Space Bound" is "a clear night in June" when Mathers becomes a self-destructive killer. The song functions as a note whose purpose is to explain the death. The song describes Mathers as transcendent, headed for the hereafter or "space bound," and as damaged (i.e., mortified), someone with a "hole" in his heart. Other parts suggest that he is a victim, betrayed by a lover and tired of being misunderstood. The video for this song (2011) supplements the drama by providing additional explanations and motives for Mathers's behavior. In fact, the video provides so much supplemental information that it was branded "evil" by Mothers Against Violence and named the second most controversial video of the year 2011 by *Metro*.

Co.Uk.[7] The video, about a lovesick and unstable man who chases after a woman who means everything to him, declares what the song only implies: that Mathers is unlucky in love, that he might have multiple personalities, and that he might be possessed. The video explains that Mathers lost control of his identity to someone or something else and aims a bullet at his head in order to take control back.

As the drama in "Space Bound" unfolds, Mathers exhibits the classic symptoms of someone with multiple personalities. This dramatic theme allows him to explain what kind of person is capable of taking a life and how such a person could reach that point of desperation. To begin with, there are two versions of him in the video dramatized via split screens. One version is Slim Shady and the other is Mathers. Each version is different from the other, and each is dominant at a particular time. Whichever personality is dominant at a particular moment determines the rules that will be broken. Several times throughout the video it is as if one personality is waking up from a dream and cannot believe what the other appears to be doing. Whether Slim Shady is choking his girlfriend, yelling misogynist insults, checking her phone for texts from other men, or Mathers is treating her like a stranger even after stalking her, it seems that each personality is complex and integrated with its own unique patterns of behavior. And what one personality knows about the other could range from everything to nothing. Even if Slim Shady and Mathers are completely dissociated, their bond cannot be dissolved. Consequently, they both feel guilty for whatever acts of aggression are committed.

Mathers is the persona that appears to be aware that the other exists, and he wants to break the relationship. From what he tells us about his roller-coaster relationships with women in songs like "Oh Foolish Pride" (1992), " '97 Bonnie and Clyde" (1999), "Anger Management" (2003), "The Warning" (2009), and "The Reunion" (2011), it is easy to imagine his conversations with Slim Shady and his girlfriend in "Space Bound" as a metaphor for the futility of breaking up. In light of the above, we must remember that "Space Bound" is just one of Mathers's many dramas laced with feelings of guilt, attempts at redemption, and strategies for purification. This transformation occurs in any of three ways—transcendence (blaming higher powers), victimage (blaming other people), and mortification (blaming himself).

"Space Bound" could be seen as Mathers's latest attempt at transcendence by destroying the "evol"[8] love that just will not let go. Evol love is impatient, selfish, wants what it cannot have, forces itself on others, flies off the handle, enjoys suffering, keeps score, always replays situations, and refuses to trust. Mathers and Slim Shady demonstrate evol notions about love when they display aggressive behavior toward their girlfriend (i.e., invading her privacy, stalking her, abusing her). Slim Shady is possessed by evol love and will not let go, Mathers is possessed too but can see one way to restore some sort of order. He must kill the person who cannot let go of evol love—Slim Shady. From this perspective Mathers does not commit suicide but is a killer who also self-destructs because of evol love. Even though Mathers pulls the trigger, Slim Shady's death is not his fault. He was driven to the murder by evol love and by Slim Shady's blind faith in evol love. Mathers shot Slim Shady in the head in "Space Bound" because it was the only means of breaking away from evol love.

But purging his soul through transcendence—condemning evol love and its hold on Slim Shady—is not the only redemptive strategy at work here. Victimage, in the form of condemning Slim Shady and their girlfriend, also plays a role. In "Space Bound," Mathers kills Slim Shady because Slim betrayed him and chose to be possessed totally by evol love. And Mathers depicts his relationship with his girlfriend in the same dysfunctional ways he relates with Slim. Their girlfriend's multiple betrayals are not just suspected infidelity, but they are temptations that cause Slim to behave badly. In this way the girlfriend is just another manifestation of evol love, another demonic force. According to Ebony A. Utley, author of *Rap and Religion: Understanding the Gangsta's God,* the devil often manifests as feminine. Utley argues, "Eminem's exchange with the devil follows an obsessive/possessive pattern where intimacy is fraught with violence and love is complete possession."[9] The recurrence of these themes and the failures to achieve nonviolent stability in his relationship and trust in his girlfriend cause feelings of guilt and lead Mathers to seek redemption by purging himself of Slim Shady and the hold his girlfriend has over them.

As the video concludes, however, Mathers admits that killing Slim Shady and ending their evol love relationship is not enough to purify his spirit. The spiritual drama can only be resolved fully by purging guilty feelings through mortification. Slim Shady's death and the alleged murder of his girlfriend in "Space Bound" are Mathers's fault by his own admission. Mathers managed to achieve momentary purification after killing Slim Shady because he also, ultimately, killed (a part of) himself. In "Space Bound," Mathers's painful purification results in the ability to accept blame for his inability to control Slim

Shady, their girlfriend, or manage the temptations of evol love. Although not without its violent flaws, this underlying message suggests that taking responsibility for engaging in evol behavior is necessary for growth. The fact that the drama is only resolved by Mathers's self-condemnation, despite the different paths offered in "Space Bound," indicates that everything hinges on what is to be gained through seeing a killing as redemptive and as an act of purification.

Like the rewind visualized in the video, this killing forces us to go back to the beginning of the drama, to the dark deserted highway, accompanied by music, and ask what Mathers is really getting at through its depiction. Is it the chance at a better life? Is it an eternal afterlife? Is it power and control over the future? Is it sacrificing oneself so that others may live freely and happily without him? Is it an attempt to rethink right and wrong? Is it an attempt to communicate a different kind of spirituality? Because the video enhances (rather than resolves) uncertainty, the answers are difficult to discern. What is clear is that dysfunctional relationships, devils, and split personalities cannot be destroyed with a single bullet to the head. Their holds seem unbreakable no matter how much blood is spilled. All are powerful enemies capable of returning to remind us of the guilt that is always already within and the redemption that is needed. Whether it is splitting a body with Slim Shady, clinging to a love that is already lost or being possessed by evol itself, one of Mathers's many messages in "Space Bound" is that everyone and everything has more than one persona—even love. And in this drama, the path to love, the greatest expression of human goodness and kindness, finds dramatic expression in the depths of guilt, the heights of redemption, and the pains of purification.

Despite the lessons to be learned about drama and the guilt–redemption–purification cycle from Mathers in "Space Bound," there is sufficient cause for alarm. Critics argue that the Marshall Mathers persona is a vehicle for graphic depictions of violence at the hands of an attractive perpetrator. Furthermore, critics claim that Mathers's acts appear real because they are committed with a gun and contextualized with blood. Not only does he go unpunished by legal and moral authorities for killing within "Space Bound," the video has reaped great financial rewards for Mathers in real life by becoming one of his most downloaded. Critics assert that these factors all heighten the probability of aggression for viewers, and especially young male viewers.[10] Thus, they fear that in becoming the voice of a generation, a modern-day Everyman, Mathers has also become an attractive perpetrator of violence who teaches youth that guilt-inducing behaviors are not only an acceptable means of solving conflict but are also likely to go unpunished and may even be rewarded. In order to understand these concerns, and understand exactly what the critics are missing, I now turn to additional examples of guilt-inducing behavior and redemption–purification embedded therein.

LOCATING ADDITIONAL THEMES OF GUILT-INDUCING BEHAVIOR AND REDEMPTION

The controversial nature of the behaviors described in Mathers's music and enacted in his videos is not of his own invention. For decades, hip hop has focused on rebellion against the status quo and depicted life's suffering. However, the rate at which Mathers's music is consumed suggests that he is embedding underlying themes beneath his dark rebellious streak that resonate strongly with listeners. In order to understand these themes and their effects, 200 of the rapper's songs were identified and evaluated for their depictions of guilt-inducing behavior and its consequences. Although songs were sampled in their entireties, only Mathers's verses were coded in songs where he did not perform alone. Therefore, the sample includes only Mathers's lyrical content. A segment was defined as all of Mathers's lyrics within a particular song. The goal of the sampling design was to select the maximum number of segments directed to as many audience members as possible.

Songs were located using four reference sources. First, I used all of Eminem's known albums, beginning with *Steppin' into the Scene* (1990) and concluding with *Straight from the Vault EP* (2011). Second, I searched the top Eminem fan sites for lists of his songs that may not have been released on his own albums from 1990 to 2012. Third, I initiated an electronic keyword search to verify each of the identified Eminem songs in Google as well as on YouTube and, when possible, Billboard.Com charts. Fourth, I cross-referenced the songs found through electronic keyword searches with the discographies published in Eminem's autobiographies and biographies. The resulting sample consisted of 200 songs released by the artist between the years of 1990 and 2012.

Lyrics were either obtained from the liner notes on the albums or transcribed by hand. Then, all lyrics were coded for guilt-inducing behaviors under the following rubrics identified by previous studies of

Eminem's lyrical content and MTV music video messages: violence, sex, substance use, and insult.[11] Violence was defined as "any overt depiction of a credible threat of physical force or the actual use of such force intended to physically harm a person or group of people."[12] Violence also included certain depictions of physically harmful consequences against a person or persons that results from unseen violent means. Sex was defined as the "portrayal of sexual feelings and impulses" that are not considered socially acceptable.[13] Substance use was defined as the use of any substance for mood-altering purposes.[14] Insult was defined as expression or behavior that is considered degrading, offensive, or outrageous.[15] The amount of violence, sex, substance use, and insult were measured in terms of frequency, which refers to how often these behaviors are featured in each lyrical segment.

In keeping with Burke's dramatistic perspective and guilt–redemption–purification cycle, the consequences of each guilt-inducing behavior (i.e., violent, sexual, substance use, or insult incident) were also evaluated and measured in terms of frequency. Consequences were defined as those verbal or nonverbal signs of condemnation and blame that were expressed by the perpetrator for engaging in guilt-inducing behavior. Each segment was coded as mortification (self-condemnation), victimage (other condemnation), or transcendence (social–scientific–spiritual condemnation). Coding followed the recording industry's judgment about the overall lyrical content, relying on the Parental Advisory Explicit Content labeled versions of lyrics.

UNDERSTANDING ADDITIONAL THEMES OF GUILT-INDUCING BEHAVIOR

The results pertaining to guilt-inducing behavior indicate strong emphases on physical violence, sex, substance abuse, and insult in lyrics. Violence was by far the most prevalent guilt-inducing behavior represented. Overall, violent acts were depicted 195 times, or in 97.5 percent of lyrics. Seven types of violence emerged: fighting/physical, murder, dismemberment, vandalism, suicide, self-mutilation, and terrorism. Fighting/physical violence occurred 116 times, or in 83.0 percent of lyrics. For example, in "The Apple" (2011), Mathers refers to himself as his mother's rotten fruit that acts out because of her influence. And, in the popular song "Love the Way You Lie" (2010), he explains what it is like to perpetrate and survive domestic violence.

Murder occurred 74 times, or in 37.0 percent of lyrics. For instance, "'97 Bonnie & Clyde" is essentially a murder ballad sung to his daughter Hailie as they drive to the beach to bury her mother at sea. In "50 Ways" (2011), he confesses to murdering a girlfriend he cannot bring himself to leave by any other means. And titles of songs like "Murder Murder" (1997) and "Kill You" (2000) just about say it all. For Mathers, it seems that violent murder is the only way to end negative drama caused by others in love relationships through victimage, making it a positive act in his worldview.

In comparison, terrorist acts occurred 19 times, or in 10.3 percent of lyrics. Interestingly, this theme emerged after the actual terrorist attacks of September 11, 2001, suggesting that Mathers engages with and responds to current events in his art. In songs like "Doe Rae Mi" (2003), "My Dad's Gone Crazy" (2002), "Business" (2002), "Invasion: The Realest" (2004), and "Seduction" (2010), Mathers compares his communication to bombs dropped by terrorists. He also likens himself to Osama Bin Laden and Saddam Hussein. The prevalence of this behavior also indicates that, for Mathers, victimage still works. It is almost as satisfying to kill collective enemies as it is to kill them one at a time.

Killing the most hated enemy, Mathers himself, is only depicted in terms of suicide, which occurred 18 times, or in 9.0 percent of lyrics as evidenced in "Music Box" (2009) where he nearly kills himself through an overdose, "Rock Bottom" (1999) where he describes his real-life suicide attempt ingesting up to 20 Tylenol 3 tablets and "The Way I Am" (2000) where leaping off of a skyscraper is the only escape from fame. The pattern of suicide-oriented lyrics suggests that mortification does hold significant appeal for Mathers as a way to break the guilt–redemption–purification cycle. However, all attempts at staying dead are unsuccessful. This suggests that purging guilty feelings through mortification is ultimately no more successful than victimage or transcendence because they are always only temporary solutions.

Closely related to the futility of suicide is self-mutilation, which occurred 14 times, or in 7.0 percent of lyrics. Although not the most prevalent or intense theme in Mathers's lyrics, the fact that it appears is further evidence that self-mutilation, a form of mortification, is a pervasive public health problem. Psychologists at Harvard and Yale Universities found that self-mutilation occurs at a rate of 4 percent in the general adult population and at rates of 14–39 percent among adolescents.[16] The fact that Mathers's audience is largely comprised of

adolescents suggests that self-mutilation could be a purification seeking and/or identification mechanism that merits additional attention
mortification in the public's consciousness.

Mathers does complicate matters by alternating between self-
mutilation and dismemberment, or the mutilation of others. Dismemberment occurred 8 times, or in 4.0 percent of lyrics as identified in
"Wee Wee" (2011) when he addresses the media effects of horror films
by way of the sick thoughts and violence they provoke. The alternating pattern between self-mutilation and dismemberment suggests that
the expression of self-mutilating behavior in Mathers's lyrics could be
intended to highlight victimage, including the solicitation of assistance
from others and removing the perceived expectations of others. But
Mathers's lyrics are not limited to mutilating himself and others. Physical environments are also affected by vandalism, which occurred six
times or in 3 percent of lyrics. For example, in "The Real Slim Shady"
(2000), Mathers raps about random acts of destruction he intends to
perpetrate when he is ultimately put away in either a nursing home or a
mental institution. The low rates of harming others and their property,
compared to the higher rates at which self-mutilation and suicide behaviors appear suggest that a mortification strategy is preferable when
it comes to guilt induced by violence. Harming oneself rather than
harming others is a more just means of coping with life's limitations.

Sex, depicted nonviolently and violently, was the second most prevalent guilt-inducing behavior represented in Mathers's lyrics. Seven
types of guilt-inducing (i.e., socially unacceptable) sex acts emerged:
sadomasochistic sex, same-sex sexuality, infidelity, unprotected sex,
rape, masturbation/masochism, and animal sex. Guilt-inducing sex
acts occurred 162 times, or in 81 percent of lyrics. Sadomasochistic sex acts occurred 68 times, or in 34 percent of lyrics. Same-sex
acts and epithets were mentioned 46 times, or in 23 percent of lyrics.
Eminem has come under fire for his references to same-sex sexuality
and homophobia as in "Criminal" (2000), where he uses derogatory
terms to refer to gay and lesbian individuals. In "Rain Man" (2004), a
duet with Dr. Dre, Mathers asks what kind of homosocial and homosexual behaviors could be considered gay. In "Stan" (2000) he rejects
a gay fan's homosexual advances. Here Mathers uses transcendence
as an appeal to higher powers so that he understands guilt-inducing
sexual behavior. Infidelity occurred 20 times, or in 10 percent of lyrics.
Women are generally portrayed as unfaithful partners in songs such
as "Oh Foolish Pride" (1992), "Maxine" (1996), "I Love You More"

(2003), "Spend Some Time" (2004), and "The Reunion" (2011). Each act of infidelity committed against Mathers deserves punishment (i.e., victimage). Closely tied to infidelity is the theme of unprotected sex, which appears 20 times or in 10 percent of lyrics. Typically, Mathers treats unprotected sex for men as a form of expertise, as in "C'Mon Let me Ride" (2012) when he says, "condoms are for practice, man I skip practice." For women, unprotected sex appears most often along with rape, which was committed 12 times, or in 6.5 percent of lyrics. In each instance the victim did something to deserve this form of punishment (i.e., victimage). Masturbation was mentioned eight times, or in 4 percent of lyrics. In the song "313" (1996), Mathers likens his poetry to masturbation. And in "No Apologies" (2006), he describes the highs of masturbation when practiced in conjunction with poetry and masochism as a form of transcendence. Animal sex or bestiality was mentioned five times, or in 2.7 percent of lyrics, for example, in "Wee Wee" (2011) when he suggests that he could star in his own "bestiality porno." Animal sex is often contrasted with same-sex sexual relations as the worse of two evils when Mathers uses mortification and appeals to higher powers.

Substance use was the third most prevalent guilt-inducing behavior represented 126 times, or in 63 percent of lyrics. Two types of substance use emerged: drug use and alcohol use. Drug use was mentioned 81 times, or in 40.5 percent of lyrics. Representations of drug use range from outright abuse, as in "I'm Having a Relapse" (2009) to comparisons with the recording industry as narcotic in "Cocaine" (2010). Mathers almost always blames his drug abuse on his mother and upbringing (i.e., victimage). Alcohol use was mentioned 46 times, or in 23 percent of lyrics. Representations of alcohol use also ranged from abuse, as in "Still Don't Give a Fuck" (1999), to actual recovery and sobriety, as in "Not Afraid" (2010). The prevalence of substance use is significant as a theme that has not only touched Mathers and his family directly but also potentially resonates with young audiences and their families. For instance, in 1999, the same year Mathers was introduced to mainstream popular culture, the National Council on Alcoholism and Drug Dependence reported that "approximately 8% of the nation's eighth graders, 24% of tenth graders, and 32% of twelfth graders have been drunk during the last month; 12%, 23% and 25%, respectively have used an illicit drug."[17] This is especially important because, among teens and undergraduate college students, alcohol is estimated to contribute to an increasing number of sexual assault cases involving acquaintance or date rape. This finding is not surprising given the social acceptability of victimage as an explanation for rape when boys force themselves on girls if they are under the influence of drugs or alcohol as depicted in Mathers's "Guilty Conscience" (1999). The relationship between substance use and sexual assault has become increasingly relevant to our political culture in recent years. For instance, in January 2012, House Republicans removed the controversial "forcible rape" provision from their "No Taxpayer Funding for Abortion Act." Therefore, it can be argued that public policy is in conversation with mediated representations that link substance use and guilt-inducing sexual activity under a strategy of victimage. Unfortunately, more often than not, these links take us back to a time when just saying no was not enough.

Accordingly, insult was the fourth most prevalent guilt-inducing behavior represented in Mathers's lyrics. Insult was mentioned 111 times, or in 55.5 percent of lyrics. Four types of insults emerged: offensive speech, lying, theft, and dropping out of school. Offensive speech was referenced 57 times, or in 28.5 percent of lyrics. For instance, in "Stimulate" (2003), he discusses how young audiences hear his music and want to do what he says as a way to highlight how others use victimage against him when youth break society's rules. This kind of public speech is presented in contrast to offensive speech acts (aka "disses") aimed at other entertainers. An example is "I Remember" (2000), a dis rap in which Mathers targets another white rapper from the group House of Pain named Everlast. As mentioned above, in many other songs Mathers likens his offensive and politically incorrect speech acts to transcendence. His need to tell the truth from his perspective trumps any concern for others' feelings.

Lying arose 36 times, or in 18 percent of lyrics. All references position Mathers as a truth-teller and position others as lying to and about him. Half of these occurrences emerge in conjunction with themes of terrorism. The remaining half of Mathers's allusions to lying arise in the context of personal relationships with his mother as in "My Name Is" (1999) and "Cleaning Out My Closet" (2002) and with his ex-wife Kim as in "The Reunion" (2011), "Kim" (2000), "I Love You More" (2003), and "Jealousy Woes II" (1997). These more personal references to lying suggest that adult women are deceitful creatures who need to be punished. Women are never to be trusted because they never feel guilt for their deceitful acts. As a consequence women are in need of punishment (i.e., victimage) so that they can be purified and redeemed.

Theft was mentioned 14 times, or appeared in 7 percent of lyrics. For example, in "Criminal" (2000) and "Mockingbird" (2004), Mathers refers to stealing as a strategy of last resort for overcoming poverty, changing its meaning from negative to positive. However, there is another side to this argument about theft. For Mathers virtually all of the guilt-inducing behaviors mentioned so far are versions of theft. Murder is taking a life. Rape is taking someone's body against his or her will. Lying is taking someone's right to the truth. Infidelity is stealing trust. In order to restore order, Mathers explains the punishments he doles for theft using victimage and transcendence. Liars must suffer for their actions (i.e., victimage) and he must punish them because they've broken his most important commandment (i.e., transcendence).

The final insulting behavior, dropping out of school, was mentioned four times or in 2 percent of lyrics. In songs like "Our House" (1999) and "White America" (2002), Mathers discusses the effects of an educational system that fails some of its brightest students, including himself, and contrasting it with hip hop geniuses like LL Cool J, Ice-T, and Dr. Dre who turned out to be his lifelong master teachers. Utilizing a victimage strategy, Mathers notes several main predictors that led to his dropping out: low test scores and grades in high school; poor academic achievement in middle and elementary school (i.e., not being "book smart"); bullying; domestic instability that caused him to switch schools often throughout his educational career and being held back at least three times in the ninth grade. The connection between dropping out and insult here is profound. Mathers argues that access to material sources as well as social resources in the form of supportive relationships with families, teachers, and friends could have changed his fate as a student. Overall, insulting behaviors are used in lyrics as victimage to blame traditional models of power, prestige, and perfection for failing him and all those who come from disadvantaged backgrounds.

UNDERSTANDING ADDITIONAL THEMES OF PURIFICATION AND REDEMPTION

The results pertaining to consequences indicate strong emphases on victimage and transcendence and a weaker emphasis on mortification. Analysis reveals that an overwhelming majority of songs, 184 out of 200 (92 percent), dramatize guilt-inducing behavior and attempts to purge feelings of guilt and avoid consequences by enacting the guilt–redemption–purification cycle. Mathers summarizes this cycle in

"My Life" (2012) when he raps, "This is like a vicious cycle, my life's in a crisis . . . I'm running in circles."

Of the 200 songs analyzed, 144 (or 72 percent) purge guilt by blaming a variety of people for Mathers's own bad behaviors. For example, in "Going Crazy" (2011), Mathers says that he "can't stop" battling and fighting because "too much blood's drew." In "Guilty Conscience" (1999), he blames his victims for the theft, murder, and dismemberment he inflicts upon them. In "My Name Is" (1999), he is surprised to discover his dysfunctions are hereditary because his mother "did more dope than I do." And, in "Criminal" (2000), he says that his mother's substance abuse while being pregnant created "a seed who would grow up just as crazy as she." He repeats the theme of being his mother's "bad seed" in "The Apple" (2011) and in "I'm Back" (2000) when he says "I been crazy way before radio didn't play me." In addition to blaming his mother, many of his most popular songs describe abusive, obsessive love–hate relationships with women and are accompanied by attempts at purging guilt through victimage. Several songs blame the mother of his children for her own death, divorce, and dismemberment, including the controversial "'97 Bonnie & Clyde" (1999), "Kim" (2000), and "Love You More" (2004). In "Things Get Worse" (2011), he blames his ongoing deceit, violence, substance use, and offensive speech acts on post-traumatic stress disorder, which has been caused by the stresses fame placed on his life and marriage(s). In "Love the Way You Lie Part II" (2010), he describes a dysfunctional love relationship that has reached its boiling point because his partner always makes him hurt her even though it is not the desire of his heart to do so.

In 40 (or 20 percent) of the 200 songs examined, Mathers's lyrics are primarily transcendence-oriented. In these lyrics Mathers professes to follow a higher calling that cannot be avoided given life's circumstances. In songs such as "It's Ok" (1996), "Cleanin' Out My Closet" (2002), "Cinderella Man" (2010), and "Cold Wind Blows" (2010), Mathers seeks redemption and renewal for his actions by offering prayers to God. Conversely, several other songs are indeed odes to the Devil like "Murder Murder" (1997), "Demon Inside" (2008), "My Darling" (2009), and "Hell Breaks Loose" (2009). Sometimes feelings of guilt are purged by blaming fate or destiny. In "As the World Turns" (1999), for instance, he writes, "I don't know why this world keeps turning. . . . But I wish it would stop and let me off right now." And in "Drug Ballad" (2000), he raps that no matter what happens today, destiny is inevitable: "tomorrow you'll be boys again."

As in all of Mathers's victimage- and transcendence-oriented lyrics, the message comes shining through: no matter what he does, the only real agency is violence. He can damage or end the lives of others who cause him pain and he can stop his own pain through suicide. But Mathers's brand of violent agency is, like the purification it achieves, often only temporary. For despite his many interventions his lyrics suggest that he cannot affect the future, he cannot change what he will turn out to be, and he certainly cannot change his fate or what the world has in store for him. Thus, according to 92.5 percent of Mathers's lyrics, he is Everyman, a spiritual hero who must resign himself to making the best of the hand he was dealt. Even when what seems best to him seems wrong to everyone else.

Of the remaining tracks, only 14 (or 7 percent) purge guilt through mortification. More than half of these songs appeared since 2010, which is important since that year marks the release of his *Recovery* album and his attempts at purifying himself from his drug addiction. Exactly half of the total mortification songs—"Talkin' 2 Myself," "On Fire," "Going Through Changes," "Seduction," "Space Bound," "Despicable," and "Love the Way You Lie" (2010)—appear on Mathers's recent and best-selling solo album *Recovery* (2010). In each of these songs, the persona of Marshall Mathers takes responsibility for guilt-inducing behaviors such as physical violence, substance abuse, and offensive speech. Only one song that employs mortification appeared early on in Mathers's career, "My Fault," from the *Slim Shady LP* (1999). In it, he apologizes to God and to Susan, a woman who dies from an overdose of drugs he gave her without thinking it through. It must be noted, however, that Mathers's tone may be a very powerful antidrug message that appears each time the song is heard. His apology resounds with sorrow and desperation over a senseless loss of life. The remaining pre-*Recovery* mortification-oriented songs—"Yellow Brick Road" (2004) and "Rain Man" (2004)—appear on the album *Encore*. The pattern of increasing the use of mortification in lyrics suggests that the victimage-oriented messages responsible for Mathers's initial popularity and success are in need of an update. When he entered popular culture, his messages were based on refusing to take responsibility for the irreverent, indecent, and guilt-inducing content found in his lyrics. The rapper's new trend of taking responsibility for his actions suggests that blaming others for one's sins may no longer resonate as strongly with a maturing audience.

CONFESSIONS

This chapter is about finding the spiritual message(s) communicated through guilt-inducing behavior and redemptive strategies in Marshall

Mathers's lyrics. Analysis confirmed critics' claims that Mathers's lyrics are filled with violent acts, sexual content, substance abuse, and insulting behaviors. However, analysis also confirmed that such critics are not completely informed. As has been shown, Mathers's songs can be considered spiritual dramas that present strategies for coping with guilt-inducing events and suffering encountered in his and his audiences' lives. Although lyrics rely mostly on victimage and transcendence to purge guilty feelings caused by breaking society's rules, victimage takes precedence. Sometimes, victimage is presented as a reason for giving the victim what she really deserves, as was the case for Mathers's ex-wife Kim who deserved to be slain for her lies, infidelity, and unprotected sex. At other times, victimage is offered as a way for Mathers to pardon himself for abusive behavior based on the bullying and injustices he experienced in his youth. Although Debbie Nelson, Mathers's mother, carries most of the blame in victimage-oriented lyrics, teachers, other rappers, fans, politicians, bullies, babysitters, and lovers are also indicted to justify his behavior.

Although transcendence is not employed as often as victimage, it also proves to be an effective tool for purging feelings of guilt and absolving responsibility in Mathers's lyrics. The underlying theme here is that Mathers feels out of control and that his circumstances are doomed to failure and repetition. Consequently, the guilt-inducing behaviors about which he raps become the only way to deal with a bleak and unchangeable destiny. As some critics have argued, this message carries important implications for young audiences because it suggests that they may see themselves and their circumstances in a similar light and also blame others as a way to escape condemnation and consequences.[18] But these critics are also missing something—mortification. The fact that Mathers's current redemptive strategy relies predominantly on mortification suggests that change is possible and can be considered a form of agency. Perhaps change even indicates that his and his audiences' attitudes, morals, and tastes are evolving as they move further toward and into adulthood. Now, an increasing number of Mathers's lyrics argue that recognizing one's responsibility and taking the blame are means of attaining spiritual and mental health, sustaining positive interpersonal relationships and resolving conflicts.

Mathers's increasing use of mortification-oriented lyrics indicates that he maintains social relevance by dramatizing spiritual development through the guilt–redemption–purification cycle. In *Gods Behaving Badly: Media, Religion and Celebrity Culture,* Peter Ward argues that spiritual development is critical to continued relevance for celebrities in today's popular culture. Audiences do not want their favorite celebrities to keep singing the same tune. They are "always waiting for the next act. They want to see a happy ending."[19] And Mathers is *slowly* giving audiences what they want. Whereas he used to "not give a fuck," he now takes some responsibility for the guilt-inducing content which figures so prominently within his work. Audiences will have to stay tuned in order to find out what will happen next. Based on the critical acclaim and popular success of *Recovery,* and the great anticipation for his upcoming solo project, we can rest assured that new dramas of guilt and redemption are on the way and that audiences will continue coming back for more.

Most important to understanding the rapper's spiritual persona, however, is the idea that his music may be a complex call to change social norms and spiritual values rather than a simple example of bad behavior modeling. The fact that Mathers continues to revisit the same guilt-inducing behaviors and redemptive strategies could mean that society has not yet understood his purpose. In addition, analysis suggests that there are benefits to looking at his work as a safe space for re-examining social rules and spiritual values through tales of guilt, redemption and purification. For instance, Mathers's uses of victimage and transcendence may be more than ways to shift blame onto others. Victimage and transcendence may be calls to look directly at narrow and rigid standards of justice, ideals of perfection, and hierarchies that do not allow for understanding "guilt-inducing" behaviors as anything but deviant and wrongful. In this way Mathers may be arguing for a way to transcend the guilt-redemption-purification cycle all together. Such transcendence cannot be achieved immediately or in isolation. Rather, transcendence is achieved as people listen to each other, encounter actions that induce guilt, and undermine the rules with which they have always tried to secure their existences. Only then can a spirituality that accepts stark realities, embraces bold sinners, and provides a permanent understanding of purification be heard.

CHAPTER 5
Angels and Demons and Mathers

Eminem is not exactly famous for having a spiritual side, especially when he inhabits the Slim Shady persona. In fact, as Slim Shady, Eminem is known for being at odds with everything sacred and being passionate about anything profane. But as Marshall Mathers, Eminem describes a spirituality through which he connects with higher powers and people around him and asks big questions about the meaning of life and afterlife. In the process, his music and lyrics operate on a spiritual but not religious level. As spiritual persona, Mathers represents Eminem's moral compass and personal struggle that is best observed when rules are broken and guilt is induced. In a 2009 interview for *Vibe Magazine*'s June/July issue, Mathers explains why and how: "Spirituality is definitely a part of [the rehab] process. They tell you in recovery to pray to your higher power—God is my higher power and He always has been. I definitely pray a lot more than I used to. I don't feel like I'm crazy religious where I'm at church four days a week or anything like that—not to say that that's a bad thing for anyone who wants to do that. But I do believe in God, and I do pray." The photograph accompanying this quotation is of Mathers wearing a contemplative facial expression, a black tank top, and a silver crucifix around his neck. The photo represents Mathers as one of many Americans who wish to be spiritually left alone, without the hassles of organized religion.

Mathers does express a kind of "Christianity without religion," a solidarity with Christ and Christian values rather than with the church.[1] In "Eminem: The Best Emcee Since Jesus," religious studies professor Marie W. Dallam finds that Mathers frames himself within a mainstream Christian value system, and that understanding his lyrics requires an understanding of that value system and its limits. Popular culture expert Gordon Lynch agrees. In *Understanding Theology and Popular Culture,* Lynch notes that Mathers presents at least two versions of a

Christian God in his music. According to Lynch, sometimes God can inspire an intense and noticeable change in a person's whole life, including his or her beliefs, values, surroundings, or associations. In this sense God gives Mathers the strength to transition from relapse to recovery by translating his thoughts, reactions, responses, and insights about spiritual matters into lyrics. Other times, God provides what is needed for survival from day to day. Mathers offers prayers in lyrics to ask his benevolent God to provide material resources, protection, and forgiveness in a harsh world. Prayers and allusions to prayer appear in many songs, including "Infinite" (1996), "It's Okay" (1996), "Till I Collapse" (2002), "Never Enough" (2004), "Evil Deeds" (2004), "A Drop in the Ocean" (2008), "Beautiful" (2009), and even the profanity-laced tracks "Still Don't Give a Fuck" (1999) and "Cold Wind" (2011). For Mathers, spirituality is a natural aspect of everyday life; a personal struggle to relate to the supernatural in the midst of tough situations. In this way Mathers's spirituality also becomes a process of understanding what God is, what God does, and where God resides. In light of this, it becomes necessary to think seriously about what spiritual messages about God are actually being sent in his music.

Because Marshall Mathers invests most of his energy being Slim Shady's and Eminem's moral compass, actions and discourse about the Devil also get a fair share of attention. The Devil usually appears as a wicked spiritual adversary, liar, and tempter. For example, in "5 Star Generals" (1998), Mathers says that he is taking orders from the Devil. In "Say Goodbye to Hollywood" (2002), he confesses to making an irrevocable deal with the Devil by selling his soul. In "Sing for the Moment" (2003), he mourns missing a part of his soul. And in "Lose Yourself" (2002), he mentions a desire to become part of a "New World Order." A couple of years later, Mathers says that he is still possessed in "Rain Man" (2004). And when the rapper refers to himself as hip hop's "G.O.A.T." (2011), he also alludes to the ways in which *Satanism* can take hold of the poet's spirit and can unleash the symbolic goat whose horns, thrust upward like two raised middle fingers, represent duality and defiance. But the Devil also takes on other forms in Mathers's music. Sometimes he is a manifestation of society's ills—poverty, segregation, alienation, misogyny, masochism, jealousy, and ignorance. The Devil takes the form of these social ills in "Murder Murder" (1997), "Demon Inside" (2008), "Hell Breaks Loose" (2009), "Space Bound" (2010), "25 to Life" (2010), and "Angelic Demons" (2011). Other times, the Devil looks exactly like Mathers. "My Darling" (2009), perhaps Mathers's most infamous Devil-themed song, enacts a conversation about and presents a relationship with the Devil in the mirror.

Some scholars believe that Eminem uses his music to dramatize a deep and intense spiritual battle. He admits as much in "Must Be the Ganja" (2009) when he confesses that he can identify with both the Dalai Lama (as good) and Jeffrey Dahmer (as evil). As he seeks deeper spiritual commitment, Marshall Mathers, the redeemed or spiritual Everyman wrestles against the sinful Slim Shady persona. In *Rap and Religion: Understanding the Gangsta's God,* Ebony A. Utley suggests that the Slim Shady persona is downright demonic. Utley writes that "in the introduction to the *Slim Shady EP,* a foreboding voice not unlike the one attributed to the Devil in 'My Darling' taunts Eminem even though he repeatedly states, 'I thought I killed you,' 'what do you want from me?,' and 'leave me alone!'"[2] Jeffrey S. Victor looks at the larger cultural context of possession and Devil rumors in popular culture in *Satanic Panic: The Creation of a Contemporary Legend.* Victor writes that "these claims . . . exploit widespread fears, particularly the anxieties parents have about their children."[3] Victor argues that Devil-worshipping claims like those made against Mathers and his music are probably unfounded but culturally "significant . . . because they are . . . symptoms of serious problems in American society, which affect a great many people."[4] Some of these problems are addiction, war, poverty, civil rights, sexual revolution, and immigration.

The popularity of Satanist claims made against Eminem over the past 15 years, a period of great demographic, social, economic, political, and technological change in the United States, proves Victor's point. Conspiratorial theories asserting that Mathers is either a Satanist or an Illuminati pawn have reached a broad, mass audience through the Internet. For example, a quick Google search for the key terms "Eminem" and "Devil Worship" yields 541,000 results. These include message board threads, Wikipedia posts, and YouTube videos, many of which have been viewed anywhere from 5,000 to 300,000 times. Mathers (or Slim Shady) fans the flames by appearing to legitimize these rumor stories, which reveals audiences' values and social connections. As these Satanist rumors are generating appeal among spiritual zealots and mass-media audiences alike, it is important to examine his public endorsements of them as a meaningful way to draw audiences in through passionate condemnation.

A brief examination of two of Mathers's most spiritually charged songs, "Beautiful" and "My Darling" from the 2009 *Relapse* album, will help us understand the type of spirituality embedded in his music. First, we will explore how these spiritual expressions promote a sense of heaven and hell as ultimate destinations and the opposing possibilities for getting there. Then, we will see how Mathers connects with and relates to spiritual forces greater than he—equal parts proof that he walks with God and dances with the Devil.

WALKING WITH GOD

As far as spiritual selves go, the Marshall Mathers persona is not beautiful. However, he is honest and direct, and he is the soul and sanctuary of Eminem's life. Eminem enters this holy space and bares his soul more often than one might think. For instance, in "Beautiful" (2009), Mathers asks one question: What would you think if you saw someone important, like a government official or celebrity, digging around in the trash? The answer: You'd probably think that this kind of behavior was suitable for beggars only and certainly not for yourself. But this is exactly what Marshall Mathers does in "Beautiful" (2009). He looks for himself, others, and their fallen world or Eden (aka Detroit, Michigan) and finds everyone and everything in the garbage. In this way, "Beautiful" is a lovely parable. And, as with any parable, its objective is to illustrate a moral or a spiritual lesson using a simple human relation. The lesson in this case is looking for something or someone that has been lost. In Mathers's parable, there are seven ideas expressed about how to find what we have lost and develop our spiritual selves along the way: loss, light, movement, discovery, salvation, connection, and celebration. Here we will consider them one at a time.

The first verse of the song describes a person who is lost, incommunicado, and forlorn. This description can be related to the starting point of humanity's spiritual condition writ large per Christian spirituality. Some lose health. Others lose wealth. Some lose faith. Others lose heart. Even God has experienced loss, for in the Christian faith God sent his son to earth to die. Indeed, the chapter of loss in humanity's history is large, too large to write or read. Humanity has lost its state of innocence, its communion with God, its paradise and control over its environment. The song's first verse affirms such losses, especially the lost communion with a higher power, when Mathers asks "Are you calling me? . . . Are you reaching out for me like I'm reaching out for you?"

The second verse of the song tells us that the lost person needs a "spark to get psyched back up." That spark is light, and it is impossible to live without light, whether it is light for the eyes or for the heart. Mathers affirms this when he raps that he can no longer exist in the darkness of loss. He is depressed, in a slump, has fallen and wants to rise. For Mathers, words are the light: "So I decided just to pick up this pen." Similarly, in the beginning, God created light from darkness through words. Jewish and Christian scripture tells us that "God spoke: 'Light!' And light appeared. God saw that light was good."[5] This light converted many of history's darkest souls, such as Saul (aka the Apostle Paul) who saw the true condition of his heart and mind inside the light. At this point in the song, Mathers is like the Pharisee Saul before he becomes the Apostle Paul, and he embodies the many ways of being without light. To begin with, he cannot see very clearly. However, it can be argued that he cannot see because the light he carried into his solitary confinement has gone out and cannot be relit. Or, we can say that he is without light because he has nurtured his own selfishness through sorrow and addiction for too long and cannot see the world through the eyes of another. Or, he might be without light because he does not understand the things of God.

The chorus and third verse of the song are an invitation to see, somewhat dimly, through Mathers's own eyes. Mathers expresses this change of perspective by asking his audience to change places with him, to move, and "walk in my shoes, just to see." The call to movement is both secular and sacred. Biblical history tells us that during the time that Rome was the power in the known world, a Roman soldier could legally require anyone to carry his pack for a mile. And in The New Testament, the Apostle Paul suggests that we carry our brothers' and sisters' burdens even further as a sacrifice, gift, or to have a greater understanding of their life experiences.[6] Mathers references both of these perspectives along with an updated variation based on a Lakota Native American proverb: "Never criticize someone else unless you walk a mile in his moccasins." He then simplifies matters by saying that physical movement is not really even necessary. If we would just set our eyes to see and our ears to hear the story he is telling without judging him, it would be enough to share in the reality of human suffering and pain he describes.

The next verses are about discovery. Mathers tells listeners they can find him and those his story represents in low places. Let's face it: Low places are easy to find. You can see them, smell them, and hear them. And low places are easy to get lost in. Most people who get lost in low places usually suffer and die there. Mathers is saying that we must not be afraid to open the doors and windows to low places and meet one another at the bottom. After all, that is where God looks for and meets us: at the bottom of the world's low places—in immorality, in political garbage, in intellectual garbage, and in social garbage. And what Mathers now sees by inhabiting his own low place is that God could be looking for someone exactly like him, a pornography-watching, foul-mouthed, high school dropout turned gangsta rapper. The song implies that someone like Mathers can be redeemed and used by God to turn conventional wisdom on its head and reveal so-called experts and critics as crackpots. These lyrics confirm Mathers's previously expressed spiritual perspective in songs like "Criminal" (2002), where he offers up an example of insincere prayer by a televangelist. Describing the song in an interview, he says, "we've got all these preachers going 'Jesus, Jesus!' And then they're molesting kids. I'm taking stabs at crooked motherfuckers in the system."[7] Mathers's remarks in "Beautiful" and about "Criminal" suggest that one of his spiritual goals is to communicate positive values based on his evolving spiritual identity, which stands in direct contrast to the ways he has been portrayed by the hypocrisy of mass media and the religious right.

In "Beautiful," Mathers is proposing that society would be wise to rethink the ways that people can forge spiritual connections. In other words, perhaps we should drop some traditional religious practices in favor of creating a new culture of communication with the world, with each other, with the gospel, and with God. This spiritual interpretation of Mathers's work can be affirmed through scripture. The Apostle Paul writes that since worldly wisdom never seems to have a clue when it comes to the things of God, God in his wisdom takes delight in using whatever the world considers irreverent to bring those who will trust him into the way of salvation.[8] In this case, it is Mathers's gangsta rap that is considered irreverent. But Mathers is not alone here. Like other so-called gangsta rappers, including DMX and 2Pac, Mathers is clearly communicating that he did not learn any of the values he is expressing here by going to church. Instead, he learned them from God, who taught him in a personal way through his life's experiences that he is sharing with whoever will listen in the same firsthand, personal way.

Having found God, Mathers is able to end "Beautiful" on a relatively joyful note. He rejoices because he has been found in a low place and is in the process of being cleaned and made "beautiful" again. And he shares his joy by connecting with his children and listeners "even if it sounds corny." He lets us all know that we are beautiful too, and he uses that beauty to remind us that the moccasins God gave each of us will always fit beautifully because they are already broken in (by Jesus Christ). Those moccasins will be just the right ones we need to cover our feet as we walk into the light, embracing recovery, and away from the Devil's temptations, avoiding relapse.

DANCING WITH THE DEVIL

The experiences and encounters inherent in Mathers's alternative spiritual portrait, "My Darling" (2009), still emphasize personal struggles between light and darkness, finding a purpose in suffering and seeing a connection between societal and supernatural powers. Only this time, the supernatural power belongs to the Devil. Yet, unlike other songs in which he does battle with the Devil or suffers for his sins through eternal damnation in hell, "My Darling" is about a soul living in hell right here on earth. In this way, "My Darling" is both a lamentation and a dark parable whose moral complements that of "Beautiful." While God's salvation is a gift that can be accepted freely as we walk into the light, those who sell their souls to the Devil face dire consequences and eternal darkness. Those who sell their souls do get what they want in the short run. But they also pay for it later by suffering attack, oppression, or even possession. Mathers shares this moral in "My Darling" through six ideas about what happens when a person is losing his or her battle with the Devil and the demons he or she carries inside. These ideas are uncertainty, possession, darkness, harm, wholeness, and lament. We will now consider them one at a time.

In the first verse, Mathers brags about his public status as rap royalty because of his spiritual uncertainty and insecurity. He states that he is secure in the rap world even though there are a couple of good white rappers selling records like Paul Wall and Bubba Sparxxx. One reason Mathers sings his own praises here is because he is empowered by the Devil to dispose of all people who are willing to "sell their soul for this rap game." The underlying message here is that the only way for a white rapper to be totally respected and successful in a black art form, would be to make some sort of dark deal with the Devil. Another reason Mathers sets himself apart is because he is the only one really willing to sell his soul and say something about it. As he put it to journalist Chuck Weiner, "my thoughts are so fuckin' evil when I'm writing shit. . . . My thing is this, if I'm sick enough to think it, then I'm sick enough to say it."[9] We know Mathers is willing to go the extra mile in "My Darling" because he earlier announced on

"Infinite" (1996) that he has "a monster" within, later selling his soul in "Murder, Murder" (1997). Lastly, on the "Greg Freestyle" (1997), which was delivered on the *Sway and Tech Show,* he confessed, "It's only fair to warn I was born with a set of horns." Those horns are why he has never been afraid to document strange, frightening behaviors in his lyrics. And, as we will see, these include dramatic personality shifts accompanied by marked changes in behavior, voice tone, and speech content. Slowly but surely, Mathers's lyrics in "My Darling" refer to a part of himself—the Slim Shady persona—as a specific demon or spirit.

Mathers confirms the relationship between his decisions, lyrical prowess, and demonic possession when he checks microphone three times in "My Darling," saying, "one-two-three." Hip hop's conspiracy theorists suggest that this microphone check is actually an incantation or invitation for the Devil to enter the song's spiritual space for two reasons. First, because they believe that Satan is inherently musical with instruments built into his body and was even heaven's choirmaster before he was excised. This belief is supported by Christian scripture, which says, "the workmanship of thy tabrets and of thy pipes was prepared in thee in the day that thou wast created."[10] Second, conspiracy theorists believe that Mathers's microphone check is a Satanic incantation because the numbers, one-two-three, whether added or multiplied, total six-six-six when he recites them three times. This numeric pattern is commonly referred to in apocalyptic circles as the name of "the beast," which is never really named but represented by the 666 numeric pattern. Mathers implies that he wants his audiences to understand that 666, which is couched in a mysterious codified microphone check, is really the name of the higher power that continues to persecute him.

The beast hears and accepts Mathers's invitation and appears in his mirror, where he whispers seductively for Mathers to draw close. Although the mirror in which the beast manifests is warped and cracked, it is still painfully revealing. The Devil's wit and distortion, expressed through his chuckles, contain serious analysis of how humans' souls work. The Devil laughs when he intimates that humans are self-interested, interested in appearances and notoriety, and fearful of failure, rejection, and death. Although the Devil's reflection and commentary make Slim Shady smirk, they also make Marshall Mathers squirm. For Mathers, then, the Devil attacks from the outside as well as within by way of the conflicting personas both parties seek to control.

Not only does Mathers believe in the Devil, but he also believes that, as Slim Shady, he can be the Devil.

As we saw in "Beautiful," Mathers is still on a quest for spiritual intimacy, perspective, and release, only this time in "My Darling," his hymn about possession demonstrates the Devil's ability to pick at the cracks in any person's public image and private life. Satan knows that Mathers needs love, so he serenades, "you're my darling 'cause I possess your soul, your mind, your heart and your body." The possessive–obsessive relationship that controls every fiber of Mathers's being in "My Darling" is presented in direct opposition to the relationship between humans and God alluded to in "Beautiful" and described in Christian scripture. For instance, Jesus says that a person should "Love the Lord your God with all your heart and with all your soul and with all your strength and with all your mind'; and, 'Love your neighbor as yourself.'"[11] The point is that love of God and for others is what is missing in Mathers's spiritual connection with the Devil. Love and life have been exchanged for money and superstardom.

The increasing intensity and harm of the spiritual exchange between Mathers and the Devil are reflected in their verbal back-and-forth. Their souls, minds, and bodies are increasingly connected as they exchange more and more words. As in earlier songs like "When I'm Gone" (2004), at two different points in "My Darling," Mathers attempts to free himself by killing the Devil in the mirror, who looks and sounds more and more like Slim Shady. Obviously, the first attempt failed. This failure suggests that death is the only acceptable or known means of freeing Mathers from the Devil's tightening grip. That is why Mathers ups the ante the second time by taking himself out as he tries to do away with the Devil for good. Mathers awakes on the other side only to find the Devil there too, laughing as he taunts, "You can't kill a spirit even if you try to." Mathers has accidentally made their bond stronger by executing himself. Then he realizes that death is not enough to break the bond with the Devil. Only God can break the pair.

The Devil anticipates Mathers's revelation and intercepts any potential cry Mathers may make to God when he asks him to recall "that night you prayed to God you'd give anything to get a record deal." The Devil is reminding Mathers that possession may even occur in sacred settings such as prayer sessions because no space is truly safe. These remarks also indicate that Mathers's gains (fame and fortune) and losses (best friend and family) are consequences of his relationship with the Devil and not God. There is nothing Mathers can do to change anything. The Devil has taken hold within him and is now beyond his power to control. At the end of the song, Mathers submits. He comes to understand that he and the Devil are one as the Devil's final chorus becomes a duet with Mathers. The two have become one through a relationship of exchange and possession. Despite their opposing beginnings and endings, "My Darling" and "Beautiful" demonstrate that Mathers is influenced by a spiritual point of view. The moral raised by "Beautiful" is that God's salvation is a free gift given to those in low places who are not afraid to confront oppression and dispossession. The moral of "My Darling" is that fear of oppression creates opportunities for possession, which has a high price even as it takes the possessed to high places. These messages evoke public moral judgment and open a space for spiritual innovation. In order to reconcile what that innovation entails, and to understand what, if any, coherent spiritual messages are intrinsic to Mathers's work as a whole, I now turn to additional examples of spiritual beliefs, actions, and discourse embedded in his lyrics.

LOCATING MATHERS'S SPIRITUALITY

Paying attention to the spiritual themes found in Mathers's music is an important part of understanding how the perception of God and the Devil are active in today's popular culture. It is also a way of understanding whether Mathers himself attributes human suffering and success to these parties as supernatural forces. Mathers has admitted to a belief in God in interviews and he is not alone. According to a 2004 Gallup poll, Mathers is one of an "increasing number of individuals who believe in heaven, hell, the Devil, and angels."[12] Yet many of his lyrics suggest that he also contemplates and explores spirituality as an important part of everyday life. In order to find these themes and understand what they mean, 200 of the rapper's songs were identified and evaluated for their depictions of spirituality. The sample was obtained according to the same criteria and method outlined in Chapter 4.

Lyrics were coded for expressions of spirituality. Spirituality was initially defined as the feelings, thoughts, experiences, and encounters with God or Angels and Satan or Demons that arise when rules are broken and guilt is induced. The definition of spirituality was defined more narrowly for purposes of measurement as an awareness and relationship with God or Angels and Satan or Demons. Awareness of

God or Angels was defined as perception of the existence of a "spiritual force," God or Angels, "which may exert an active role in mediating human affairs and influence everyday life outcomes."[13] Relationship with God was defined as "the ability to interact with God or a Higher Power rather than being impersonally influenced by them."[14] Conversely, awareness of Satan or Demons was defined as "perception of the existence of a spiritual force," Satan or Demons, "which may exert an active role in mediating human affairs and influence everyday life outcomes."[15] Relationship with Satan was defined as the "ability to interact with" Satan or Demons "rather than being impersonally influenced by them." Belief was defined as "the mental action, condition, or habit of trusting or having confidence in" God, the Devil, and their manifestations.[16] The degree of awareness and relationship were measured in terms of frequency, which refers to how often these themes are featured in each lyrical segment.

THE GOSPEL ACCORDING TO MARSHALL MATHERS

Spiritual themes emerge in all of Mathers's albums and in a majority of his guest appearances and unreleased and/or underground recordings. In fact, Mathers's recently recorded solo album *Recovery* (2010), also his most commercially successful album, contains an overwhelming majority of his overall spiritual content. *Recovery* boasts a total of 68 references to, or 34 percent of, spiritual awareness and relationship. The album's visual communication affirms this spiritual theme as the CD is covered with a white cross in a red background, indicating that Mathers might be sharing an interest in the theme of resurrection. The solo album released just prior to *Recovery, Relapse* (2009) contains the second highest number of spiritual references, 43 or 21 percent of Mathers's overall spiritual content. That 56 percent of Mathers's overall spiritual content has emerged since 2009 suggests that his spiritual persona is developing in the wake of his recovery from drug abuse and as he continues to mature as a recording artist.

These general spiritual references indicate that Mathers's lyrics are influenced by a spiritual standpoint. However, in order to understand how these references form a thorough spiritual perspective, we must uncover what, if any, specific emphases on awareness and relationship exist.

Awareness of God

Awareness was the most prevalent aspect of spirituality represented in Mathers's lyrics. Spiritual awareness—knowledge of higher powers or realms that influence human affairs—was mentioned 130 times, or in 65 percent of lyrics. References to five types of spiritual forces, higher powers, or supernatural realms emerged: God (including Jesus Christ and the Holy Spirit), Angels, Satan or the Devil, Demons, and Hell. Explicit references to God occurred 46 times, or in 23 percent of lyrics. For example, in "It's Ok" (1996), he raps that he's "found . . . Christianity through God." And in "Say Goodbye to Hollywood" (2002), Mathers expresses gratitude to God for the gift of his daughter and the motivation she provides. He repeats the theme in "Never Enough" (2004) and "Never Over" (2010) when he declares that he is thankful for the life and talent God gave him, and he cries out to Jesus to save him from hellish torment in "3 AM" (2009). The frequency of explicit references to God suggests that God is the supreme personality or power in Mathers's spiritual picture. In several songs, such as "Infinite" (1996) and "Angels Around Me" (2004), Mathers paints himself as a Christ-like figure that is being crucified or otherwise attacked unjustly. In "Lose Yourself" (2002), he presents his journey from working-class Detroit to global superstardom as a parallel of Christ's journey from humble beginnings in a Bethlehem manger to becoming Lord and Savior of all. Therefore, no one should be surprised that young audiences listen to him religiously.

Explicit references to angels occurred nine times, or in 4.5 percent of lyrics. An example is provided in "Hellbound" (2000), where he states that "angels greet me but I don't reply back." This example is consistent with the idea that Mathers's spirit is influenced by demons and comes from hell rather than heaven. However, references to angels as guardians and protection from evil forces also emerge. In songs recorded after 2006, the year that his best friend Proof was gunned down, Mathers begins talking to angels and asking for their support. In particular, he assigns status as guardian angel to his deceased buddy in "Difficult" (2010), "Not Afraid" (2010), and "Cinderella Man" (2010).

Awareness of the Devil

With God and angels firmly situated it is fitting that the Devil would make an appearance. The spiritual power referred to as either Devil or Satan comes up 21 times, or in 10.5 percent of lyrics. Clearly, the Devil does not appear as often as God does. However, as demonstrated by the previous discussion of "My Darling" (2009), Satan's power over and impact on Mathers's lyrics is to be taken seriously. Essentially, the Devil is portrayed as God's opposite. Sometimes the Devil is a version of Mathers himself as in "Renegade" (2001) or "Murder Murder" (1997), when he raps, "money turned me into Satan." Other times the Devil is his master as in "5 Star Generals" (1998) or his father as in "Evil Deeds" (2004). Still other times, as in "Bad Influence" (1999), Mathers describes his listeners as the next generation of devils who are empowered to do evil things after hearing his music. And when the Devil comes down to earth, he becomes a she. Yes, she. When women are devils, they represent both threats to and objects of Mathers's masculinity. Although Mathers certainly is not the only rapper who makes this gendered correlation (think Kanye West), in his lyrics, women tempt him to commit sins for which all parties must burn in hell. Because his personal failures are her fault, she deserves whatever violence he commits against her. By Mathers's own admission in his official autobiography *Angry Blonde* (2002), this is one way to interpret his murder ballad "Kim" (2000). An example of the woman as the Devil's helper is "Cocaine" (2010), in which he takes a bite out of Eve's apple and must suffer the eternal consequences. It should also be noted that women are relegated to the status of devils whenever they assert their independence and disobey Mathers's orders, as in myth when the angel Lucifer became Satan because he thought himself to be God's equal and not God's servant. A primary example of this latter characterization is "Fastlane" (2011), in which Mathers decapitates a long-legged, busty animated woman who disobeys his demand for instant sexual gratification.

When the Devil appears as or within Slim Shady, as in "My Mom" (2009) when he says that he is his mother, we see that the woman some men fear most is the woman within. If we believe that all good and true leaders are masculine and heterosexual, then this woman within must be dominated by any means necessary, especially sexualized violence. Mathers addresses the need to dominate and excise the female Devil within in "Kill You" (2000) when he humiliates her verbally and talks of raping her. And if we believe that the Devil is mostly female, as Mathers does, then we also believe that she needs to be contained, controlled, and destroyed because of her evil desires and deeds. Therefore, she deserves whatever punishments males, acting as God's soldiers and representatives, inflict on her. When we consider the largely demonized spiritual view of women in Mathers's lyrics in light of the fact that "one in four women (25 percent) has experienced domestic violence in her lifetime,"[17] we begin to see an emerging spiritual rationale for sexism and misogyny. If women are influenced by a satanic force, then there is not much point in showing them any respect or empathy. After all, all is fair in spiritual warfare.

Demons, the next figures in Mathers's spiritual drama, appear 20 times or in 10 percent of lyrics because they are personalities through which the Devil's presence manifests. In general, Mathers describes demons as cruel, evil, destructive, and tormenting. Mathers does most of his spiritual battling with demons because they remind him of the habits and Devil he is attempting to leave behind. In "Wee Wee" (2011), he screams that he should "let them demons out!" Other times he becomes a demon, as in "I'm Having a Relapse" (2009) when he returns to drug use. In "Music Box" (2009), demons speak to him and encourage him to worship Satan by committing violent sins. In "Lose Yourself" (2002), he references the eerie Stephen King novel *Salem's Lot*, which describes a man and a town under siege from the forces of demons. Like Satan, demons appear in many forms. Sometimes they appear as the power or influence of alcohol and drugs. Sometimes demons are the cause of mental illness, fear, anger, and depression. And in rare cases, Mathers suggests that demons can even cause epilepsy and Parkinson's disease. The point seems to be twofold. First, demons are to blame for much of what is wrong in the world today, and second, that when people believe that evil forces are attacking them, there is a great need to somehow find freedom from the torment even though there is not much information given on how to do so.

Relationships with God and the Devil

Mathers's lyrics also express his relationship with supernatural powers. References to relationship with God appeared 39 times, or in 19.5 percent of lyrics. Sometimes Mathers sees himself as godlike. In "Infinite" (1996), he refers to Jesus as a rapper who battled against phonies and to himself as the greatest rapper to appear "since the burial of Jesus." Other times he sees himself as made powerful by God. For instance, in "You're Never Over" (2010) and "Not Afraid" (2010), Mathers asks God for the strength to overcome oppression. In "Any Man" (1999),

"My Fault" (1999), and "Cold Wind" (2010), God is the only one who can grant forgiveness of sins. In "Lose Yourself" (2002), God is his friend, the only one who can know the trouble he has seen. In "Till I Collapse" (2002), he admits to being saved, "I showed ya the spirit of God lives within us." In "One Shot 2 Shot" (2004), God saved his life and called him to fulfill a higher purpose as a rapper. And, in "Cold Wind" (2010), God strikes Mathers with lightning and speaks from on high, reminding him of his promise to repent and be saved. Mathers's multifaceted relationship with God suggests that God has high expectations for him, that God expresses tough love through discipline, can see beyond his imperfections, is ultimately forgiving, and most importantly, that God is on his side. The frequency of references to a relationship with God suggests that Mathers may ultimately be finding himself on God's side too.

Ultimately, Mathers relates to God in terms of recovery, resurrection, and revival. In "Not Afraid" (2010), Mathers paints a portrait of his comeback by using his checkered past as a way to connect with listeners on a more authentic note. In the chorus he raps, "Everybody come take my hand. We'll walk this road together." These levels of connection with and movement in the world around him are made possible through his relationship with God. Throughout his work he credits God for his new levels of professional and personal success. Such successes are measured by his ongoing sobriety, his award-winning album *Recovery* with its record-setting successes in the digital marketplace, his improving relationships with his mother and ex-wife, and his successful lawsuits, which resulted in large donations to the recovery of Detroit through the Marshall Mathers Foundation and large-scaled changes to the global recording industry. It seems that with God's help Mathers's powers to generate profit and overcome challenges are just as he predicted on his first album. They are infinite.

References to Mathers's relationship with the Devil, occurring 29 times or in 14.5 percent of lyrics indicate that the highway to heaven is definitely unpaved. In "Still Don't Give a Fuck" (1999), "Bad Influence" (1999), and "Music Box" (2009), Mathers calls himself a Satanist. In "Demon Inside" (2008), he once again admits to selling his soul in exchange for success. Throughout his lyrics, he attributes the origin of his own sins and the sins of others to the Devil. Unsurprisingly, he does this with lyrics that describe antagonism and contain evil imagery, as in "Role Model" (1999) when he plays on the idea of celebrity as a devilish figure who can magically persuade audiences to do absolutely anything.

Mathers also depicts himself as possessed by the Devil and demons. In "Go to Sleep" (2003), he says that he will go on a killing spree because "a demon's unleashed in me." In "Demon Inside" (2008), he describes in chilling detail what it feels like to be possessed and wait for Satan to appear. And, as "My Darling" (2010) illustrates, every reference to his relationship with the Devil is rife with themes of intimacy, total possession, and exchange that could also describe his relationships with women. This suggests that while a person can fall out of and back into God's good graces, thus experiencing freedom, a relationship with the Devil is unchanging and unrelenting. Mathers's suggestion may indicate that he is still working out his salvation with fear and trembling. God gives Mathers the space he needs to figure things out while the Devil leaves him only enough room to squirm. God is merciful while the Devil is not.

REVELATION

This chapter looked at the type and number of spiritual expressions evident in Eminem's lyrics in order to better understand the Marshall Mathers persona as spiritual self. Spiritual expressions were defined awareness and relationships with God or Angels and Satan or Demons that arise when rules are broken and guilt is induced. On the surface, connections to spirituality in Mathers's lyrics may seem insignificant. However, the increasing recurrence of spiritual themes suggests that we would be wise to consider an open-minded examination of his work. Analysis confirmed previous studies' results, which indicated that there is a spiritual element to his work despite much of its crude content. Although the spiritual element exists, it does not clearly indicate that Mathers adheres to a particular religion. Rather, the spiritual element suggests that Mathers communicates a genuine awareness of God and the Devil and their manifestations and a heightened awareness of God that allows him to relate to the world at large. In this way Mathers is one of many artists whose pop culture content carries a strong spiritual dimension, confirming results of previous studies, which argue that "celebrity culture is secular society's rejoinder to the decline of religion and magic."[18]

Mathers's spiritual themes played out in terms of solidarity with God and the Devil, a mistrust of organized religion due to its inherent hypocrisy, a desire to escape hell, ambivalence about getting into heaven, and an intense personal battle between good and evil. These dynamics are important because they show Mathers's audiences not just a reflection of himself in higher powers, but a reflection of themselves in his spiritual persona. The spiritual reflections presented in Mathers's music are not just means of identification; they are also means of division that reveal how conflicted we often are about ourselves. Just as Mathers walks with God and dances with the Devil as he deals with life's challenges, audiences listening to his music are able to escape from their own worlds and find temporary refuge in his mediated spiritual world. As Peter Ward writes in *Gods Behaving Badly,* the spiritual power of Mathers's music for audiences lies in its representations of a "conflicted and complex self clothed in the metaphors of the divine and reflected back to us."[19] The popularity of Mathers's lyrics supports the conclusion that his version of spirituality coincides with the spiritual ideologies of fans that buy and listen to his messages and the larger society within which their spiritual ideologies are shaped. It can also be concluded that his work speaks to those who consider themselves spiritually committed even if that commitment is often not manifested in traditional religious activities. If the above is true, then we can take Mathers's claim, expressed via tweet on October 11, 2011, that "music has the power to heal" as a spiritual declaration.[20] And we can also take a fan's response to this tweet as an Amen: "All Eminem songs has [*sic*] a spiritual connection . . . you have to have the ear to find that for yourself."[21]

CHAPTER 6
The Thin Line

There is a thin line between love and hate for us all, and for Eminem, that line reaches its finest point. He crosses the line between love and hate in many of his lyrics, especially those about and addressed to women. Slim Shady shows open contempt for female fans and, to be fair, veiled contempt for all fans. Marshall Mathers, the moral compass, appears to make sure that fans do not lose interest or willingness to invest in his music. Mathers is able to express love as a powerful spiritual force matched only by the searing and destructive intensity of Slim Shady's hate. Mathers is always there to remind audiences that there is a "decent human being underneath" as evidenced in the lyrics of "Bitch Please II" (2000). This back-and-forth between Slim Shady and Mathers allows the rapper to follow a raised middle finger with an apology, a change of tone and tenor, and a declaration of love in "Kill You" (2000) and "White America" (2002). Slim Shady's contempt is not to be taken seriously, we are told, because Marshall Mathers really loves us. Mathers takes a similar approach to explaining several scandalous ballads like "Cleaning Out My Closet" (2002), "Kim" (2000), "'97 Bonnie and Clyde" (1999), "Drug Ballad" (2000), "Space Bound" (2010), "Love the Way You Lie" (2010), and "Love the Way You Lie Part II" (2011). He does take a more serious and respectful approach in his odes to the men he has either loved or lost in his life like Stan in "Stan" (2000), Proof in "Never 2 Far" (2010), and Dr. Dre in "I Need a Doctor" (2011). Other times, he crosses the line and expresses downright hatred for the entire world as in "Just Don't Give a Fuck" (1999), "The Apple" (2010), and "Roman's Revenge" (2010).

However, love and hate are not just opposing forces in spiritual struggles that emerge when rules are broken and guilt is induced. Love and hate are intertwined. And the web of love–hate Em spins in his lyrics keeps Debbie, Kim, Hailie, Lanie (niece and adopted daughter), Dre,

Paul Rosenberg (Eminem's manager), Ken Kanniff (an imaginary gay man from Connecticut who love–hates the rapper), a Public Service Announcer, Slim Shady, and Marshall Mathers trapped inside. Several cultural commentators have offered explanations for why these tales of love–hate are so appealing. In *Jesus and the Disinherited,* theologian Howard Thurman writes that hate is something that often becomes a powerful motivation for action and a form of protective armor. In this way, hate becomes a way of rejecting others before they can reject us because we would rather do that than get to know and experience fellowship with others. Feminist author bell hooks agrees. In *Communion,* hooks writes that everyone wants love and fellowship and that nearly everyone is unable or unwilling to talk about it. We fear that honest talk about love will force us to face what we hate most—the pain of admitting we have neither received nor given the kind of love that really satisfies us on a spiritual level. In *The Nature of Hate,* sociologists Robert J. Sternberg and Karin Sternberg explain why Thurman and hooks are right: instead of living love-filled lives, we more often experience "love-hate" as a common feature of day-to-day life. This is because "the ones we love have the most power to hurt us, and it can be those loved ones that stir hatred in us."[1] Love–hate relationships are common because they allow for the exploration and fulfillment of deep spiritual needs for intimacy, nurturance, and belonging in many ways.

As we will soon see, some of those ways of fulfilling the spiritual need for intimacy are more socially acceptable than others. The Sternbergs identify several types of love–hate relationships. Sometimes love–hate relationships appear in the form of addiction, where people are dependent on one another or on drugs and alcohol. Sometimes love–hate is a business relationship, where people see themselves and one another as investments or investors. Sometimes love–hate is depicted in terms of horror, when one partner terrorizes the other. Sometimes love–hate takes a mysterious form, where one partner is puzzling and the other tries to figure him or her out. And sometimes love–hate is, as rocker Pat Benatar once called it, a "battlefield" upon which partners get pleasure from fighting with each other. But more often than not, love–hate displays its truest colors through the lens of fantasy, in which partners take on roles and must fill those roles for each other at all costs. When partners fail to fill their assigned roles in a completely positive way, love quickly turns to hate.

Fantasy love–hate relationships are usually one-sided and can occur quite easily for celebrities' fans since fans enter into one-sided parasocial fantasy love–hate relationships by way of mass-media exposure. The more fans listen to their favorite stars, the more they create shared experiences with the celebrity persona. The more fans watch, the more they think they can predict what the persona will do. And the persona becomes increasingly reliable, even more reliable than many of the real people in fans' lives. In return, fans become increasingly loyal and zealous. Of the 200 Eminem songs evaluated in this book, only one displays the full spectrum of a parasocial fantasy-oriented love–hate relationship with a spiritual edge. That song is "Stan" (2000), whose plot is based on fan mail the artist actually received. Mathers describes Stan as a zealot, someone who is fanatical and uncompromising in pursuit of Slim Shady as his ideal partner. Mathers goes on to describe the song as an epistle "about an obsessed fan who keeps writing me and tells me he's taking everything I say on the record seriously. . . . I try to help him . . . it kinda shows the real side of me."[2]

STAN

"Stan" starts with sounds of an intense thunderstorm much like the opening of William Shakespeare's *The Tempest*. And, as in Shakespeare's play, the storm in "Stan" is full of symbolic meaning. The thunderstorm is a clash of cold and hot physical forces, an external expression of the clash between love and hate in Stan's soul and mind. Like Stan's voice, thunder resounds with instability. Like Stan's hands, lightning destroys whatever it strikes. We meet Stan in the bathroom of his run-down home, putting peroxide in his hair and watching himself turn into Slim Shady with sadistic regard (love–hate). He is already dressed like Slim Shady, wearing a white wife-beater tank, black jeans, and dog tag. This wardrobe choice indicates Stan's high levels of identification with Slim Shady. When his girlfriend enters the bathroom to find out what is going on, he screams that he does not want to be called "that" (Stanley or Stan) anymore.

Stan has obviously been sexually intimate with his girlfriend recently because she is pregnant. However, he treats her with contempt when she interrupts his one-sided relationship with his favorite idol. When his girlfriend questions Stan's fidelity due to his desire to take his love for Slim Shady "too far," Stan leaves her in the bathroom and descends to his basement underworld. There he has plastered the walls with pictures of Eminem in an attempt to bridge the very real social, economic, and spiritual gaps between them. Stan paces. He is crazed. He looks at the two stamped letters on his desk ready to be mailed to Eminem's Fan Club. Then he sits down to write another. Stan looks up from his letter at the television where he sees Slim waving at the camera. Stan, taking this image as a personal address, waves right back and keeps writing. Soon, we see Stan looking in the mirror and seeing Slim's reflection staring back at him, just the way Mathers himself will later see the Devil's reflection (as Slim) in another mirror in "My Darling" (2009). Could Slim have possessed Stan and added a letter to his name? Is Stan becoming Satan? If so, this could mean that when Slim possesses Stan and takes over, evil things are going to happen and that whatever happens is not Stan's fault. By making himself over in Slim's image, Stan could be calling the Devil forth in the mirror. But even if this is not the case, the video explains that Stan's obsessive neurosis is fed by the demon of substance abuse, which shows the dark and hate-filled hold on his life. The point is that Slim, and neither Stan nor Mathers, will be to blame for whatever comes next.

Meanwhile, Marshall Mathers (Eminem's spiritual persona) is on a tour bus sitting still and thinking, waiting for fan mail to be delivered. We know it is Mathers because he is alone (not social self Eminem), and he is not wearing the typical Slim Shady uniform (not material self). He puts his glasses on and sits back in his seat to really concentrate on Stan's letter while shaking his head, indicating that he is both intrigued and disgusted by what Stan has written (love–hate).

The letter Mathers reads, Stan's latest letter, is the first verse of the song. It is a love–hate letter but mostly expresses love. In it, Stan writes that he admires and approves of Slim's music, identifies with the domestic instability and violence he experienced and expects a response in the form of a phone call from the rapper. Stan also expresses and fights off feelings of abandonment over Slim's lack of response by blaming it on his own bad handwriting and errors at the post office. We later learn that Stan was right. The post office lost his first letter, so the rapper is not unresponsive. Stan moves on to say that he cares about Slim's family and well-being and tells him about how things are going in his own life. Mathers learns that Stan is from a single-parent household, has a six-year-old brother named Matthew (played by Mathers's cousin Korey Nelson), and is expecting a daughter with his girlfriend, who he will name Bonnie after Mathers's deceased uncle Ronnie. Incidentally, Ronnie committed suicide because a desired mate rejected him. Mathers quickly sees that Stan's attempt at loving identification and approval carries the potential to turn to hate-filled harm. As if anticipating this reaction, Stan continues by repeating how much he loves the rapper's music. Slim Shady's music is sacred because Stan takes refuge in it from life's pursuits, dangers, and troubles. He proves this when he signs the letter expressing his devotion, "Truly yours, your biggest fan. This is Stan."

Stan's next letter comprises the second verse of the song. It is another love–hate missive but Stan's hate is beginning to replace love. Although the note begins with a loving "Dear Slim," the tone quickly changes to express Stan's feelings of abandonment at the lack of response. Stan lets Slim know that he is not fulfilling his proper role as Stan's partner in this relationship. Then Stan explains that he has filled his role as a loyal fan by waiting outside in the snow after an appearance to get an autograph for Matthew for "four hours." He also reminds Slim about their meeting at a record signing in Denver when Slim promised to write back to Stan. Again, Stan emphasizes that he has been the perfect partner in this relationship but Slim has not. We know from Stan's return address that he drove 12 hours and over 700 miles to Denver, Colorado from Portland, Missouri just to meet Slim at the album signing. We also know that Stan shakes Slim's hand and hugs him when they meet but Slim does not hug Stan back. That is when Stan writes that he still holds Slim in high regard because of their intense bond and shared experiences of parental abandonment, infidelity, and poverty. To demonstrate this, Stan writes that he has gotten a tattoo of Slim's name across his chest just as Slim got a tattoo of Kim across his chest. He then tells Slim about the pleasure he gets out of listening to his music while cutting himself. Stan sees self-mutilation as a kind of blood offering to Slim. He also sees his unnamed girlfriend's concern for him as jealousy over his intensity and devotion to Slim. Stan's contempt for his girlfriend increases as her perceived envy and meddling increase.

Next, Stan remembers another Eminem concert where he and his younger brother are up front and are the only males. Stan and his brother are fixated on the rapper and not on the many females who surround them as they are dancing to the music and vying for the rapper's attention and affection. Stan is disgusted by the women's attempts at tempting Slim. In his eyes, the women's impure physical response to the music is displayed by their willingness to shake their bodies and show Slim some kind of erotic expression of love. However, Stan and his brother share a deeper and purer love connection with the star.

We know that Slim looks in Stan's direction from the stage and smiles, but we do not know that the rapper even saw Stan among the sea of girls dancing. After the concert, a crazed female groupie thwarts Stan's attempt to get an autograph. Stan is enraged. Again, women keep getting in his way. Stan's mother also becomes an obstacle when she yells at Matthew because he is following in Stan's and Slim's footsteps with peroxide blonde hair. Women are always trying to break the sacred connection between Slim and his most adoring male fans, so they must be punished.

Because all women are obstacles, and because they all hate the love connection between Stan and Slim, we are not surprised to learn that Stan's contempt for his girlfriend grows. Stan tells Slim that she just does not understand the bond they share because of their similar upbringings. All she wants to do is interrupt their communication. Now, seeing himself as a version of Slim Shady, Stan gets back to writing and ends the letter by pleading for a response, signing it "sincerely yours." Only this time, Stan also reveals his increasing desire for Slim by adding an erotic postscript: "we should be together too." To make sure Slim gets the message, he includes a picture of himself and his girlfriend that he has altered to be a picture of himself with Slim. In Stan's mind, the picture displays his devotion to the star and will make Slim feel really sorry if he ends up losing out on a chance to know his number one fan.

The tide now turns swiftly. When the chorus plays, Stan's girlfriend goes to the basement while Stan is sleeping and looks around. She finds the photo and feels afraid, betrayed, and disgusted. Stan finds her and puts her in the trunk of his car. Then he goes back into the house and destroys his shrine. The song/video then transitions quickly to its third verse, Stan's final love–hate letter. We see that Stan is reciting it into a tape recorder while driving drunk in the rain. Stan looks longingly at the Slim photo hanging from his rearview mirror and begins. He coldly dictates his resentment and anger at Slim's refusal to respond for six months. Stan has run out of patience and wants Slim to hear the sound of his voice because he is longing for a connection. He talks about the pleasure he is getting out of driving around with his girlfriend screaming in the trunk of his car and of the excitement he is feeling because he is about to do something evil.

Stan makes one last attempt to identify with Slim, asking him if he remembers Phil Collins's song "In the Air Tonight" (1979). This song, written out of the love–hate Collins felt after divorcing his first wife Andrea, is about a man who could have rescued another man from drowning but chose not to. Stan paints Slim as a villain who has chosen not to save him. Interestingly, even in this accusation, Stan does not refer explicitly to any of Slim's own violently themed love–hate songs. Of course, both he and Slim know that he is acting out "'97 Bonnie and Clyde." But Stan refers to one of the many other recording artists who have expressed similar themes before Slim became famous. Through Stan, Mathers's subtle message here is that Slim really is not doing anything new and therefore cannot really be held responsible. Although Stan's final act appears to be premeditated and inspired by Slim's murder and suicide fantasies, Stan is careful to remind Slim that they are not very much alike after all. For instance, Stan did not slice her throat but chose instead to tie her up. In Stan's mind, this proves that he is no longer Slim's greatest fan. He has actually become the real Slim Shady because he will cause more suffering to his girlfriend than Slim did to Kim in "'97 Bonnie and Clyde." Stan's girlfriend will die a slow and painful death by suffocating. Stan will even kill himself and his unborn child in the process, which are things Slim might say but Mathers would never have the courage to do. Their blood will not just be on Slim's hands, but it will also be on his soul. Stan quickly snaps out of his hate only to see a very real roadblock and utter his final words, a last ditch effort to bridge the gap between himself and Slim: "I forgot, how am I supposed to send this shit out?" Stan cannot know it then, but Slim will learn about and connect with him soon enough through mass-media coverage of his and his family's death.

The last verse of the song is the response Stan has been waiting for but never has the chance to receive. However, it is not Slim who responds, it is Marshall Mathers. This persona shift is important because it suggests that some fans do not realize that there is no real Slim Shady or that they really do not know Marshall Mathers despite the fact that they may identify strongly with his music. Answering Stan as Marshall Mathers makes the point that Slim Shady is a false idol and Stan is an idolater. Stan's idolatry is serious business for many reasons, not the least of which is that it is a breach of the first commandment. In Exodus 20:4–6 (The Message) God warns, "Don't bow down to [false gods] and don't serve them because I am GOD, your God, and I'm a most jealous God, punishing the children for any sins their parents pass on to them to the third, and yes, even to the fourth generation of those who hate me." This punishment certainly applies in Stan's case as his girlfriend and unborn daughter die and his little brother is left only to mourn and repeat his mistakes.

Mathers starts writing his love–hate letter to Stan with this idea about idolatry in mind. He starts with an attempt to make Stan feel more secure. Mathers writes that he respects their shared backgrounds. We are reminded that the two do reflect each other in many ways when we see that Mathers writes with his left hand while Stan writes with his right hand. Mathers goes on to explain that his busy schedule kept him from writing sooner. He wants Stan to know that he really cares about his fans and would not miss out on an opportunity to sign an autograph or otherwise attend to their needs. He then expresses his concern and disgust (love–hate) at Stan's self-mutilation. He suggests that Stan get some therapy. He also expresses his concern and disgust at Stan's erotic desire for them to be together. Mathers tells Stan that if he keeps writing things like that, he will lose out on the chance to get to know his idol better. He tries to explain that the bond Stan feels is one-sided because he cannot tell the difference between fantasy and reality. For instance, Mathers only takes on the Slim Shady (straight) persona to create controversy. Mathers returns to writing and realizes that because of Stan's increasing instability, he needs to get this letter out urgently. He is afraid that Stan will do something violent. At this point, Mathers remembers seeing a news report about a young man who drove off a bridge and connects the dots. The thunder claps. It was Stan . . . "Damn!" The lightning strikes, and we can see Stan's haunting reflection over Mathers's shoulder in the window of the tour bus.

The song/video "Stan" is a demonstration of spiritual dimensions of love–hate for many reasons. The most obvious is that it takes the form of an epistle, or a poem in the form of a letter or series of letters. This style of communication is found in many sacred texts including the *Holy Bible* and the *Holy Qur'an*. This epistle presented in "Stan" dramatizes the perils of love–hate relationships and punishments for idolatry. "Stan" also demonstrates that despite their best attempts, Stanley Mitchell and Marshall Mathers were never able to make a real spiritual connection. The only connection the pair could ever share is through mass-media representation. Stan knows Mathers's Slim persona through his music, videos, and interviews. Mathers recognizes Stan because of the televised news coverage of his tragic death. Mathers does not know Stan by the Slim Shady persona he adopted because the news did not report it. And neither Mathers nor Stan can really ever know the other's true spiritual self based on the information mass media reveals and conceals about their Slim Shady personas. The media's broken connection is symbol-ized by the fact that the bridge Stan finally drove off while dictating his final words was blocked. In this way, "Stan" argues that media exposure is no substitute for old-fashioned human communication. To put it plainly, the "Stan" epistle's message is that only true interpersonal interaction between equals creates authentic and sustainable love connections. Loving by way of parasocial interaction too easily disintegrates into love–hate relationships because of real gaps, like the need for authentic human fellowship, which media imagery just cannot bridge.

Critics and colleagues have acknowledged "Stan" as one of Mathers's most influential and controversial compositions. Most recently, Lil' Wayne admitted that he was so haunted by the song's portrayal of celebrity–fan relationships that he wrote "Dear Anne" (2011) as a response. In this song, Lil' Wayne pens an epistolary ode to his "number one fan" Anne, telling her that he appreciates her support, wants to know more about her perspective, and does not want her to suffer Stan's fate. "Dear Anne" broaches many of the same themes as "Stan," suggesting that one way of understanding attempts at spiritual fellowship between rappers and fans is through detailed description, interpretation, and evaluation of themes of love and hate in rap lyrics. In order to recognize these themes, and to understand what, if any, coherent spiritual messages about love and hate appear in Mathers's work as a whole, I now turn to a content analysis of his lyrics.

UNCOVERING THE LOVE–HATE IN EMINEM'S LYRICS

When tracing the thin line between love and hate in Eminem's lyrics, we must be detailed and careful. To begin with, we must define love and hate as spiritual conditions. According to Rev. David Hino, from a spiritual perspective, love is based on value held for the person or object of our desire.[3] Love generates intimacy, and lovers ensure the well-being of the person or object of desire. Hate destroys intimacy, and haters devalue or destroy everything they hate.

As we have seen in "Stan," love and hate can coexist. Research in communication and psychology supports this perspective and suggests that love and hate share six types of expression. According to John K. Rempel and Christopher T. Burris in "Let Me Count the Ways: An Integrative Theory of Love and Hate," the six types of love are erotic, dependent, enrichment, companionate, regard, and altruistic. Erotic love or *eros* makes us feel excited and is "an intense longing for a sexual and emotional union with a desirable mate."[4] Dependent love is like an addiction. It is "a love based on need" that cries out for "nurturance . . . the ongoing soothing of one's felt deficiencies by the loved other." In contrast, enrichment love is based on security. In enrichment love, the secure partner wants to make the beloved happy and create a safe space for the relationship to grow. Companionate love, what theologians describe as *philia* or brotherly love, is the kind of love that seeks out "cooperative, mutually rewarding relationships."[5] It is similar to erotic love but does not include the sexual–passionate dynamic. Regard love looks for a good catch and can even involve hero worship and parasocial relationships. As a result, love relationships based on regard are more self-oriented as lovers are really looking for social approval from and identification with a particular person or object rather than a mutually rewarding relationship. Altruistic love, also referred to as *agape* love, is unadulterated love. It is completely selfless, based on empathy, caring, and responsiveness, and its only goal is to promote the well-being of the beloved person or object. Most people, except for maybe some very self-absorbed types, operate in erotic, and companionate love. When people encounter altruistic relationships, they understand how better to operate in all other types of love.

In counterpoint to the six types of love, Rempel and Burris also introduce the six types of hate: sadistic, mutiny, tethering, denigrating, redress, and nihilistic. Sadistic haters get their thrills from interactions that cause the hated other to suffer. Mutiny haters feel trapped and resent feeling that way, so they assert autonomy by lashing out against whomever or whatever is around. Examples of mutiny hating are child abuse and domestic violence. Tethering hate has the opposite effect of mutiny hate. Instead of trying to separate from the hated person or object, the tethering hater draws increasingly closer in order to fight off feelings of fear, loss, and abandonment. Denigrating haters are generally led by jealousy and disdain and want to bring others down and keep them there. The idea behind denigrating hate is that there are limited resources available and others, who are inferior to the hater, are getting more than their fair share of those resources. Redress hate is basically a form of revenge. Redress haters are characterized by their anger and disgust at the way they have been treated by others and want to make things right according to their own standards of justice. Nihilistic hate is redress hate gone wild. Nihilistic hate is "elicited by a loathing of the other and typified by a sense of the necessity of the other's injury, suffering or complete demise."[6]

In order to uncover the spiritual expressions of love–hate in Eminem's lyrics, a sample of 200 songs released by the artist between the years of 1990 and 2012 were examined (as in Chapters 4 and 5). It is to these passionate expressions that we now turn.

WHERE IS THE LOVE–HATE?

Mathers expresses six types of love–hate in the following order: dependence love–redress hate; altruistic love–nihilistic hate, companionate love–tethering hate; regard love–sadistic hate; erotic love–denigrating hate; and enrichment love–mutiny hate. The frequency with which these relationships appear raises three important points. First, that Mathers's lyrics are meant primarily to negate intimacy between him and the characters about whom he writes. Second, that his lyrics promote intimacy with audiences. Third, that it is possible to hate a loved one as the result of perceived wrongdoing and disloyalty.

Of the six types of love–hate expressions examined, dependence–regress is the most frequent, appearing 123 times or in 61.5 percent of lyrics. Dependence–regress relationships are characterized by need, anger, and disgust. As examples, Mathers diagnoses his personal relationships with women in this manner. We have seen representations in "Kim" (2000), "Love You More" (2004), "Crazy in Love" (2004), "Love the Way You Lie" (2010), and "Space Bound" (2010). He also characterizes his relationships with demons and the Devil similarly in "Still Don't Give a Fuck" (1999), "Crazy in Love" (2004), "Rain Man" (2004), "Evil Deeds" (2004), "We're Back" (2006), "3 AM" (2009), "Demon Inside" (2008), and "My Darling" (2009). These songs show the total dependence and disgust that take over when women, devils, and demons fall in love with an angry addict. Mathers's trick is using disgust to his advantage by presenting hateful descriptions without being so revolting that listeners stop loving him. Here's how it works: younger audiences love the same disgusting content in Mathers's lyrics that angers older audiences. Young females who listen to the music may become vulnerable in the eyes of young boys who either act macho or feign indifference to the gore presented. The idea here is that if boys can withstand the disgust violation presented, they will be more attractive in girls' eyes even if they act out the disgusting behavior and ultimately harm girls. Like anger, disgust is aimed at maintaining a social order that too often makes women dependent on men.

Altruistic–nihilistic expressions appeared second most often, 115 times or in 57.5 percent of lyrics. In these expressions "selfless, other-oriented compassion"[7] is matched with "simmering" hate and total destruction.[8] This type of relationship appears in songs that refer to unfaithful females like "'97 Bonnie & Clyde" (1999), "Guilty Conscience" (1999), "Kim" (2000), and "50 Ways" (2011), when he plots and/or carries out the murder of an unfaithful female (who could be either a lover or his mother). In such expressions, the female is elevated as a possible object of affection while promoted as a source of sadistic pleasure. Generally, Mathers's pleasure is often derived from narrating the loved one's total destruction after describing the missed opportunity to pursue and sustain a stable, secure long-term love relationship. It seems that for Mathers the idea of a stable love relationship based on empathy and caring is, ironically, experienced as one that causes permanent emotional and physical harm.

The third most frequent love–hate expression in Mathers's lyrics is companionate–tethering, appearing 112 times or in 56 percent of lyrics. This type of relationship seeks a sustainable and mutually beneficial relationship while grappling with intense fear of abandonment. Such expressions are designed to keep the love–hated other close while disabling her through physical, emotional, psychological, or economic channels. The most dramatic depictions of tethering can be found in the songs that deal with masochism and domestic violence. For instance, in "Love the Way You Lie" (2010), Mathers begs the partner he abuses not to leave, and he continues pleading in "Love the Way You Lie Part II" (2010) when he asks her to "hug me then tell me how ugly I am . . . then after that shove me." In "50 Ways" (2011), a psychiatrist tells Mathers that only he can choose to disconnect his desire for a mutually rewarding relationship from his fear that opening up will make his partner want to leave. Because he knows he is unable to dissociate companionate love from tethering hate he warns potential girlfriends that they would be better off not getting involved with him because he exhibits abusive behavior in songs like "Pills" (1999) and "Superman" (2002).

Expressions of regard love–sadistic hate appeared 101 times, or in 50.5 percent of lyrics. These expressions take on two forms: idolatry and interpersonal attraction. As demonstrated by "Stan" (2000), idolatry is one-sided whereas interpersonal attraction requires mutuality. Conversely, in "Crazy in Love" (2004), Mathers describes his regard for Kim metaphorically. She is "the ink to [his] paper," the force that brings him to life. These expressions indicate that the objectives of regard love are approval and identification which, when withheld are transformed into pleasure at another person's suffering. Most often, Mathers provides graphic depictions of sexualized violence against Kim and other women who withhold approval and identification. The most notorious examples include "Just Don't Give a Fuck" (1999), "Guilty Conscience" (1999), "Kill You"(2000), "Amityville" (2000), "A Drop in the Ocean" (2008), "Medicine Ball" (2009), and "Stay Wide Awake" (2009). These rape brags take on additional significance in light of The Center for Public Integrity's 2010 report, indicating "roughly one in five women who attend college will become the victim of a rape or an attempted rape by the time she graduates."[9] Many of these victims, who comprise Mathers's core target audience, drop out of school while perpetrators go unpunished and are rewarded.

Some critics suggest that Mathers's rape brags inflict additional punishment on the victims by glorifying their abuse. An attempt to counter this line of criticism is provided in "Insane" (2009) where Mathers describes what is presented as his own sexual assault at the hands of a stepfather. As a younger version of himself, he narrates many of the classic symptoms of the abused: broken trust, unjust coercion, parental abandonment, dysfunctional parent–child relationship, feeling trapped, internalized guilt, change of behavior, and chilling silence after the incident. Whether Mathers's depiction is fact or fiction, it remains important as an example of giving a voice to abused youth everywhere and the hatred they feel toward their abusers who were supposed to love them. According to the U.S. Department of Health and Human Services' Child Welfare Information Gateway, in 2011 there were 63,527 reports of child sexual abuse. That means nearly 1 in 10 children in the United States and Puerto Rico reported sexual abuse. Sadly, Mathers's lyrics also demonstrate what can happen when the abused, who need acceptance and approval, are unable to resolve their complex emotions. They lash out at those who they perceive as weaker or at those who they feel were supposed to protect them from such abuse.

Erotic–denigrating expressions appeared 83 times, or in 41.5 percent of lyrics. These expressions pair love focused on a strong desire for a lover with perceived competition and punishment. For the most part, Kim is the beloved but other women do make brief appearances. These women include Nicki Minaj in "Fastlane" (2011) and Mariah Carey in "Jimmy Crack Corn" (2006), "Bagpipes from Baghdad" (2009), "The Warning" (2009), "We Made You" (2009), and "Cold Wind Blows"

(2010). Scores of erotic partners go unnamed in songs like "Superman" (2002) and "Seduction" (2010). Although Nicki and Mariah and countless anonymous lovers are objects of Mather's erotic or sadistic desire, Kim is the only woman for whom the preservation of well-being (erotic love) is ever mentioned. However, odes to Kim like "Searchin'" (1996) and "Love You More" (2004) are often overshadowed by the rage expressed in ballads composed in her honor like "Kim" (2000) and "'97 Bonnie & Clyde" (1999), in which she is the victim of his wrath or, as in "Puke" (2004), the object of his disgust. The message here is that women, the key to his happiness, are also a constant source of problems and a threat to his ultimate happiness.

Enrichment–mutiny expressions appeared 69 times, or in 34.5 percent of lyrics. These expressions pair a desire for safety, comfort, and growth with desire to assert one's autonomy because of forced dependence. Interestingly, it is not a person but hip hop that is the beloved in the majority of these expressions. For example, in "Our House" (1999), "8 Mile" (2002), "Run Rabbit Run" (2002), "Lose Yourself" (2002), "The Sauce" (2003), and "Stimulate" (2003), Mathers describes hip hop as a place of refuge in times of trouble. Hip hop provided everything his mother could not—nurturance, room for growth, identification, and approval. In "25 To Life" (2010), Mathers expresses hate for hip hop because she is a fickle and overly demanding lover, yet he always returns to her. He returns to hip hop because only she can provide the safety, security, and fulfillment that cannot be found anywhere else. In his autobiography, *The Way I Am,* he plainly admits it: "hip hop became my girl, my confidant, my best homie."[10] Mathers's love for hip hop suggests that the goal of enrichment love is enhancement, which makes life worth living, but he is trapped by fame and drug addition as the effects his love for hip hop produced.

CONCLUSION

This chapter uncovered and explored expressions of love–hate in Eminem's lyrics in order to better understand the motives for Marshall Mathers's expressions as a spiritual persona. Analysis confirmed that Mathers's spirituality does not pretend that life is beautiful or carefree. Instead, spirituality is a personal struggle that is best observed when brokenness is emphasized and love-hate is induced. In the process, he reveals that love and hate are not oppositional forces, but forces that coexist and overlap as each song analyzed depicts at least three types of love–hate relationships. Sometimes, love–hate relationships are dramatized in terms of biological families where Mathers is bound to people (like his mother and ex-wife) who cannot be easily avoided. Other times, love–hate relationships are portrayed as one-sided between fans and their versions of celebrity personas as in "Stan" (2000). And still other times, as in "Space Bound" (2010), love has an "evol" dark side. Analysis also confirmed that although love can be evol it is much less likely that hate can make an about face. As Mathers's lyrics indicate, the demonically possessed—those who abuse women and children—are nearly impossible to love. Mathers is also suggesting that abusers (and victims) like him are ultimately unloved because they fail to love themselves. Mathers's love–hate expressions revolve around the value clashes and moral conflicts confronted in his life and the struggle to define a spiritual perspective. Unfortunately, his spiritual expressions do not yet articulate any well-formed methods of breaking the love–hate pattern or bridging the very real social gaps between the characters brought to life in his lyrics. Instead, they express a bottled up bitterness that has the danger of being an essential component of spiritual identity.

There is hope, however. We can imagine that at some point the opportunity to forgive those who have done him wrong might be taken. He has opened the door to his own forgiveness in "Evil Deeds" (2004) when he asks his Heavenly Father to forgive him while using the metaphor of his earthly father's abandonment as justification for his sins. However, as yet, Mathers has failed to express that the road to forgiveness is open to two-way traffic. In "Evil Deeds" (2004), he acknowledges the Lord's Prayer in Matthew 6:9–13 (The Message), but does not acknowledge the second part of the equation: we must ask God for forgiveness while we are "forgiving [of] others." For Mathers, then, the road to forgiveness starts with asking God for forgiveness. It continues with acknowledging his brokenness and forgiving himself for the wrong he has done. And forgiveness is not about forgetfulness. It is about remembering that even the most vile offenders are human beings who, despite all the suffering and misery they impose, are worthy of love as much as they are worthy of hate.

If Mathers is to ever forgive his offenders, we can rest assured that he will tell us about in fluid poetic form to represent the fluidity between love and hate and between imagination and reality. In this way, he will remind us that love and hate are not emotions but powerful spiritual decisions and reasons for action. To avoid being victimized or victimizing others in the names of love or hate, we must always choose to love by combining its erotic, enriching, companionate, dependent, regard, and altruistic forms with real forgiveness and open communication. By humanizing and personifying his own love–hate filled "yellow brick road," Mathers provides audiences with an opportunity to see whether complete forgiveness can be granted through his eyes while imagining more peaceful and loving relationships through our own.

CHAPTER 7
The King of Controversy

Whether it is the disruptions Eminem's white body and high-pitched voice bring to hip hop, his repugnant "genderphobic"[1] and homophobic rhymes, his crude bodily noises and excretions, his drug abuse, or his often blasphemous stance on religion, just about everyone has found a reason to object to his music or behavior at some point since he took center stage back in 1999. In fact, many people have done more than object over the years, having publicly recounted the many ways in which they find him repulsive. Some say he is profane and puerile, while others claim he is violent and bigoted. Some even go as far as to say he is mentally unbalanced, a menace, and a cultural exploiter. However, everyone seems to agree that Eminem's gift to curse really is a curse. His loathsome and offensive vocabulary and disagreeable temperament have earned him notorious nicknames like "the Pied Piper of disaffected youth," the "sworn enemy of 'concerned parents' everywhere," "rock-and-roll's biggest pain in the ass," and, as he calls himself sometimes, "Mr. Potty-Mouth King."

Each of these labels expresses an important partial truth about who Eminem is and what Eminem does, and each of these monikers misses a larger point the rapper is making throughout his work, a point that the great Roman orator Cicero made centuries ago: "the greatest pleasures are only narrowly separated from disgust." Or, as Eminem remixed it in songs like "Role Model" (1999), "The Way I Am" (2000), and "Without Me" (2004), it is audiences' and critics' uncontrollable desire to criticize him that makes him "disgusting" rather than any actual obscenity he may deliver. According to Eminem, he is "whatever" we "say" he is because that is what we want him to be. By embodying the worst of what we say about him, he turns the tables on all of us. He knows he is no role model, and if we do not know that, then we are the crazy ones. If we listened to him as much as we talked about him, we would get it, or so it goes. If Eminem is right, that it is our thoughts and remarks about him that make him disgusting rather than his own indecency, then he is really asking us to address some bigger unspoken questions about the value we place on identity, realness, expression, and performance as a society. If Eminem is right, then he might be one of our society's most misunderstood commentators and critics.

Take the song "Role Model" (1999). Here, the rapper addresses the issue of what effects music has on the listener, especially when the listener is a child or adolescent. Eminem begins by likening himself to the Great Houdini, who performed death-defying stunts to arouse audiences' pleasure and disgust. The video for "Role Model" adds a silent film-styled caption that reads "You Can Be Just Like Me," subtly introducing the metaphor of contagion. And just in case audiences do not pick it up there, the first words of the song say it loudly. Eminem is "cancerous." He spreads like a disease that cannot be seen. Just like we are preoccupied with eradicating invisible cancer cells, we are preoccupied with eradicating Eminem because even though we cannot see cancer cells, we are disgusted by their visible and audible symptoms. When applied to Eminem, these symptoms are the millions of youth who consume his music by buying or downloading it and the millions more who ingest and regurgitate his "sick" lyrics at shows (potential carriers of disease), graphic images of social and biological deformity in his videos like when he implies that he has HIV and other sexually transmitted diseases (reminders of disease), and evil deeds like pedophilia and obscene words directed at his mother (evidence of disease). And because he is "diseased," Eminem becomes public enemy number one. Our urge to distance ourselves from the disease that is Eminem comes from our feeling of disgust. According to Rachel Herz in *That's Disgusting: Unraveling the Mysteries of Repulsion,* "disgust is . . . a special type of fear that evolved to help us evade slow and uncertain death by disease."[2] In other words, our disgust for Eminem indicates that we want to reject everything he represents because we are really afraid of what he represents. We are afraid that his words will sink into our children's minds and hearts and skew their moral fiber and ethical perspective. Ultimately, we believe that Eminem is cancer. We want to get rid of Eminem because we are afraid that if we do not, he will get rid of us by inspiring other members of our body politic to do his dirty work for him. According to this logic, "healthy life" as we define it will no longer exist if we allow Eminem to thrive. Here's the thing: Eminem cannot be rejected or done away with because he does not exist. He tells us that he is not real. Even at his deadliest, he is just a projection, a figment of our indecent imaginations.

In "The Way I Am" (2000), he provides further evidence as he describes his clear invisibility. He reflects on the public's need to eradicate him and his diseased, profane artistry by going back in time and backstage to shed some insight into how celebrity works. According to Eminem, it is kind of like chemotherapy because everything hinges on invading his space and everything to which he has grown attached. First, fans intrude upon his solitude and seclusion by taking his presence as an invitation for conversation, photography, autographs, and the like. Second, the media, and other celebrities in the know, release unauthorized private information about his life and family without his consent. Third, haters and critics publicize him in a false light and create a false impression of him as disgusting. Finally, corporations appropriate his identity for commercial purposes. For example, Eminem successfully filed suit against Apple for "exemplary damages" when in a television ad for its iTunes pay-per-download music store aired on MTV in 2003, featuring a young boy with an iPod portable music player singing the lyrics to "Lose Yourself," the theme song for the rapper's hit movie *8 Mile*. This suit was settled out of court for an undisclosed financial sum. In 2007, Eminem sued Apple again for copyright infringement. The ruling in this case was that record labels do not have the right to turn an artist's recordings into digital music download sales on the Internet without permission from music publishers who hold the licenses. Translation: A minimum of $50 million in additional royalties for Eminem and his production over the next decade because of this case. Not too shabby.

Returning to "The Way I Am," we can see how Eminem is eagerly protective of his image even as he claims the opposite. In the song he remarks on the rough road he took to get to where he now is, suggesting that Eminem is at times trapped by fame, by industry constraints, and by the never-ending sonic loop from which neither time-travel nor death can provide relief. Before he begins rapping, he asks listeners to "shut up and listen." Then, he starts the first verse explaining how his profanity is actually a personal form of relieving stress and a way to direct his pain at its source—society at large. In fact, it is the public, rather than Eminem, that is indecent because it just will not leave him alone. He is disgusted and offended because those who are searching for the man behind the lyrics invade his privacy constantly. Fans' interest is abetted by media coverage that points the finger at Eminem rather than at the failed social institutions (i.e., education, religion, family) that produced him. He uses this song to turn the tables on a condemning media and tell them to leave him alone. He goes on to attack concerned parents everywhere who blame his music for violent outbreaks in upper-class high schools like Columbine. These parents are hypocrites who have failed to care for their children by turning them over to Eminem without supervision in the first place. He continues by turning these parents' attacks into "fuel" for even more offensive rhymes. Finally, he says that he is "glad" if we refer to him as "an asshole" because he just wants to be left alone and in peace. He does not want to be a conventional rapper and he definitely does not want to be a pop or a rock star. He wants to be himself. But since it does not appear that society will let him, he will settle for being "whatever" we call him.

By the sound of the lyrics of "Without Me," it appears that we have chosen to call him disgusting and offensive. Eminem laments the fact that his true identity is considered "chopped liver" because audiences only want to hear his disgusting and offensive rambling under the label Slim Shady. As such, he addresses by name those who have taken his lyrics to Congress for obscenity like Mrs. Lynne Cheney. He says that the Federal Communications Commission (FCC) tried to ban his music from MTV but proved unable because audiences cried out in support of him. In addition, he curses his mother Debbie who sued him for defamation of character after his lyrical references to her allegedly made her life a living hell. He ends the song by taking on recording artist Moby, who criticized him for his woman-hating and gay-bashing lyrics. After addressing these beefs, he turns on the audience, reminding us that without him, our world simply lacks controversy. He continues by cursing all those who are offended because he is a white man in a black cultural and artistic scene. It seems that he settles one controversy only to be engulfed by another. Translation: "Everybody only wants to discuss me. So this must mean I'm disgusting, but it's just me; I'm just obscene." Remember, according to Eminem, the controversy is not his fault. If anything, he is trying to avoid it and us. We are at fault because we have made him famous by finding him offensive and disgusting.

Eminem takes time out on his 2009 chart-topping comeback album *Relapse* to remind us that we are still the problem, and he does so sonically and visually in the song "We Made You." Set in a psychiatric asylum, the song samples portions of "Without Me" to make clear that he is still supporting the argument made therein. In the video version, he takes on the iconic roles of Mr. Spock, Rain Man, Norman Bates, and Elvis Presley to demonstrate that we can find traces of his character flaws in a long line of media personalities. He also places the widely known Guitar Hero track in the background while he delivers the song's chorus. This layering suggests that Eminem has been dropped into the game and is inviting others to participate in his authentic expression by imitating him. Recall the song "The Real Slim Shady" here? The point is clear: reality stars, politicians, pop stars, and rock stars are equally inauthentic and should not be trusted.

Perhaps these intertextual references also indicate that Eminem thinks video games are as controversial as the complicated game of celebrity, especially as it is played on reality television. What is certain is that Eminem plans to keep giving us reasons to stir up controversy because offense is what we have come to expect from all of our media. He makes this argument clearly in the video for "We Made You" when he battles a warrior on Planet Womyn who tells him that no one can really blame him for his disgusting behavior because "we" (women perhaps) made him who he is. He reminds us that only he can satisfy our desire for revulsion, regardless of the violent, gross, sexual, or unjust form it takes. This time, Eminem is punished as the inhabitants of Planet Womyn tear his body limb from limb at the end of the song. But there is more here: In keeping with Eminem's theory about the nature of disgust, the video and song generated additional layers of controversy and increased the size of his audience as the celebrities depicted and referenced responded. Kim Kardashian's response appeared in her blog: "I am a huge Eminem fan and find it flattering that he would rap about me . . . Personally, I'm honored."[3] Sarah Palin allowed Fox News's Bill O'Reilly to respond for her when he said, "Eminem is obviously on an obscene rant . . . All I want to do is repeat that Eminem means nothing. The video means nothing. It's played for kids that are confused."[4] Eminem commented only by way of sampling "We Made You" in "Cold Wind Blows" from his 2010 album *Recovery,* implying that his theory about being disgusting because people are discussing him still holds water.

To test Eminem's theory about the purpose of controversy and the nature of disgust, I did some crowdsourcing during the summer of 2012. I asked my Facebook, Twitter, and Google+ friends to tell me what Eminem sounds like in their ears today. Here is a representative selection of the more than 200 responses I received: "fast-talking musician," "in need of anger management," "brilliant but sad," "honest

and raw," "satirical," "intense with a groove/swagger," "angry," "attention seeking," "steel-edged," "self-aware," "hypermasculine," "trying
to cope," "complicated," "biracial," "prophetic," "cartoonish," "young
boy gone wild," "woman-hating," and "passionate." These vastly different takes on Eminem represent a sharp contrast to the first wave of
dialogue that overwhelmed the rapper when he came to fame. I was
surprised to see how few of these more recent descriptions reflected
disgust and outrage. For this reason, in this chapter, I look at three
rounds of controversy concerning sex, sexuality, and gender to figure
out why. Why does Eminem no longer seem to disgust us? What has
changed? Is it him, or is it us?

BATTLE I: EMINEM VERSUS TORI AMOS

When Eminem's first album, *The Slim Shady LP,* dropped in February
1999, fans and critics pounced. The album debuted at No. 2 on the Billboard Top 200 Chart (U.S.) on March 13 and maintained that position
for over a month. Criticism started over the cover art, which brought
the terrifying scene of his then wife's imagined murder to life. Critics
said that this imagery, coupled with Eminem's gross lyrical content,
portrayed him as a dangerous gangsta. Gender studies professor Anna
Hickey-Moody writes, "Eminem successfully sells a version of gangsta that deviates in some ways from the imploded tropes of thug, hustler,
and pimp/player."[5] This remixed gangsta frame gave the rapper's debut
album an edge that helped it win two Grammys and go multiplatinum
in 12 short months. It also contributed to many people's opinion of
Eminem as a raging woman hater.

Critics found support for their perspective in the song "'97 Bonnie and Clyde." The song's title refers to the notorious criminals of
the Great Depression era Bonnie Parker and Clyde Barrow and to the
late 2Pac's "'96 Bonnie and Clyde (Me and My Girlfriend)" (1996).
In this song, Eminem is silent. He uses the persona of Slim Shady to
narrate the murder of his wife and kidnapping of his infant daughter.
The song begins as Shady explains the purpose of their late-night car
trip to his little girl. It continues as he tries to tell his daughter what he
has just done in very simple terms, attempting to cover up the truth all
the way through. It concludes when the pair reaches the water, dumps
the body, and Shady declares unity with and undying love for his child.

Interestingly enough, it was not just old folks and politicians who
raised their voices in protest when this CD hit record stores and topped

the charts. Award-winning recording artists like Tori Amos did too. Amos just did not buy the fact that Eminem did not exist in this song. She resented the way he used his infant daughter as a symbol to represent innocent listeners who are under his control and (unwittingly) forced to witness his crimes. What proved most offensive to Amos about this song was that its physical violence attempted to mask a hateful disregard for the victimized woman's humanity. Listening passively to "'97 Bonnie and Clyde" was not an option for Amos because listening passively to the song would mean that she accepts the messages about men, women, and children that it sends.

Amos's protest took the form of a chilling cover version of "'97 Bonnie and Clyde" on her album *Strange Little Girls* (2001). In her version of "'97 Bonnie and Clyde," Amos critiques Eminem's version for interweaving a horrible act of violence into a narrative where an innocent child participates unwittingly and the normal for her is the abnormal. She does not let Eminem get away with trying to lessen the abnormal violence that ensues by using baby talk and simple language for the child's (or listener's) benefit. Rather, Amos shows us that something in the child dies in this song along with her mother, and the fact that she is an infant suggests that she may never even know the true nature of her loss. For this reason, Amos also calls out Eminem's use of the Slim Shady persona as a cowardly act that tries to explain the song and the social effects it reflects away as "not real."

By taking on Kim's voice and perspective, Amos presents a powerful counter-narrative. Amos breathes life back into Kim, making listeners reckon with her experience and her deep longing for her daughter. The deep humiliation that comes from dying without benefit of cause or purpose is finally spoken. At least this time, Kim goes down to her watery grave with something more than a splash. In this way, the situation is no longer dissonant. Amos rendered it as complicated, uncomfortable, and dysfunctional as the actual violence that is occurring throughout the song. Musicologist Alyssa Woods's review captures its essence:

> Amos's contrived shift in narrative perspective from murderer to murdered casts new meaning over the lyrical content. She explains, "You're hearing her listen to him tell their daughter lies." In other words, in her version of the song, the listener bears witness to the dead mother as she listens to her murderer's justification of the murder. Amos considered her cover a form of activism that gave voice to Kim's side of the story.[6]

Amos released her version of the song after its prequel "Kim" (2000) was released. In "Kim," Eminem paints himself as the true victim of Kim's emotional violence and infidelity and provides a rationale for the crime of passion he commits. After hearing the terrorizing scenario through which Kim met her imagined end in Eminem's song, Amos said she was compelled to give Kim a voice. Kim's humanity is restored, and she is no longer an adulteress, but a woman and a person who has regained her essential dignity and worth. Amos takes on Kim's voice from beyond the grave to bring attention to the fact that women in Eminem's music are portrayed as voiceless because that condition makes it more difficult for them to prove that they have been victimized. Amos suggests that there is something worse than death, even a violent death like the one imagined for Kim in this song. That something is what happens as Eminem denies his own human integrity by making himself a channel for an increasing level of violence against women endemic to our society.

According to professor Jennifer Stoever-Ackerman, author of *The Sonic Color-line: Race and the Cultural Politics of Listening*, Amos's cover is more than a potent critique of the original or a fiery charge of disgust against one rapper. In an interview, Stoever-Ackerman remarked that Amos's cover "paints Eminem as an angry prophet, who is accurately describing and predicting what will happen to women in our society in the not-so-distant future." History has proved Amos and Ackerman right. As noted in many contemporary reports of the 21st century's "war on women," there is proposed legislation that is actually trying to take away women's voices and roll back their hard-won civic and social protections. For starters, there are laws proposed which seek to redefine rape and to change the legal term for "victims" of rape, stalking, and domestic violence to "accusers"; to remove much-needed confidentiality from the cases of rape and domestic violence victims; to make it legal to murder a doctor who provides abortion care; to cut nearly $1 billion of food and other aid to low-income pregnant women, mothers, and their families; to cut all federal funding from Planned Parenthood health centers; and to cut funding for senior citizens' (two-thirds of whom are women) employment services, meals, and housing. Like the scenarios presented in many of Eminem's more controversial songs, laws like these criminalize women who express their sexual desires and physical needs. According to Ackerman, such scenarios and the laws that they echo present "a political wrangle whose key has changed, like Eminem's lyrics, from indifference to downright cruelty." Perhaps that sonic and social harmony is why MTV compared Eminem's lyrics with sound bytes from ultraconservative Republican Rick Santorum in March 2012 and found it difficult to tell them apart.[7]

Thinking about Eminem as a social commentator who is both a manifestation of a violent misogynistic history as well as its prophet and provocateur allows us to think both about how society teaches men to hate women and about how society teaches women to hate themselves. In "'97 Bonnie and Clyde" and "Kim," Eminem shows how a woman's self-hatred can flourish in the tolerance of an abusive relationship. Since women have nearly no voice in Eminem's lyrics, women and girls who hear them are not afforded the experience of realizing how their own personal problems fit into larger political structures. Women's representation as voiceless victims within Eminem's lyrics is itself an important form of social critique, for it draws attention to constraints placed on women's sexuality and publicizes issues such as physical and sexual abuse and rape that are too often ignored by media and law. By adding one woman's whispering voice to Eminem's cacophony, Amos effectively emphasizes the importance of placing taboo subjects such as kidnapping, domestic violence, sexual and emotional abuse, violent murder, and their cause—male insecurity—out in the open. In the process, Amos also gives girls ideas about how to make their own music that expresses their anger at a world that is out for their blood. Eminem had no response. After all is said and done, the winner of this round of battle is Tori Amos. Knock out.

ROUND 2: EMINEM VERSUS GLAAD

Amos's critique of Eminem's misogyny came on the heels of the May 2000 release of *The Marshall Mathers LP*, which broke sales records in its opening week, debuted at No. 1 on the Billboard Top 200 Chart (U.S.) and became the world's fastest selling album. *The Marshall Mathers LP* portrayed Eminem as poor white trash and an underdog, signaled by images on the back and inside front covers of the liner notes and on the CD. In these black-and-white semi-realistic photos, Mathers is shot from above, signaling his low social status. He is also shown wearing his signature white T-shirt and dark jeans, only in these photos, he also wears the apron of a food-service worker and is shown taking out the trash. Autobiographies and interviews released in conjunction with the album explain that this is exactly the attire and role he donned when he was a short order cook at Gil's Lodge outside of Detroit, Michigan only a few years before.

But when the public looked beyond the pop packaging and opened the album, they found that Eminem took his themes of mayhem and murder from "Kim" (2000) and "'97 Bonnie and Clyde" (1999) to new homophobic heights.[8] Controversy ensued and Gay and Lesbian Alliance Against Defamation (GLAAD) was at the forefront. The organization issued many statements of protest to the press like this one: "From the day Eminem's *The Marshall Mathers LP* was released . . . GLAAD has worked toward a singular goal: to increase public awareness by initiating a high-profile national dialogue about the impact of hate lyrics and the continued glorification of violence against lesbian, gay, bisexual and transgender people."[9] The epistolary song "Stan" was specifically placed under the microscope as being about an overzealous fan that Eminem rejects because of his psychotic fixation and homosexuality. Interestingly, critics from GLAAD glossed over the rapper's appeal to the First Amendment and the rapper's critique of his own misogynistic and dysfunctional familial themes, instead focusing on how Stan responds to Eminem by killing himself along with his girlfriend and unborn daughter as an indictment of Eminem and the effect of his lyrics on his young fans.

When *The Marshall Mathers LP* was nominated by the National Academy for Recording Arts and Sciences (NARAS) for four Grammy awards including Album of the Year in 2001, an even bigger national debate sparked over its musical content and the line between hate speech and artistic license. Eminem supporters pretty much fell into two main camps: those who said he was a gifted satirist, adept at giving full frontal exposure to society's ugliness and injustices, and those who said he was a brilliant lyricist whose attitudes could use some adjustment. Either way, supporters agreed that his lyrics were protected as free speech. Eminem detractors were unified. They said it did not matter how great he was at spitting rhymes. He was exploiting misery and bigotry for commercial gain. Eminem's lyrics were not just disgusting. They were hate speech. Period.

Most mainstream coverage of the controversy seemed to take the side of Eminem's detractors. While many newspapers relegated the controversy over Eminem's nomination to the "Entertainment," "Arts," "Style," "Life," and "Features" categories, the *Miami Herald* and *Los Angeles Times* ran it as front-page news. As such, the story was reported to be about the impact of Eminem's nomination on the national dialogue over explicit lyrics in rap music. Key terms used to grab readers' attention within the articles included "controversy," "violence," and "shocking."[10] Coverage also employed terms to trigger readers' disgust such as "slasher film fantasy" in the *Chicago Sun-Times* and "potty-mouthed" and "naughty" in the *Washington Post*. The *New York Times* is the only mainstream newspaper that focused more on the nominees and the voting process rather than on the outrage over Eminem's nomination though its coverage refers to *The Marshall Mathers LP* with a negative valence by using key terms like "naughty" and "misogynist."[11]

In an ironic demonstration of Eminem's perspective, that it is talk about him that makes him "disgusting" and controversial rather than his own lyrics, mainstream press coverage basically blamed Eminem for composing a "disgusting" (aka misogynist, violent, gay-bashing) album. An article in *Vibe Magazine* summarizes the media content perfectly: "Every article ever published on Eminem can be paraphrased thus: Mother, Libel, Guns, Homosexuals, Drugs, Own Daughter, Wife, Rape, Trunk of Car, Youth of America, Tattoos, Prison, Gangsta, White Trash."[12] Going further, Eminem's nomination was framed as proof that his album represented rap music's best offering for the year. NARAS's president Michael Greene is oft quoted in these reports, mainly because of his status in the industry and his defense of Eminem's nomination. Greene said that the nomination was meant to acknowledge the rapper's excellent lyrical skill and not to cosign on his lyrical content. He declares, "I hope the public realizes that by recognizing the album, we're not honoring the subject matter,"[13] and "You've really got to view this in the context of art being a pretty extreme medium sometimes."[14] The defensive frame in which Greene's comments are offered supports the stereotypical view that rap music and its predominantly black and Latino creators are distinct from normal (read white-oriented) values and culture. Additionally, it provides an excuse to further marginalize these populations because they are framed as choosing to be out of step with mainstream norms instead of telling the truth about institutional and structural discrimination that has marginalized them historically.

Taken as a whole, this kind of media framing has several subliminal effects: (1) It discourages readers and listeners from identifying with Eminem or his music, thereby preventing them from encountering his alternative perspective on free speech, media effects, and the nature of disgust. (2) It solidifies rap music's status as negative and uncritical ranting, which has a lot to do with the stereotypical ways black and

Latino youth are presented and dismissed in media and politics. (3) It fuels white supremacy and privilege. The nomination of Eminem's *The Marshall Mathers LP* for "Album of the Year" at the time implies that this white rapper is superior to so-called dumb and profane rappers of color who created the disgusting musical genre in the first place—even if his superiority makes him even dumber and more disgusting than those people of color could ever be. (4) It limits Eminem's homophobia to gay-bashing and ignores how his use of words like "faggot" and "lez" often refer to the complicated ways in which people are punished for presenting their gender identities non-traditionally in today's culture. (5) It refuses to acknowledge how class and race play into Eminem's representations of sex, sexual orientation, gender, family, and violence. And, as a result, larger issues about the intersections of structural oppression and personal identity formation are left unasked and, more importantly, unanswered.

A clever attempt to ask and answer at least some of these questions came through a song mocking Eminem and "Stan" called "The Night I Fell in Love" (2002), recorded by British dance-pop group the Pet Shop Boys. Essentially, "The Night I Fell in Love" takes a twist on the plot of "Stan" by having a male teenager provide the narration about his love affair with an Eminem-like rapper. Like "Stan," the fan is eager to meet his rap idol, but this time the rapper is the one who makes the homosexual advances. The rapper asks the teen if his name is Stan and invites him backstage for a private performance after the show. They start out having a nice conversation, and the young fan is surprised by how nice the rapper is. Once the pair has gotten to know each other a bit, the rapper gets a video camera. This scares the young, inexperienced fan for a moment and then the rapper reassures him that they are going to make a memory. The young fan wakes up the next morning and realizes he has just made love to his favorite rapper. When the young fan asks the rapper why everyone thinks he is a homophobe, he shrugs, suggesting that it is because nobody knows who the rapper really is. He responds by telling the young fan to keep their sexual encounter a secret.

"The Night I Fell in Love" is a creative rebuttal of what goes unspoken in the controversy between GLAAD and Eminem over "Stan": (1) That rap music like Eminem's is at its core about same-sex relationships because its most devoted fans are young, white suburban males. (2) The voyeuristic relationship between Eminem and the Stans of the world signals the privacy that a racially segregated culture provides as these young white men idolize and emulate (mostly) black rappers from a safe distance. (3) That Eminem's and his young white suburban male fans' aggressive masculinity could be just a show because they are all really gay, or at least heteroflexible, behind closed doors. (4) If the real Eminem really is not mean, offensive, or homophobic, because Marshall Mathers is nice, shy, and gay/heteroflexible, then Eminem is the ultimate passer. Eminem can be whatever we say he is because that is exactly what Eminem is—a public persona. Marshall Mathers, Eminem's real self, only comes out in private.

The Pet Shop Boys' critique was also obviously a response to Eminem's performance of "Stan" at the 43rd Annual Grammy Awards ceremony in Los Angeles. Eminem surprised many when he performed "Stan" with none other than openly gay British musician Elton John. John's decision to perform the song "Stan" with the rapper brought criticism from GLAAD, who organized protests of the awards ceremony because they considered Eminem's lyrics to be homophobic. The group's Executive Director Joan M. Garry released a statement saying,

> We are disappointed that Sir Elton John will be performing with Eminem at the Grammy Awards. John has played an enormous role in educating the world about AIDS and gay issues through his music and charitable work. GLAAD is appalled that John would share a stage with Eminem, whose words and actions promote hate and violence against gays and lesbians.[15]

In spite of GLAAD's best efforts, which included an organized protest of the awards ceremony outside its Los Angeles venue on February 21, the show went on. The performance, which admittedly was neither John's nor Eminem's finest, did accomplish its larger political objective of silencing the critics. *Entertainment Weekly* put the occasion on its end-of-the-decade "best of" list, saying: "It was the hug heard round the world. Eminem, under fire for homophobic lyrics, shared the stage with a gay icon for a performance of 'Stan' that would have been memorable in any context." John is reported to have remarked that he gets Eminem as a social critic who is fixing the attention of rap music's global audience on serious problems, like homophobia and closeted homosexuality, in U.S. culture.

Collaborator Sir Elton John agreed, and wrote the following when he described Eminem as one of "The Immortals" for *Rolling Stone in* 2004.

> From the start, I've always admired Eminem's thinking. That's the reason I wanted to appear on the Grammys with him when I was asked, despite all the nonsense talked about his being homophobic and crap like that. Let the Boy Georges and the George Michaels of the world get up in a twist about

it if they don't have the intelligence to see his intelligence. Eminem has the balls to say what he feels and to make offensive things funny. That's very necessary today in America, with people being muzzled and irony becoming a lost art. Artists like Eminem who use their free speech to get a point across are vitally important. There just aren't many people in the world with balls that big and talent that awesome.[16]

In an article called "Eminem's Lyrical Personae: The Everyman, The Needy Man, The Hegemon," gender studies scholar Anna Hickey-Moody takes John's comments to their logical conclusion. Hickey-Moody writes that Eminem's critical irony—calling attention to the fact that without the attention of the mainstream media his music would have a much smaller audience and impact—may have gone over the heads of mainstream media, making the rapper's commentary even more significant to his core (male) audience.[17]

A decade later, Eminem remembered the performance as a turning point in his career. In an interview with entertainment marketing icon Steve Stoute, the rapper referred to this performance as the biggest creative risk he ever took because its evidently homophobic content was challenged by something else going on beneath the surface: "You've got what people perceived as this homophobic rapper. And then you've got his audience and his fans and supporters and how they could have reacted—and some of mine could have been like 'Yo, you're gonna go on the stage with this openly gay guy?' Now it wouldn't seem as crazy. But if you go back nine or ten years, it was."[18] Since that performance, the rapper's opinions on homosexuality and same-sex marriage appear to have evolved. As proof, in a recent interview with *New York Times Magazine,* Eminem expressed his updated take saying, "I think if two people love each other, then what the hell? I think that everyone should have the chance to be equally miserable, if they want. It's the new tolerant me!"[19]

Eminem is not the only public figure whose opinion about same-sex relationships has progressed. In May 2012, President Obama announced that he now fully supports same-sex marriage rights. Several other rappers who support the president publicly have followed suit including Jay-Z, Immortal Technique, and T.I. In a brief interview with CNN, Jay-Z backed Obama's stance on marriage equality, equating discrimination against the LGBT community with discrimination against the African American community. "I think it's the right thing to do," Jay said, "so whether it costs him votes or not—again, it's not about votes. It's about people. It's the right thing to do as a human being." Along with Eminem's, these recent social and political endorsements of same-sex political equality suggest that as society grows and changes, rappers do too.

Only time will tell whether these endorsements will spark enough change in the social realm to alter the commonly held idea that to be a gay male means that one cannot also be a man. Take the following as examples: an emerging trend of inserting the phrase "no homo" after lyrics, just to make sure listeners know that the rapper is absolutely not gay and the rise of Berkeley-based rapper Lil B. The rapper released an album called *I'm Gay* (2011) and, with intended irony, swears that he is heterosexual. The rapper and his album's title have since endured a backlash, as Lil B told MTV he gets threatening messages from some ex-fans saying "I'm gonna bash your head in," "you faggot," and "I'm gonna kill you." This homophobic response means that, to date, no openly gay male rapper has achieved mainstream success. It also indicates that Lil B's queer dream of fostering diversity and acceptance has yet to be realized even as many rappers express their support for same-sex marriage rights. In light of this, it seems that the larger culture war of hip hop's homophobia and free speech in rap music is ongoing. However, the unique battle duked out by Eminem and GLAAD (with some help from the Pet Shop Boys, Elton John, and the popular press) goes to Eminem. It was a close one. And it took over 10 years to render the final decision.

ROUND 3: EMINEM VERSUS MARIAH CAREY

Sadly, Eminem's opinion of heterosexual, sexually active women as a class of people has not evolved as far as his political opinions of the LGBTI community over the years. He admits it himself in "Cold Wind Blows" (2010) when he says, "Homie, I'll be nicer to women when Aqua Man drowns and The Human Torch starts swimming." Nowhere is this more evident than in his public feud with legendary pop star Mariah Carey, whom he also calls out as defeated in song. Eminem met Carey in 2001, when they began to make plans for collaborating on Carey's *Charmbracelet* album. Although a song was recorded, it never saw the light of day because of a reported love affair gone wrong between the duo. Rumors surfaced in 2002 when, in an interview for *Rolling Stone,* Eminem said that the pair did indeed have a romantic relationship, adding, "on the whole personal level, I'm not really feeling it. I just don't like her as a person." Carey fired back in December 2002 when she appeared on CNN's *Larry King Live* to promote her album. Carey said, "I hung out with him; I spoke to him on the phone. I think I was probably with him a total of four times. And I don't consider that dating somebody."

But the different stories did not stop there. *The Eminem Show* album, which debuted on The Billboard 200 in the No. 1 spot, included a song called "Superman" (2002), referring to the nature of the duo's relationship in a sexually charged manner. Basically, Eminem says that he rejected Carey's advances to take their relationship beyond a sexual level and into the realm of commitment. Carey responded in song by way of "Clown" (2002), which suggests that the rapper is not who audiences think he is. He is definitely not the "meanest emcee on this earth." Rather, as Carey put it, he is "just a puppet show, and the little boy inside often sits at home alone and cries." Through her lyrics, Carey lets us know that she has gone backstage with Eminem and therefore knows things that the public does not. While she does not provide many details about her insider knowledge, it is clear that she is calling Eminem a liar and a fake. Not only does she accuse him of lying about the nature of their relationship, but she says he is also lying about his identity. He is not whatever we call him. In fact, what we call him (i.e., "disgusting" and "offensive") could not be further from the truth. The truth, according to Carey, is that Eminem is nothing but a clown. He is a comic entertainer in a hip hop circus, wearing his traditional baggy costume and an exaggerated persona called Slim Shady. Meanwhile, Marshall Mathers is a soft, scared, child who sits alone at home crying. This is a double-edged critique. On one level, Carey is saying that Eminem's masculinity is a performance within and by the rap genre, and that it is based on a false foundation. Furthermore, it suggests that rap music itself is just a big carnival that serves the purpose of controlling crowds by making them dance to beats that too often mask the fact that traditional ideas about women are being reinforced. On another level, Carey is saying that Eminem's many personas have effectively isolated him from the rest of humanity, leaving him at the mercy of his many insecurities, fears, and confusion.

Eminem did not take well to being Carey's "clown" or to being criticized for using his different personas to do anything but be a real man who criticizes rather than supports mainstream thinking. Carey's opposing viewpoint left room for others to ask larger critical questions: Why it is so important for Eminem to maintain this particular performance of masculinity? What would it mean if rap music itself stopped being about a real hard masculinity that sought to subordinate women? What would happen if rap music started respecting women as equals? Eminem fired back as only he could. He showed his disgust for Carey and her commentary at concerts by dedicating the song "Puke" (2004), which he originally wrote about Kim, to the pop diva. When that did not prove satisfying enough, the rapper began playing personal voice messages from Carey on stage at concerts. The *New York Post* described these messages as "weird and graphic" and included Carey speaking in "a baby voice." Carey responded immediately through the *New York Daily News* by questioning Eminem's masculinity. "I don't know what the hell he's doing," Carey said. "It's a little excessive. Doesn't it seem a little bit girly? Like we're in a catfight." True to form, Carey went for Eminem's jugular.

After having his masculinity questioned yet again, the rapper took his time responding. He finally fired back through an interview on his uncensored hip hop channel on Sirius Satellite Radio station Shade 45. There, he said that Carey was the real liar because she denied their relationship. According to Eminem, they were dating for six or seven months, but it did not work out because he was just not that into her. And several years later, in "Bagpipes from Baghdad" (2009), he made reference to her mixed race beauty, expressed his desire to get back with her, recounted her romantic exploits with ex-boyfriend Luis Miguel and now-husband Nick Cannon, and finished by detailing how he was going to make her pay for her public betrayal through violence. After Cannon responded through a series of tweets and blog posts, Eminem admitted that he did take things a bit far in the song and publicly wished the newlyweds well.

For her part, Carey was not buying it. She released the song "Obsessed" (2009) as a response. Despite denials from her representation, the song is clearly directed at Eminem. She referred to the rapper as an amateur entertainer and as a Stan-like fan who was stalking her. But in this scenario, a city bus hits the infatuated fan while he is snapping pictures of his beloved idol on his smart phone. To bring the point home about Eminem's fake-masculinity, Carey portrayed Eminem herself in the video by donning his signature baggy pants and T-shirt costume. She suggests that there is nothing but a confused girl underneath the hard masculine appearance. Interestingly, "Obsessed" became a genuine hit single by debuting at No. 11 on the Billboard Hot 100 chart.

One reason for the song's success, in addition to its vivid satire, is that it broke with gender conventions that associate women with pop music and commercial entertainment and men with rap music and authenticity. Carey turns the tables on Eminem personally and publicly in this song with her sharp social commentary and performance in drag.

Eminem responded shortly thereafter with the song "Warning" (2009) on the *Relapse* album where he asks if Carey was really playing him in her video by donning a goatee and baggy sweats. For this, he calls her a "whore," "psycho," and "liar" and describes their sexual encounters in graphic detail as the song grows increasingly intense. Carey is depicted as an impatient and prudish lover. As a way of reminding her who is the real man and who is not, and noting her proper role as a heterosexual, sexually active woman, he tells her to back off. He warns her that if she fires back, he will release tapes and videos featuring her that will ultimately hurt her career and marriage. Putting a coda on his warning, Eminem brings up his beef with Carey in "Cold Wind Blows" (2010) to ward off attacks from those who would contemplate composing songs about him or any of his personas in the future. To date, Carey has not issued a formal or informal response.

The details of Carey's and Eminem's relationship are less important than what the feud itself suggests: Eminem's gender identity as a heterosexual, hypermasculine, and authentic man can be challenged. For example, by transforming herself into Eminem as an icon of sexuality and heterosexuality, Carey highlights the feminine and homoerotic themes that quietly permeate rap, particularly through rap performance. Because Carey hit the nail on its head, each of Eminem's responses to Carey, and "Warning" especially, make it clear that the rapper may be a sexual deviant who ejaculates prematurely and sometimes crossdresses but that he is neither a liar nor a homosexual. He is a real and authentic heterosexual man even when he takes on the whiny persona of Slim Shady and the soul-searching spiritual persona of Marshall Mathers. Furthermore, the feud shows that what Eminem finds disgusting about Carey, and about all heterosexual sexually active women for that matter, is that they can be heard through artificial pop music. Additionally, they can be heard even as their gender identities are performed in a fluid manner that the more authentic genre of rap does not allow for men like Eminem. Remember, rap masculinity, at least according to Carey, is one that deals with femininity by making fun of it, getting rid of it, or absorbing it in sexual terms.

On that note, a final point to be made in the battle of Eminem versus Mariah Carey regards the issues of unity and coalition. The good thing is that Carey certainly gives girls ideas on how to make their own music and about how to spot a man who claims to be the real thing but is not. The bad thing is that as entertaining and smart as Carey's songs are, they do not make lasting connections with other girls and women that build a long-term feminist and political consciousness. One reason is that Carey's songs are essentially about one man in particular rather than about male stereotypes in pop culture and the system of patriarchy in general. As a result, these songs turn out to be only slightly kinder to and respectful of women than Eminem's. For this reason, round three goes to Eminem, reluctantly.

CONCLUSION

Let's review the tally. In the battle of Eminem versus Tori Amos, Amos wins. In the battle of Eminem versus GLAAD, Eminem ekes out a victory. And the eight-year-long battle of Eminem versus Mariah Carey finally goes to Eminem though he definitely had to fight for it. This 2-to-1 scorecard suggests that Eminem's failure to fully include women's and gay men's voices, consent, and lives in his lyrical content is overshadowed by outrage over his challenges to rigid scripts and gender identities for men. For even while he is angry, violent, and deranged with the women he loves most, he is also terrified.[20] He is so terrified that he often demotes them, along with gay, lesbian, bisexual, and transgender people, to a lower order of being. And he never ever tells us why. This is one of many conundrums and contradictions that make Eminem so popular—if by popular we mean both disgusting and enjoyable.

In this context of disgust and pleasure, any meaningful analysis of Eminem's social critique must focus on his many affronts to good taste and decorum. Those who do not take time to discuss these topics find themselves treated like "Minimes" (mini-Eminems) who become targets for having ignored the only things that supposedly make Eminem the real Slim Shady. But a strict focus on Eminem as a disgust trigger when it comes to progressive views about sex, sexual orientation, and gender is not the only story to be told.

Remember, the persona we think we know as Eminem is about social critique on the grandest scale imaginable. Eminem is about placing opposing viewpoints in close proximity so that they cannot help but to create friction and start a fire, and watching that fire burn provides some light with which to illuminate schisms in our society.

This combustible brand of social commentary requires Eminem to contend with opponents both onstage and offstage over time. On one hand, this style of critique stems from the criticism and censure he receives from liberal media coverage and conservative political pundits alike, which means that Eminem is right. He is disgusting because that is what we say he is. On the other hand, Eminem is part of something bigger—rap music and hip hop culture—and is making important critical commentary on their behalves in terms of disadvantage and discrimination on the bases of race and class. This leaves the winner in the battle of Eminem versus everyone else undecided. But it will not stay this way for long.

CHAPTER 8
Losing Himself

Beneath the disgust Eminem generates in many ears with regard to gender, sex, and sexuality is an undertow of race-oriented criticism that paints him largely as a minstrel figure. To many, Eminem is nothing more than a rapping Elvis who would use white privilege to rape and profit from black culture because he really hates black people. Although always lurking behind the scenes, this racist portrait of the rapper gained serious traction from 2002 through 2004. This time period marks Eminem's enormous success with the chart-topping album *The Eminem Show,* released on May 29, 2002; his first feature film *8 Mile,* released November 8, 2002; and the film's soundtrack, released October 29, 2002. The album, film, and soundtrack generally garnered positive reviews for being less homophobic and genderphobic and more introspective and explanatory than the rapper's earlier work.

In fact, the first single from the *8 Mile* soundtrack, "Lose Yourself," was a phenomenon in and of itself. The song was Eminem's first U.S. No. 1 hit, the first rap song to win an Oscar in 2003, winner of the 2004 award for Most Performed Song from a Motion Picture, and the first song to break the digital download record when it was downloaded for the four millionth time in 2011. The song continues to resonate with audiences today because it makes them feel closer to the artist and the life he lived before he became a rap phenomenon. The song also resonates because it speaks to Eminem's strategy of identification, of "losing" himself. However, not everyone was buying what Eminem was selling. The rapper's increased introspection and explanation led many critics to question his motives for becoming a rapper in the first place. Therefore, in this chapter, I look at two rounds of controversy concerning the untold story of Eminem's racial identity to find out why. What was really so threatening about Eminem's talent, love for, and success in rap music? Was it that Eminem was trying to be black? Or, was it that he was trying to be not-quite white? Did Eminem lose himself in the music for real?

EMINEM VERSUS MARSHALL MATHERS

Marshall Mathers had a complicated racial identity even before his dreams of becoming Eminem were made a reality. As noted by Debbie Nelson, the rapper's now-estranged mother, Marshall Mathers was never really a regular white guy in the first place. According to Nelson, she and Nathan Kane Mathers (Marshall's half-brother) were reunited after winning a custody battle by appealing to the Indian Child Welfare Act. As identified by Debbie, the pair claimed to be of mixed race white and Native American ancestry and was recognized under the Cherokee Nation as part of the regional Echota tribe of Alabama. Marshall chose not to identify as mixed race white and Native American and instead chose to identify only as white. Depending on whom we ask, this could be considered the beginning of Marshall's "passing." For those who may not be familiar with what the term "passing" means, I refer to the definition I offered in *Clearly Invisible: Racial Passing and the Color of Cultural Identity.* There, I defined passing as a social phenomenon through which people present themselves as "other" in order to succeed, survive, influence public policy, find love, or seek communities of common interest. Based upon this definition, Marshall Mathers could be considered a racial passer, a multiracial person passing as white. If this is the case, then the question of the rapper's racial identity is answered as much by what he exposes as it is by what he hides.[1]

From the very beginning of his mainstream career, the rapper was sure to let shrewd audience members in on the fact that he was hiding something. For example, in the song "Role Model" (1999), Eminem reveals that he is neither black nor white and that he really is more of a gray ghost, a multiracial combination that is as clear as it is invisible. In doing so, the rapper makes stark social commentary about the nature of racial and multiracial identities. His presence explodes censures on interracial romantic and platonic relationships because these kinds of relationships exist and produce a long cultural and musical history of which he is a part. He also betrays how little his fiercest critics and the entire mainstream media understand about what a multiracial and

Native American identity can be, where they come from and what they can look like. Eminem hints at the fact that people understand multiracial Native American identity even less than they understand multiracial African American identities in songs like "Our House" (1999) and "Yellow Brick Road" (2004), where he talks about the difficulty he faced from white and black communities alike as he tried to fit in during his teenage years. In "The Re-Up" (2006), he talks to critics in racial terms they can understand by telling them to "kiss" his "black ass." In "The Apple" (2011), he explains why he was really "the black sheep" of his family. And, in "Evil Deeds" (2004), he makes the statement most directly: he is without a racial home because Americans understand racial identities in black and white instead and in terms of the "one-drop rule," which says that no matter what a person's actual racial background may be, that person must identify as either white or black. For Eminem, the idea of being "predominantly" white or black blots out any other way of imagining racial identity. Consequently, it can be concluded that Eminem chose not to identify publicly as a multiracial Native American because a vast majority of his audience would not be able to grasp such an identity. He wisely foresaw that critics would scrutinize both his mother's romanticized claims and his decision to identify differently (which, conveniently, leaves him unable to provide proof that he really is anything but white). More importantly, he understood that such scrutiny would reveal that America still has not grasped the real fictions upon which all racial identities are based. If whatever Eminem's race is does not exist—either because no races exist or because we simply cannot grasp the full complexity of racial identities—then Eminem is also implying that race is not a biological trait at all. Rather, it is a set of social traits—a way of thinking and acting—that is created, fluid, overlapping, and changeable. This knowledge that race is a social trait that a person can define and redefine throughout life in order to succeed and survive is at the center of the various racial and racist controversies Eminem has encountered over the years.

We must remember that Marshall Mathers came of age in an era that was largely unwilling to recognize the complex racial and ethnic identities of those who were averse to choosing only one box on the U.S. Census.[2] As Marshall Mathers was becoming Eminem and was recording and promoting the album *Infinite* (1996), the nation booed Tiger Woods for referring to himself as "Cablinasian" on *The Oprah Winfrey Show*. Popular culture also had trouble knowing what to do with emerging actor Vin Diesel, as his critically acclaimed independent film *Multi-Facial* (1995) was brought to life. Diesel chose to use his racial ambiguity to his advantage by refusing to make additional public comments on his ancestry and playing characters from a wide variety of racial backgrounds. Marshall Mathers was obviously taking notes while trying to carve out a unique racial identity among these high-profile stars' experiences. In "G.O.A.T." (2011), Eminem spells it out. Since he did not look black like Tiger Woods or ambiguous like Vin Diesel, he would have to figure out a different way to tap into and express a multiracial identity. It seems reasonable for Eminem to have concluded that there was barely space for him to claim as a white rapper in hip hop culture, let alone as a multiracial Native American and white rapper. Although good Native American rappers certainly exist—like Supaman (aka Christian Parrish Takes the Gun), Litefoot, and Junior Harvey—they were not getting much airplay in the 1990s. Marshall Mathers realized that if he were ever to successfully embody an identity as Eminem, he would have to figure out a way to stay white on the outside and appear in audience's minds as racially mixed. But even this presented a challenge as Eminem would need to appear authentic in audiences' minds as mixed white–black rather than white–Native American.[3] Enter Slim Shady.

According to best friend Proof, Slim Shady is "a mask" for Eminem "to hide behind." Eminem goes on to explain exactly how Slim Shady was born: "I was sitting on the toilet and *boom,* the name hit me. I started thinking of all of these words I could rhyme with it . . . I went and called everybody I knew."[4] But Slim Shady was not just a poetic tool; he was a way for Eminem to get the final stamp of approval from his D12 comrades, who would later go on to describe the persona racially as both white and black. When Slim Shady got D12's approval, Marshall Mathers went to the tattoo parlor and paid $50 to have his new alter ego's name tattooed in his left arm. This tattoo was a counterpart to the "Eminem" tattoo he already had on his right arm. A multiracial Slim Shady is exactly what Marshall Mathers needed to ensure Eminem's success as a white rapper.

As much as he is a catchy name, mask, or tattoo, Slim Shady is the product of Eminem's intense study of the roads that successful white rappers traveled to gain popularity within hip hop. First came The Beastie Boys, who had black management and audience acceptance. With the help of Russell Simmons, they fashioned the formula for white emcees to attain success while remaining authentic innovators and not imitators: black production and management, a-political lyrics, and a rock-oriented crossover style. In the tradition of The Beastie Boys, Eminem would be sure not to challenge the pro-black rhetoric that fills many hip hop lyrics.

The black–white interracial trio Third Bass was also a major influence on Eminem as they made sure everyone knew that they were authentic members of the hip hop community because they came from New York and understood hip hop's cultural and social history. MC Search, the group's white front man, earned his stripes because he emphasized his strength and skills as an emcee over his racial identity. Everlast (aka Whitey Ford) and his Irish American rap group House of Pain tried a different strategy. Instead of playing down their whiteness, they tried to tie it to a part of African American struggles in songs like "Jump Around" (1992). This was certainly more politically correct than what other white rap acts would go on to do, but the strategy ultimately failed because audiences felt the group was actually trying too hard to be black and really was not. Eminem would later win a battle against Everlast as he became famous, which is one reason why House of Pain's biggest hit now gets heard mainly at the NBA Playoffs as a literal description of taking jump shots in basketball. Meanwhile, three-time league MVP LeBron James inspires himself before his biggest games by reciting the lyrics to "The Way I Am" in front of cameras in the locker room. Perhaps Eminem's lyrics reflect how one of the most-scrutinized men in sports is now handling the limelight.

But before Eminem could inspire famous fans like LeBron James, he was influenced by the successes of The Beastie Boys and Third Bass. The rapper was equally inspired by the failures of House of Pain, Marky Mark, and the infamous Vanilla Ice. Eminem admitted as much to *Rolling Stone* when he said, "Look at Vanilla Ice. Yo, he got exposed. You can only put up a front for so long before people start coming out of the woodwork . . . White rappers . . . should play off it like, 'Hi! I'm white.'"[5] Eminem realized that Vanilla Ice was not the only white rapper to make this mistake. While Vanilla Ice failed as a class passer, and Marky Mark failed because he and his music were pop passing as hip hop, the Young Black Teenagers (YBT) failed as racial passers. YBT was a controversial all-white hip hop group from the early 1990s that came under fire for trying to present themselves as other than what they really were in order to succeed in hip hop. YBT's response was that the group's name was really a comment on the members' relationships with and a tribute to rap's many black pioneers. It was also a way for them to expose what they saw as the limited ways society had for thinking and talking about race. Even though YBT had the support of the politically oriented all-black rap group Public Enemy and were signed initially to Hank Shocklee's label Sound of Urban Listeners (SOUL), songs like "Tap the Bottle," (1993), "Proud to be Black" (1991), and "Daddy Called Me Nigga Cause I Liked To Rhyme" (1991) were interpreted as stereotypical and offensive. Most critics now agree that these songs were not intended to come off as racist and agree that YBT's real mistake was thinking that black was an identity that could be appropriated and declared rather than experienced and communicated with historical and contemporary nuance. In other words, YBT's real offense was promoting the idea that hip hop could change a person's race. Eminem learned two lessons from YBT. One is that "for white rappers, there's such a fine line between shit you can and can't do."[6] The other is that he could never make the mistake of renouncing his whiteness because doing so would ultimately serve to stabilize the racial barriers he was trying to undermine with the privilege that whiteness offered.

Eminem's rap racial tutoring also took place closer to home in Detroit, Michigan, with white rocker Kid Rock and rap duo Insane Clown Posse (aka ICP: Inner City Posse). Kid Rock did not announce himself as black nor did he really try to rap either though he did feel free to occasionally drop the "N" word. Kid Rock expressed himself as a rocker with a rap edge because the majority black environment of Detroit influenced his artistic sensibility. This gave Eminem the idea to introduce himself as a rapper with a rock edge. ICP, however, were a different story. ICP were different because they were Eminem's direct competition as they too were working their way up Detroit's underground rap ranks in the 1990s. ICP doled out horrorcore rap lyrics in full clown face under the names of Violent J and Shaggy 2 Dope. Some say that the black-and-white makeup is a gothic gimmick used to draw attention away from the fact that the rappers are white and suggest that they are really black and white. But Eminem realized that ICP's approach could be too dicey. Even though Eminem dished out shocking lyrics of his own as Slim Shady, he was definitely not going to change the color of his face.[7]

The white rapper that came closest to what became Eminem's style is Cage, who was part of New York City's underground rap scene and accused Eminem of biting his style when the rapper went public as Slim Shady. Obviously, Eminem denied this and replied by way of "Role Model" (1999) when he said that he purchased Cage's record and taped over it. Eminem also hurled insults at Cage through a variety of other lyrics including "Tony Touch Power Cypha 3 Freestyle" (1999). Cage reportedly concluded that Eminem copied his style because he knew it would sell, and, since Eminem had the support of Dr. Dre, there could only be room for one highly skilled white rapper. Cage insulted Eminem and Slim Shady in several songs, including "And So Kiddies" (1999) and "Bitch Lady" (1999). But when asked in an August 2000 interview with MVRemix.com how the rivalry began and where it currently stood, Cage said that there was no rivalry: "If you want to know the deal, look around the net and run with the one you like the most!"[8] One thing cannot be denied: the two rappers identify themselves racially as fitting in best in something of a gray racial area.

Eminem learned from YBT's fundamental attribution error, Kid Rock's success, ICP's stage presence, and from Cage's taste for racial ambiguities, and he combined these lessons by collaborating with Dr. Dre in his debut single "My Name Is" (1999). On its surface, "My Name Is" introduced Eminem as a white rapper whose upbringing on the wrong side of the tracks gave him a unique view on and way to communicate with mainstream white culture. Eminem would return to this theme over the course of his career in songs like "The Real Slim Shady" (2000) where he says that people do not believe he is white, "White America" (2002) where he says that if he were black, he would not have sold so many records and "Yellow Brick Road" (2004) where he says that he lived on the margins of black and white.

But underneath that white surface, "My Name Is" was the equivalent of a wink. The single introduced Slim Shady to rap's national and global audience as the dysfunctional multiracial (aka white and black) offspring of Debbie Nelson and Dr. Dre (see Chapter 2). Slim Shady existed on the margins of society like any stereotypical multiracial kid represented in mainstream media. His name said it all. Slim Shady was disadvantaged and marginal. He had difficulty fitting in because he was so slim and existed like a ghost in the shade between white and black racial spaces. He was angry and confused, was bullied because he was different, and, as a result, he was a deranged junkie awaiting his clinic results. Slim Shady was the personification of centuries' worth of racist theories, which said that multiracial people inherited the worst traits of the racial groups from which they descended in order to discourage interracial relationships. Or, as professors from Yale, Harvard, and the University of Chicago put it in a 2008 research report called "The Plight of Mixed Race Adolescents," multiracial youths are as bad as whites when it comes to abusing drugs and alcohol and as bad as blacks when it comes to watching too much television, using mobile technology instead of doing homework, fighting, and getting sexually transmitted diseases.[9] Translation: Slim Shady is just a regular dysfunctional black–white multiracial kid. Therefore, Slim Shady is someone whose racial identity and behavior Americans can understand, regardless of whether they approve.

But Slim Shady is not only a stereotype, he is an "other" Eminem and Marshall Mathers use so that they can identify in contrast and criticize all racial identities in the process. Eminem's name itself supports this perspective, as it is as much a racial manifesto as it is a play on Marshall Mathers's initials. Eminem is Marshall Mathers turned inside out. A version of the multiracial identity that existed privately for Marshall Mathers became public for Eminem through the introduction of Slim Shady. Therefore, Eminem is a symbol that works because it indicates that the rapper is darker on the inside than he is on the outside, allowing him to take on whatever racial flavor he chooses through the use of personas. It also suggests that audiences have a taste for racial passing just like they crave the M&M candy, so Eminem is packaged and colored differently on the surface depending on the expectations of his audiences.

Eminem acknowledges this type of identification in "The Way I Am" (2000) when he reminds us that he identifies according to the racial identity we assign him. Eminem is real in so far as he can fit into the box in which audiences want to place him. In light of this strategy, it becomes more difficult to argue that Eminem is a kitschy minstrel who devours and performs nonwhite racial identities but cannot ever experience them. And it becomes easier to imagine that Marshall Mathers became Eminem due to a clever multiracial sensibility, one that Eminem used to give birth to Slim Shady and exercise the right to identify differently than Marshall Mathers's parents and siblings, identify differently in different situations, change his identity over time and repeatedly, have loyalties to many racial and ethnic groups and decide of whom he will include in his inner circle as a true friend or business partner.[10]

By presenting himself as willing and able to identify with multiple racial identities, Eminem marked his point of entry into the rap scene by carving out a position that would allow audiences to imagine a black–white multiracial identity for Slim Shady. A quick glance at Eminem's first three solo album covers makes the point visually. The rapper's racial identity is ambiguously black-and-white on the cover of the *Slim*

Shady LP (and especially on the cover of the Limited Edition version). His racial identity looks white but is represented in sepia (reddish-brown) tones on the *Marshall Mathers LP*, indicating that something other than a white and black context is at play. And the rapper's racial identity is extremely white in the context of a full-color hip hop performance on the cover of *The Eminem Show*. Translation: Eminem can look white onstage, Slim Shady can manifest as black-and-white from a distance, and Marshall Mathers can be someone whose race is kept a secret while he reveals more about his class status and spiritual beliefs. As Eminem perfected this strategy of representation over the years, he solidified his win in the battle versus Marshall Mathers. Even though the label "Eminem" does not refer cleanly to a real individual, the label refers to a powerful performer who can wrestle with Slim Shady and control Marshall Mathers by embracing and challenging the notion of racial passing and the concept of multiracial identities at the same time.

EMINEM VERSUS THE RACE POLICE

Opinions about Eminem's polyethnic strategy of racial identification vary. Some, like PitchForkMedia.Com writer William Bowers, see Eminem as the enemy of everything polyethnic or multiracial. According to Bowers, Eminem is a white man and a white supremacist: "When he (as Rabbit) rules that all-black room, it's not just a underdog victory-fantasy, but a victory-fantasy for whitey, winning another race's game/element."[11] Bowers concludes that Eminem's music and image are feeding into an ideology that is working hard to give new meanings to whiteness as an oppressed minority group in the face of a "tanning" America. Others, like *The Nation*'s Richard Kim, saw Eminem as the prophet of a conservative racial politics who resonates with a kind of white male pain and negativity. Others, like communication studies professor Eric King Watts, saw Eminem differently. For Watts, Eminem was not a white supremacist or white rage-a-holic; instead, he was a white man who was using his working-class status to pass as black and repair a credibility issue in light of racist accusations. Still others, like the *Village Voice*'s R. J. Smith, saw Eminem as a social commentator from white America whose obviously complex racial identity got turned into a promotable product when he wrote, "They have taken a question mark and turned him into a logo."[12] The *New York Review of Books*' Andrew O'Hagan agreed and offered an optimistic twist when he wrote that Eminem's public journey from alienation to acceptance created an opportunity to redefine what it means to be a modern-day American. In a *New York Times* article, cultural sociologist Orlando Patterson provocatively suggested that Eminem is an example of what a post-white and polyethnic American racial identity (i.e., willing to identify with racial groups other than one's own) might be. This commentary suggests that it may be most appropriate to understand racial identity as social and changeable rather than biological and fixed.

Other artists and cultural critics saw things more negatively. Some critics painted Eminem as the Elvis Presley of rap, a moniker even he used sarcastically to refer to himself in "Without Me" (2002) and "You Made Me" (2009). These critics argued that Eminem would be more authentic if he were marketed as what he really was: an imitator of black style who was out to gain only fame and fortune. According to these critics, Eminem is not a rapper, he is a rock star. After all, Eminem looks white and rock music sounds white. And, if we really listen, we will hear that Eminem raps with a white high-pitched rock sound and samples from heavy metal and emo, which would be more suitable (in stereotypical terms) for white rock audiences. The blogosphere took this line of race music critique a step further as many began to suggest that Eminem could be considered a minstrel—an entertainer that performed songs and music of black American origin in a black way—minus the blackface. Some bloggers went so far as to say that Eminem was even performing whiteface minstrelsy by overemphasizing a white trash identity to gain black acceptance and attempt to "keep it real."

However, those who promoted such views on Eminem were wrong on several counts. First, the critiques simply are not nuanced enough to grapple with the rapper's increasingly complex racial representations. For instance, the minstrel critique ignores the subtle changes to the form that occurred over time. If we concede that Eminem is a "white" minstrel that goes for extreme representations of whiteness, we must also concede that his representations, however controversial, have ultimately made room for Shady 2.0, the next generation of "white" rappers who are able to express themselves differently.[13] This part of Eminem's legacy is demonstrated most effectively in his protégé Yelawolf (aka Catfish Belly; aka Michael Wayne Atha). In a January 2012 interview with *Vibe Magazine,* Yelawolf openly discusses how Eminem's music and mentorship has impacted the way he approaches life. Specifically, Yelawolf discussed why and how he identifies with his multiracial white–Native American ancestry, and how it impacts his approach to making music: "My father has Cherokee [blood], and my mom got Cherokee and Blackfoot," he says. "Yela represents hunger, life, light, fire, power. Wolf speaks to my fighting spirit. The soul I put in my music."[14] The fact that Yelawolf can identify unambiguously as a white–Native American rapper from Alabama traveling in Eminem's footsteps suggests that more rappers who do not fit into the black-and-white box can be taken seriously. Eminem confirmed this expansion as one of his objectives when he said, "Since I went through my personal thing as far as getting myself right, our only plan was to reestablish the label. And I've got a lot of faith that Yelawolf is going to be pretty damn big. It's always exciting for me because I love hip hop so much to try to bring a new artist along and help them get where they want to be. But also it's almost like I feel I'm helping to give back to hip hop."[15] The touch that Eminem is giving back to hip hop culture, the idea that we can identify as whatever we want rather than what others say we are, is now playing out in youth culture and demographics nationwide. As the tanning of America deepens with the birth of its first "majority-minority" generation, perhaps more Americans will, like Yelawolf, also feel comfortable to identify with the whole rather than a part of who they are. And, in so doing, they will hopefully introduce a broader and more progressive view of social and political issues—such as immigration reform, education reform, and civil rights—that are based on changing ideas about race and ethnicity.

Second, critics and lay people alike should also exercise caution when interpreting Eminem's so-called whiteface, or use of "white trash" stereotypes, as a way to pass as black. A closer inspection of his songs reveals that his work reflects a trajectory of class identification and mobility. The *Slim Shady* and *Marshall Mathers LPs* and the *8 Mile* soundtrack came from a lower working-class consciousness. The third album introduced a white middle-class story, which the rapper failed to sustain when he ended *The Eminem Show* and, somewhat ironically, returned to a lower-class story on *Encore*. So, Eminem's story of class identity is more accurately described as a downward social mobility or stasis. This tells us that Eminem will never be a rich person but that he will always represent himself as a poor person with money. In this way, he makes his own white trash background an ongoing and authentic musical trope, so it then makes sense for this background to show up on his fifth and sixth solo albums, which suggests that he has not changed despite his ever-increasing net worth. Instead, the ongoing references to a white trash identity on the *Relapse* and *Recovery* albums indicate that he is still grappling with this part of his roots as it represents both the source of his troubles and road to his redemption.

Third, critics who chose to liken Eminem to Elvis Presley were wrong because they failed to acknowledge that though Eminem shares a similar origin story with Elvis in some ways, his success has not sidelined black artists from hip hop the way that Elvis sidelined black rockers. Rock became "white" when white artists, like Elvis, who got their starts working with and in African American musical communities, were able to take center stage and push black musicians to the sidelines. It has been 12 years since "My Name Is" (1999) was released and hip hop is not "white." Although some critics are offended that *Rolling Stone* named the rapper "The King of Hip Hop" in 2011, others point out that Eminem's success has revived and sparked the careers of many black hip hop artists, two of whom are among the top five wealthiest rappers of 2012 according to *Forbes Magazine*.

Take 50 Cent (aka Curtis Jackson) as an example. In 2012, *Forbes Magazine* named 50 Cent the fifth richest rapper in the world, with a net worth of $110 million. This is no accident. 50 Cent's success was carefully constructed since his first hit single "In Da Club" (2003) hit the airwaves. In the video for "In Da Club," polyethnic pair Eminem and Dr. Dre design, oversee, regulate, and approve 50 Cent's persona in three distinct settings: in the laboratory in which he is literally built out of mechanical parts and tested, in a nightclub where he interacts with a predominantly black audience, and in the recording studio where he delivers the lyrics that will become his own unique expression. 50 Cent is always viewed through the eyes of Eminem and Dre to ensure his hip hop legitimacy and "groupie love." 50 Cent returns the favor by ensuring that Eminem remains the real Slim Shady.

D-12's mainstream hip hop introduction, entitled "My Band" (2004), is another example of Eminem's polyethnic strategy. D-12 capitalizes off an irreverent reproduction of Eminem's misfit Slim Shady persona and 50 Cent's thug persona to establish their credibility. This strategy translated into record-breaking sales, as the group's album *D12 World* debuted at No. 1, giving the group its second straight No. 1 release. Then there's Royce Da 5'9", the other half of Eminem's interracial rap duo Bad Meets Evil and member of Slaughterhouse, whose estimated net worth is $1 million. And let us not forget about Eminem's mentor and adoptive father figure, Dr. Dre, who reaps the greatest financial reward of all as the third wealthiest hip hop artist in the world with a total net worth of $270 million. We should also note that Eminem is not doing shabbily himself, with a total net worth of $120 million and counting as of 2012. The ledger speaks for itself: If you are a black hip hop artist, then being associated with Eminem as part of a polyethnic strategy of racial representation is worth its weight in gold—literally.

Fourth, critics who liken Eminem to Elvis are wrong because they are operating from a faulty assumption that music has a color rather than a culture. While it cannot be denied that rap music flows out of black and Latino racial and ethnic experiences in urban centers like New York and Los Angeles, and that these populations are underrepresented in the record companies that distribute the music, we must also acknowledge that popular music in the United States has a long history of crossing color lines, from rap and jazz, to blues and rock, even country. As Gilbert B. Rodman, author of *Elvis After Elvis: The Posthumous Career of a Living Legend,* observes, it is only useful to describe music as "black" if "black" is an adjective that refers to a style of performance and reception rather than a noun that refers to a particular brand of music in and of itself. When "black" is less about race and more about performance practice, then it is much more difficult to question Eminem's racial politics and identity based on the disruption they cause to traditional ways of thinking about rap. Instead, Rodman writes, we must ask what Eminem's particular performance of racial identity means in the world of rap and how that meaning connects with social and political realities and demographic changes happening in 21st-century America.

As the 21st century has become the multiracial millennium, Eminem's racial identity and expressions came under increased scrutiny. Eminem was most notoriously highlighted and attacked by hip hop magazine *The Source* in 2003 and 2004 for lyrics written in the early 1990s describing African American women as stupid gold diggers. The story about the rapper's alleged racism was picked up by many mainstream and music-oriented news outlets including the *New York Times, USA Today,* the *Los Angeles Times,* the *Washington Post,* the *Boston Herald,* CBS Nightly News, National Public Radio (NPR), *XXL, Vibe Magazine,* VH1 News, and MTV News.

The story goes a little something like this. *The Source* and its lead representative Benzino gave the *Marshall Mathers LP* a 2-out-of-5-mic rating because its success was supposedly hurting black and Latino rappers' chances of success. Eventually, the magazine changed this to a 4-mic rating, especially because a write-in campaign from readers exposed the hypocrisy behind the 4.5-mic rating given to Benzino's own mediocre album *Made Men*. Benzino accused Eminem of taking advantage of white privilege because he could be successful with introspective lyrics while rappers of color were pigeonholed into talking about "bling" or their aspiration for it. In all fairness, Benzino did have one valid point: Eminem has been disproportionately rewarded by the National Academy of Recording Arts and Sciences because no black artist who is as publicly and consistently angry as he has been ever reaped similar rewards, either from the academy itself or from the music industry at large.

Eminem fired back on "Say What You Say" (2002), "Nail In the Coffin" (2003), and "The Sauce" (2003) by questioning Benzino and *The Source*'s credibility, and, at the MTV Europe Music Awards in November 2003, Eminem accepted his fifth consecutive award for best male rap artist and called the mostly white audience a bunch of "racist crackers" while eating crackers onstage. He stated that he appreciated the adulation and recognition but knew that there were other and better African American and Latino artists at work in contemporary hip hop. This is but another example of how Eminem effectively addresses the inherent contradictions of hip hop as a polyethnic and increasingly multiracial form of entertainment.

Unfortunately, Benzino was not satisfied, so he capitalized on the controversy by putting out two response tracks, "Pull Ya Skirt Up" (2003) and "Die Another Day" (2003). Eminem responded by making it clear that he had Benzino's number. Eminem let it be known that Benzino is a hypocrite because Benzino is multiracial (white–black) yet is passing as black, especially when he compares himself to Malcolm X and Eminem to David Duke. Many hip hop heads, including Russell Simmons and Ice-T, came to Eminem's defense once this was revealed. Simmons and Ice-T reminded the public that what we call "black" is really multiracial anyway and that failing to acknowledge this historical fact indicates a desire to ignore the racial mixing that has always been at the center of U.S. history and of hip hop's culture and creative aesthetic.

The Source and Benzino were not interested in what Simmons and Ice-T had to say, and they declared as much in issue #173, published in February 2004, where a pathetic attempt was made to gain even more publicity by releasing snippets of two of Eminem's underground tapes with a "Special Editorial Audio Supplement: Eminem's Racist Songs and the Secret Agenda to Steal Hip-Hop from the Streets" compact disc.

One snippet, "Oh Foolish Pride" (1992), featured a young Eminem calling black women gold diggers after breaking up with his black girl-friend. In "So Many Styles" (1990), an even younger Eminem used the word "nigger."

In a February 2004 C-SPAN interview for *Booknotes* entitled "The Collected Poetry of Nikki Giovanni," the famous poet Giovanni commented on this situation. She remarked, "So Eminem, you know, does not have a right to dis black women when he's making a living in a black art form and you—you get sick of that." Giovanni's sentiment coupled with Eminem's other offense—his unauthorized use of the "N" word—prompted hip hop scholars like Michael Eric Dyson, journalists like Davey D, and industry insiders like Suge Knight to demand a public apology. Eminem made a swift apology. In his statement, as quoted by MTV News, Eminem downplayed the situation. He called the whole thing

> really nothing more than blatant self-promotion for a failing magazine and one man's lifeless music career. They're scared of what can happen if the hip-hop community shows it can live without them . . . [The songs] in no way represent who I was then or who I am today. In becoming an adult, I've seen what hip-hop and rap music can do to touch millions of people. The music can be truly powerful, and it has helped improve race relations in a very real way. I want to use this negative attack on me as a positive opportunity to show that . . . So while I think common sense tells you not to judge a man by what he may have said when he was a boy, I will say it straight up: I am sorry I said those things when I was 16. And I don't want to let anybody turn this into an opportunity to promote their own bullshit agenda.[16]

Eminem continued by stating that "I'd just broken up with my girl-friend, who was African American, and I reacted like the angry, stupid kid I was. I hope people will take it for the foolishness that it was, not for what somebody is trying to make it into today."[17] As for the ac-cusation that he used the infamous "N" word, Eminem was reluctant to acknowledge the recording as his own until the release of his fourth album *Encore*. There, he sealed the deal and provided further expla-nation in "Yellow Brick Road" (2004) where he said that very few people actually felt his songs were offensive even though he did use the epithet in "So Many Styles" and was wrong for making racial, but not gendered, generalizations in "Oh Foolish Pride." He even asked for forgiveness outright in "Evil Deeds" (2004) and implied that no evil word or deed represents the full intent of the talker or doer.

But the race police were not finished with Eminem yet. For starters, *The Source* alleged that Eminem lied about his age (saying he was only 16) and lied about having a breakup with an African American girlfriend who never existed. Cultural commentators more distanced from the incident reminded Eminem, and all of us, that whenever we speak with each other, the meaning and impact of our words are determined by the relationships involved. So, rather than providing an excuse for Eminem's slur, his romantic relationship with an African American girlfriend should have provided additional reason for him not to use the infamous word. Additionally, multiracial African American critics such as Jay Smooth, founder of New York's longest running hip hop radio show, WBAI's Underground Railroad, argue that it is not a double standard for African Americans to use the "N" word while others cannot and should not. In fact, because of their unique social experience and history with the word, African Americans have a license to use it in a way that is not necessarily derogatory.[18]

Renowned cultural commentator and scholar Edward G. Armstrong agrees. Armstrong also notes how Eminem learned to get around this censorship on his racial speech. Although Eminem only used the "N" word once on tape in 1990, the many black artists who make guest appearances on his albums—like Sticky Fingaz, D12, Obie Trice, Dre, Snoop, Nate Dogg, Lil' Wayne, and Xzibit—use the epithet repeatedly and thereby give him a pass. In a 2004 article entitled "Eminem's Construction of Authenticity," Armstrong goes on to say that the real reason Eminem chose not to continue using the epithet on tape is because it would likely make his core audience of white suburban males uncomfortable or angry. And, as recently as 2009, singer Nick Cannon rehashed *The Source* controversy and called Eminem a racist in a (quickly posted and deleted) blog response to the rapper's beef with wife Mariah Carey. On the other hand Harvard law professor and author of *Nigger: The Strange Career of a Troublesome Word* Randall A. Kennedy saw the situation differently. Kennedy felt that though Eminem should not have used the word in the first place, his apologies were sincere and his vow never to use the word again was a wise decision. Case closed.

Many African American and Latino hip hop journalists, fans, and rappers continued to criticize Eminem for ignoring his role as a white man in the world of hip hop. For instance, rapper Ja Rule articulated his politics of resentment in "The Warning" (2002) when he challenged Eminem to a battle and charged that Eminem could never understand the experiences of blackness. Jay-Z also commented on a change within hip hop since Eminem's emergence in "What More Can I Say" (2003) when he remarked about the large degree to which whiteness fuels record sales. A serious implication of the kind of success Jay-Z chronicles is that Eminem can take everything from hip hop except the burden of being black.

In the face of this criticism, Eminem worked hard to publicly repair his relationship with hip hop's African American constituents and consumers.[19] In February 2003, he accepted a Grammy for *The Eminem Show* as best rap album and took the stage with an entirely African American entourage. He humbly accepted the award and paid homage to the black and white rappers that paved the way for and inspired him. These included emcees and groups such as Run DMC, The Beastie Boys, LL Cool J, Kool G Rap, Masta Ace, Rakim, Dr. Dre, NWA, KRS-One, Treach, Nas, Tupac Shakur, Notorious BIG, and Jay-Z. He concluded by saying, "Thanks. I learned from all of you." And, according to Eminem.Com, this was enough to win Jay-Z and several others over. Eminem went on to produce "Moment of Clarity" (2004) for Jay-Z as well as "Runnin' (Dying to Live)" (2003) and other posthumous tribute songs for lyrics written and delivered by TuPac Shakur and Notorious BIG.[20]

No matter whom we may think is right or why, in the annals of hip hop history, Eminem definitely won the battle against Benzino, *The Source,* and hip hop's race police. For starters, Benzino and *The Source* were forced to pay Eminem for defamation of character and copyright infringement for publishing and profiting off the 20-second samples included on the audio supplement. The magazine lost most of its advertising revenue, and Benzino lost his record deal. In 2011, Benzino was still trying to repair his identity by challenging Eminem to a battle in 2012. Finally, in the summer of 2012 Benzino conceded defeat in an interview on Rap Fix Live. "I can say it now," said Benzino, "I was wrong for it. Because at the end of the day, Em is a great lyricist and he should be able to express himself in hip hop as anybody should."[21] Benzino, who now stars in his own reality television show on VH1 called *Love and Hip-Hop Atlanta,* went on to say that Eminem has done much to foster interracial and intercultural communication throughout his career. Nearly a decade after the race police tried to put Eminem away there are few, if any, commentators left who are willing to publicly accuse the rapper of racism in word or deed. Eminem's obvious victory ultimately created opportunities for rebuttals and reconciliations through which he pulled in an even larger and more loyal audience.

EMINEM VERSUS US

The question of whether Eminem will hang on to his audience for the rest of his career does not seem to be up for grabs either. Eminem appears to have already won this battle. As we have seen so far, Eminem's adept skill as an artist makes us think hard about the ideologies of racial aesthetics and representation. Let us take stock to see if we ever stood a chance of seeing, thinking about, or doing things differently when it comes to Eminem.

To begin with, Eminem uses the Slim Shady persona to distinguish himself and Marshall Mathers. At times when he addresses antisocial behavior, he invokes humor and horror, mixed-race degeneracy, and always inhabits his Slim Shady persona. In battle raps, hip hop's traditional rhetorical situations in which he struggles for street credibility and is the racialized white other, he refers to himself as Eminem. At times that call for more biographical speech about the secrets he keeps and demons he faces, he refers to himself by his birth name, Marshall Mathers. These personas open him up to multiple meanings and directions, and they can open us up too.

Instead of losing himself, Eminem uses Marshall Mathers and Slim Shady so we can find him and find ourselves in his music. His racial passing, polyethnic and multiracial identification strategies would not make sense if he were not a rapper who defied racial stereotypes. After all, passing (emphasizing part of your identity rather than the whole) and polyethnicity (identifying with a different culture than the one into which you were born) emphasize the fact race is a changing concept. We have already seen how, like the M&M candy, Eminem reinvents himself with different packaging by surrounding himself with assorted black, white, and brown entertainers, by cross-selling through various outlets in the market of popular culture, and by taking on multiple personalities, or flavors, in music videos and lyrics. As the Real Slim Shady, he reminds listeners that there may be a million others who look like him but there is only one person who can manage this kind of complex identification strategy. So, once again, Eminem shows us exactly how unlike Elvis he is because only he can impersonate (and criticize) himself. It has been over a decade since Eminem came on the scene and his imitators have not arrived, forcing us to realize that Eminem's greatest skill is in maintaining his uniqueness. Whether he presents his identities in black-and-white, sepia, or full color, onstage or offstage, he captures pieces that can be brought together to make a whole. Yet, on the cover of *Relapse,* this whole is shattered. Conversely, perhaps the *Recovery* cover represents putting these shattered pieces together and updating his identity. On the cover of *Recovery* Eminem is walking alone in a new direction, away from us, and down a deserted paved two-way road.

To the naked eye, Eminem's music seems to have brought hip hop culture and rap music away from their urban Latino and African American roots to mainstream white America. But, as we have taken it in this chapter, a closer look challenges that perspective. In order to become worthy of *Rolling Stone*'s title "King of Hip Hop," Eminem had to first carve out a unique niche within the culture and industry, which he did by translating the indeterminacy of his (alleged) white–Native American racial identity as Marshall Mathers into a slightly less indeterminate white–black identity for Slim Shady. Only then could the rapper known as Eminem come to be known as hip hop's greatest white rapper.

Finally, Eminem's representational strategy begs the question of whether his brand of polyethnic representation, what some have called racial passing, can lead to enriching forms of bonding and interaction in the world beyond his lyrics. Echoing legendary old school emcee KRS-One, Eminem believes that the answer is yes. He asserts that hip hop is unique because it has this adhesive power more than any other musical genre. Like Eminem, hip hop too knows how to present itself differently in order to succeed, survive, and create new multiracial alliances and identities. In interviews, the rapper notes, "the fact that hip hop has so many different people, different types of people coming to hip hop shows" is incredible, positive, and progressive.[22] In the end, Eminem proves that as we continue to challenge predominantly white and black ways of thinking about race, the common ground upon which we will meet remains popular music. In that case, when it comes to tackling the racial critics, it is Eminem 3, everyone else zero.

CHAPTER 9
Eminem versus Everybody

"Eminem" wins the battle against those of us who would try to lessen the impact or importance of his career by continuing to confirm his credibility as an artist and businessman, emotionally connecting with younger audiences through digital technology and social media, motivating listeners to think critically about their identities through his audiovisual and narrative imagery, and in doing so, creating a loyal fan base. The implication of this representational strategy for Eminem is the ability to shape future demand for "Eminem"—as one of the top 100 "Greatest Artists of All Time" and as "The King of Hip Hop"[1]—and for global and generational expansion. This is where the next phase of Eminem's representational strategy begins—where popular music becomes the platform upon which Eminem can mentor other artists, market new products, and create a lasting legacy by doing battle in the courtroom.

Eminem's legal troubles began close to home in 1999, when his estranged mother Debbie Nelson sued him for $10 million for alleged defamation of character by way of her negative portrayal on *The Slim Shady LP*. The suit was settled for $25,000, of which Nelson received approximately $1,600. In 2000, Eminem pulled an unloaded gun out to intimidate Douglas Dail of Detroit rap rivals Insane Clown Posse and then assaulted bouncer John Guerrera for kissing his then wife Kim in a parking lot. The rapper was arrested and was charged with possession of a concealed weapon and assault. He was charged for both offenses and pled guilty. Further illustrating that his art does imitate his life, Eminem reenacted the parking lot assault in a skit called "The Kiss (Skit)" on *The Eminem Show* (2002). Later that year, Kim sued Eminem for defamation of character over her depiction as an emotionally abusive, cheating murder victim in "Kim" (2000) on *The Marshall Mathers LP*.

Meanwhile, *The Slim Shady LP* was almost held back because Labi Siffre, the openly gay composer of "I Got The" (1975), the song sampled in "My Name Is" (1999), objected to lyrics in which the rapper boasted of raping a lesbian among other things. In order to appease Siffre, and get the sample cleared, the rapper changed the lyrics of his breakthrough single. Unfortunately, the lyric-oriented trouble did not stop there. In fact, things got much worse in 2000 when Ontario, Canada's Attorney General Jim Flaherty declared that the rapper should not be allowed into the country to perform at the Skydome in Toronto. Flaherty said, "I personally don't want anyone coming to Canada who will come here and advocate violence against women." MPP Michael Bryant took the matter a step further when he said that the Canadian government should lay charges against Eminem for promoting the violent abuse of women in his lyrics. After all, he raps about having murdered Nicole Brown-Simpson, provided ammunition to the Columbine High School killers, and fantasizes about killing his parents and wife.

In 2000, Eminem filed a restraining order against former bodyguard Byron Williams, who was suing him for back wages. In 2001, Eminem was fined $2,000, sentenced to community service and another year of probation on weapons charges based on an altercation with a Psychopathic Records employee. Eminem went to Michigan state court again that year because childhood bully D'Angelo Bailey sued him for $1 million over the lyrics in "Brain Damage" (1999). Bailey is described in the song as a "fat kid" who shoved Eminem into lockers at school, assaulted him in the bathroom, banged his head against a urinal, soaked his clothes in blood, and choked his throat. Bailey claimed that Eminem's lyrics constituted a false-light invasion of privacy. In court, Bailey downplayed the childhood incident that put the rapper into a 10-day coma, calling it a "little shove." Bailey could not prove that the lyrics were false, unreasonable, or highly objectionable, so the charges were dismissed in October 2003 when the judge rendered her decision in the form of a rap. Bailey appealed and lost. In 2005, the appellate court said that it was obvious that the song is more fantasy than reality, and that Bailey did admit that he picked on the rapper.[2]

Legal troubles came in from across the pond when the United Kingdom nearly cancelled the rapper's three-day tour and refused to let him enter the country in early 2001. According to British writer Nick Hasted, "It's the raps on his . . . record, *The Marshall Mathers LP,* the thoughts in his mind, that disturb and distress Britain most . . . That's why . . . his hockey-masked, chainsaw-wielding image is on the cover of every newspaper . . . , why the police will barge into his dressing room after the show, only to find him vanished, slipped away in the night."[3] However, Eminem could not escape the law for long. More trouble came his way in 2002 when French jazz pianist Jacques Loussier sued him and mentor Dr. Dre for $10 million. Loussier alleged that the beat for "Kill You" (2000) was sampled from his song without permission. Loussier also called for the court to seize all sales of *The Marshall Mathers LP* and destroy all remaining copies. Although a trial was set to begin in June 2004, the case was later settled for an undisclosed sum.

In 2003, the U.S. Secret Service said it was investigating claims that Eminem planned to kill then president George W. Bush in "We As Americans" (2003). Eminem responded to the claims in the court of public opinion. In his video for "Mosh" (2004), he highlighted what he saw as the president's many failures and faults. The president's people did not respond, so the incident did not go any further, but other incidents did. In 2003, Eminem's record company, Shady Records, filed a lawsuit against *The Source* for copyright infringement. According to *PR Newswire* reports, "just two weeks before Eminem was going to have to take the stand and explain the details of a series of songs he made calling Black people 'n***ers,' 'p**ch m****ys,' and 'sp**r ch***ers,' his own company, Shady Records, withdrew [the] lawsuit . . . admitting that The Source had done nothing illegal when it played the songs at a press conference and posted snippets on its website."[4] Later that same year, 70-year-old Californian Harlene Stein sued Eminem, claiming that the rapper sampled a song written by her late husband Ronald to make the instrumental for "Guilty Conscience" (1999) without permission. According to the Court documents, "'Guilty Conscience' was registered with the U.S. Copyright Office. . . . The Registration states it 'Incorporates some material from Getting Straight' . . . Stein is given no credit on the registration as having composed any music contained in 'Guilty Conscience.'"[5] The California Central District Court dismissed the case in June 2004 due to lack of jurisdiction. Stein's appeal was denied.

All things considered, 2004 was relatively quiet on the legal front in terms of new cases forming, but things erupted again in 2005. The legal woes began when Jack and Betty Schmitt (Eminem's aunt and uncle) sued him. According to *CBS Entertainment News,* the couple said that their nephew wrongly tried to evict them from the $350,000 house he was letting them occupy and refusing to pay them to maintain: "According to the lawsuit, the Schmitts claim that Eminem had agreed to pay them $100,000 a year for five years and provide them with a house worth up to $350,000. But they say the rapper has given them only $165,000 since 2002. The Schmitts say that Eminem bought a lot for them in 2002 to accommodate a home, which was finished in March 2003, but the rapper kept the property in his own name. On July 13, the Schmitts say they received a notice telling them to leave the property, the lawsuit says."[6] Fortunately, this family dispute appears to have been resolved.

Just when the personal and lyric-oriented cases were settled, the business cases erupted. In 2003, Eminem sued Apple, Inc., and forced the company to pull an iPod ad that featured a young user rapping along to the lyrics of "Lose Yourself" (2002). Eminem and his publishing company, FBT Productions, claimed that they did not give Apple permission to use the song, and Apple used it anyway. As a public act of contrition, Apple's Steve Jobs presented the Eminem iPod at a press conference in 2005. Then, Apple released an iPod commercial featuring Eminem himself. But when that commercial aired, the blogosphere erupted with claims that Apple plagiarized a 2002 Lugz Boots commercial. Apple denied the charges but pulled its commercial anyway. Eminem and company would not forget these incidents. In 2007, Eminem, by way of his publishing company Eight Mile Style LLC and Martin Affiliated LLC, filed suit against Apple, Inc., and Aftermath Entertainment for copyright infringement. Eminem claimed that Aftermath did not have the right to negotiate a deal with Apple for digital downloads of 93 Eminem songs via iTunes. The case, which we will discuss in the next section, was settled years later.

Legal controversy over advertising erupted again in 2011. One was a small case of trademarking when Eminem's image was used without his permission to endorse a Chinese brand of whiskey. The larger case concerned Eminem copyrights. Eight Mile Style LLC, Eminem's publishing company, sued Audi on Eminem's behalf and made the international business pages when they filed a cease-and-desist order against the German carmaker in a Hamburg regional court. Eminem's attorneys alleged that Audi used an unauthorized sample of "Lose Yourself" (2002) in a commercial for the 2012 A6 Avant. Eminem's attorneys claimed that the rapper only authorized Chrysler to use the song in its "Imported from Detroit" Super Bowl ad kickoff for the new 200-model vehicle. Audi denied that the video was an advertisement and downplayed the issue since it was not shown in the United States. Joel Martin, a spokesman for Eminem's Eight Mile Style, said, "we believe Audi not only used 'Lose Yourself' to sell their product without permission, but their spot actually feels inspired by elements of Chrysler's commercial campaign."[7] The suit was settled for an undisclosed sum in the summer of 2011. According to *The Hollywood Reporter,* Audi agreed to donate to Imported from Detroit and other Detroit charities to stimulate the local economy. "Just like Imported from Detroit helped benefit charities like the Marshall Mathers Foundation, we as Eminem's publisher can give back to Detroit," said Martin. "We're looking forward to working with Chrysler on several new Imported from Detroit initiatives that will benefit the city of Detroit as well as charities within the city."[8]

Another battle sprung up while Eight Mile Style and attorneys were fiercely defending Eminem's copyrights, but this time, Eminem would be the defendant. In February 2012, Stephen Lee Pieck sued Eminem for $9 million. Pieck, a homeless man from Michigan, alleged that he gave the rapper the idea for the famous Chrysler commercial in a phone call in September 2010 while in the presence of Christina Aguilera and her ex-husband. "I designed every aspect of the commercial, and the commercial was stolen from me," his lawsuit states. "In addition, I did not receive compensation in monetary terms for the work I did."[9] The rapper's battles over copyright and royalties continued in May 2013, when Eight Mile Style brought suit against Facebook and its ad agency claiming they infringed on Eminem's copyright. According to reports, a 12-page complaint was filed alleging that a Facebook ad broadcast online April 4 copied music from the song "Under the Influence." As of the time of this writing, the Pieck and Facebook cases are under investigation.

Although there is really no way to come up with an exact monetary value to place on Eminem's legal troubles, a conservative estimate is at least $5 million in legal fees plus damages and fines that he has paid. But even this seven-digit figure pales in comparison to what the rapper stands to receive as "digital reparations" in the case of *FBT Productions, LLC; Em2M, LLC v. Aftermath Records, DBA; Aftermath Entertainment; Interscope Records; UMG Recording, Inc.; Ary, Inc* (referred to from here on as *FBT v. Aftermath*).

EMINEM VERSUS THE RECORD INDUSTRY

Understanding the breadth and depth of *FBT v. Aftermath,* and understanding Eminem's impact on the global recording industry, requires a bit of context. Let's go back to 2000, when revenue from CD sales began to decline by more than 50 percent. By 2002, Eminem was one of the top downloaded artists on iTunes. Fast-forward eight years, and Neilsen Soundscan reveals the lowest number of CD sales since 1993. Meanwhile, digital music revenues totaled at least 29 percent of record companies' trade revenues by 2010. It seemed that the record industry reached the end of an era. In all, the rise of technology and its ability to record and distribute music digitally disrupted the business model, taking power from record industry's pockets and putting power into consumers' keyboards.[10]

Here is how things looked according to a report from National Public Radio (NPR): (1) CD sales plummeted, (2) digital album sales rose (but not enough to make up for the physical album sales' drop), and (3) legalized digital track downloads flattened, which means they did not compensate for any of the losses in CD sales either. Add to this Nielsen SoundScan's statistics which track album unit sales, both physical and digital: (1) The total number of albums sold in 2010, 326.2 million, was the lowest since SoundScan began compiling the data in 1993. (2) Total album sales dropped by about 13 percent when measured against sales in 2009, the same rate of decrease sales seen in 2010 over 2008. (3) Digital track sales grew just 1 percent. "For the first time ever, overall music sales—that's the number of every unit of sales for each physical format (CD, LP, cassette) plus digital tracks and music videos—declined."[11]

However, in 2011, something changed. Nielsen SoundScan released a report that stated an 8.5 percent increase in music sales for the first two quarters of 2011, and Eminem had much to do with this. *Recovery* became the first album in history to sell more than 1 million digital albums that summer, with albums from Lady Gaga and Adele right on its tail. At 3,415,000 copies sold on CD or digital download, Eminem's *Recovery* wound up selling more in a single calendar year than any other album since 2007. What is more, *Recovery* won a Grammy for "Best Rap Album," the rapper's fifth triumph in that category. Also, the rapper's virtual video presence was soaring, with nearly 1.5 billion total video views on YouTube, 15 million Twitter followers, and now over 72 million "likes" on Facebook.

Notwithstanding this success, something was missing from Eminem's producers' perspectives. That something was tens of millions of dollars in earnings. His early production firm felt something was going wrong. It all goes back to a letter sent to each of the four major record labels in March 2004. A group of 27 prominent entertainment lawyers wrote the following: "We wish to express our concern about the manner in which major record companies are dealing with artists in the critical, new frontier of music downloads by iTunes and similar companies. Among the most sensitive issues is the royalty itself . . . [which] unjustly enriches the labels." The attorneys objected to the power and economic imbalances between recording artists and record labels.

But the real start of the case goes back to an audit of Aftermath Records that started in 2006. That audit was a eureka moment for Eminem and his team when it revealed that royalties for songs and ring tones sold via iTunes and other online services were being paid to the rapper using an improper royalties scheme.[12] FBT found more evidence and sued Aftermath in 2007 for breach of contract. Among this evidence was a widely circulated blog post by then Apple CEO Steve Jobs, which stated that the relationship between iTunes and record labels was not a sale but a license.[13] FBT ran with this idea, hiring Nashville entertainment lawyer Richard Busch to argue that FBT was entitled to half of all royalties for digital downloads because they were "masters licensed" and not "records sold." In light of the above, the Court had to evaluate and interpret the particular language of the rapper's 1995 exclusive recording agreement with FBT, which was revised in 1998 to give exclusive rights to Eminem's music to Aftermath in exchange for royalty payments. The Court found that this agreement was terminated in 2003, when Eminem and Aftermath entered into a new contract that entitled the rapper to greater royalties and advance payments. However, like its predecessors, the 2003 agreement had two different royalty provisions for "records" sold and "masters" downloaded. Universal argued that Eminem should be paid a standard 18 percent royalty rate for those sales, as he is for physical copies. FBT contended that providing a song to iTunes was actually a third-party licensing situation, similar to film and TV deals, which calls for a 50 percent royalty rate (for them and for the rapper).

The arguments ensued for years. One reason was because the Court could not wade through all of the conflicting evidence and contractual language on its own. Even the keywords used to describe the case are filled with confusing industry and technology jargon (i.e., licensed, royalty, downloads, recording, mastertone, summary judgment, settlement, medium, net receipts, cross-motions, signatory, nonparty, extrinsic evidence, streams, new evidence, etc.). To make some sense out of all this, the Court sent the case to a federal jury for decision in 2009. The jury decided in favor of Aftermath and its parent company

Universal Music Group, finding that FBT and Eminem were not entitled
to royalties as "masters licensed" because the contract was clear that
these were "records sold." Busch, FBT's attorney, was not convinced,
so he appealed the case. California's Ninth Circuit Court of Appeals
reversed the lower court's decision and ruled in favor of FBT. It also
vacated the lower court's order that FBT pay $2.4 million in lawyers'
fees to Aftermath, which meant that Aftermath had to pay up. Digital
downloads were not "records sold" after all, but "masters licensed"
to which the plaintiffs were entitled royalties at the 50 percent rate.
The Court determined the proper interpretation of the Eminem agreements as a matter of law according to California Civil Code Sections
1559, 1636, 1638, and 1641. Translation: Aftermath lost. The royalties due from downloads and mastertones needed to be paid out under
the "masters licensed" provision and not the "records sold" provision.
Aftermath filed an appeal to the U.S. Supreme Court shortly after this
decision was rendered to delay the payments. Meanwhile, the stakes
were getting even higher for the rapper and his production company
because he was breaking digital downloading records. The U.S. Supreme Court denied Aftermath's petition and refused to hear the case,
which meant that the Ninth Circuit Court's ruling was the final word
on the matter. FBT (and, more indirectly, Eminem) won. Here is what
the Ninth Court ruled:

> The agreements unambiguously provide that "notwithstanding" the
> Records Sold provision, Aftermath owed FBT a 50% royalty under
> the Masters Licensed provision for licensing the Eminem masters to
> third parties for any use. It was undisputed that Aftermath permitted
> third parties to use the Eminem masters to produce and sell permanent
> downloads and mastertones. Neither the 2004 amendment nor any of
> the parole evidence provisionally reviewed by the district court sup-
> ported Aftermath's interpretation that the Records Sold provision ap-
> plied. Because the agreements were unambiguous and were not reason-
> ably susceptible to Aftermath's interpretation, the district court erred in
> denying FBT summary judgment. The judgment in favor of Aftermath is
> REVERSED, the district court's order granting Aftermath its attorneys'
> fees is VACATED.[14]

By way of this decision, FBT and Eminem were officially entitled
to digital reparations, and they are not the only ones. According to
FBT manager Joel Martin, "This potentially readjusts the econom-
ics between the artist and the record company, and that's been long
overdue. . . . It puts Eminem in a position he should (have) been in

to begin with, which is to receive a larger portion of the download royalties."[15] All that remains is for the Court to decide exactly how much money in damages the record company owes FBT and Eminem. The pretrial motions dealing with this portion of the case began on June 25, 2012. The ruling was upheld and the case was ultimately settled in October 2012.

In addition to forcing his way onto the hip hop stage, Eminem was now part of a business revolution that is forcing record companies to face the music. His role in this revolution is not only a professional but also a personal game changer. Instead of being portrayed as another selfish celebrity and a blight on society, Eminem's music is in part responsible for transforming the music industry and boosting the fortunes of untold numbers of artists. Industry insiders certainly seem to think so, at least. Many refer to this case as "The Eminem Agreements" and to the Court's decision as "astounding" and as important as "an earthquake" because it "changes the playing field" and is "an issue of fairness" that "raps the record industry."[16] Hundreds of artists who signed contracts between the 1960s and the early 2000s never imagined this kind of opportunity would be possible. Many of them are now filing suit in order to get their fair shares of digital reparations as well. Among the most famous are the Allman Brothers Band, Cheap Trick, The Youngbloods, Kenny Rogers, Peter Frampton, Bob Seger, Weird Al Yankovic, Martha Reeves, and the Four Tops (as members of Motown Alumni Association). Along with Eminem, these artists are exposing the recording industry's greatest weakness—an analog business model in a digital marketplace. As legal scholar Lauren K. Tuner writes, "the Aftermath decision . . . will have an enormous impact on record labels' bottom lines. The major record labels collectively have sold thousands of legacy artists' recordings through digital sales and most legacy artists have similar contractual provisions to those in the Eminem Agreements."[17] Busch, FBT and Eminem's attorney, is now cracking the recording industry's code to find other ways for artists to get their fair share of the music that circulates in the digital marketplace.

FROM THE COURTROOM
TO THE BOARDROOM

As one of hip hop's foremost makers, whose commercial instincts and artistic ambitions lead to the creation of alternate realities, Eminem makes sure that the success he maintains always equals the success he has attained. One way he ensures this formula is by protecting his rights as a businessman and an artist in the courtroom. In the process, he and his team practice an increasingly complex form of reputation management. Sometimes, that management takes the form of social commentary by which the rapper walks the color line. Other times, Eminem walks the fine lines between the personal and political, between social tradition and social evolution, and now between industry and artist. By walking these fragile lines, Eminem displays an immense depth. Time and again, he exhibits the ability to win battles both onstage and offstage. For every battle he loses to another recording artist like Tori Amos, he wins battles against the recording industry itself. His outstanding record indicates that he understands when to issue a response and when to remain silent. As a result, Eminem demonstrates an ability to admit mistakes, forge ahead, accept change, and in the process, create new opportunities for himself and others to succeed. In this way, he maintains his status as an artistic innovator, as one who embraces new technologies, changing demographics, and daring sounds and images to communicate a message of recovery and rebirth. His fluidity is anything but a handicap. Instead, it is a way to capitalize on the richness of his experience and create new ways to bring that experience to a wider audience through new business ventures.

For instance, Eminem first made his mark in the fashion world in 2003 with Shady Limited Clothing. This clothing line expanded his dynasty and placed him among other rapper moguls such as P. Diddy, 50 Cent, and Jay Z, who all tapped into the fashion industry. Shady Limited specialized in casual clothes like hoodies, jeans, and polo shirts. The brand prided itself on appealing to everyone while retaining its urban feel. Jay-Z's Rocawear eventually acquired Shady Limited in 2007 and Eminem stayed on in a creative role.[18] Later that year, Jay-Z sold Rocawear to the Iconix Brand Group Inc. for a reported $204 million in cash. At the time of this writing, Iconix has not relaunched the brand, making Shady Limited apparel difficult to find and expensive. But the suspension of Shady Limited has not stunted Eminem's fashion sense. A quick click on the Shady Records Shady Store reveals plenty of T-shirts and hoodies for sale with the updated Shady Records logo.

ShadE45, Eminem's Uncut Hip-Hop Sirius radio channel, is an ongoing success. This uncensored channel has been attracting music fans since 2004 and going strong ever since. Artists listeners are likely to hear there nowadays are Eminem, 50 Cent, Lloyd Banks, Tony Yayo, Dr. Dre, Snoop Dogg, Lil' Wayne, Drake, Kanye West, Jay-Z, and D-12. Listeners can also find programming about the art, culture, and business of hip hop, where deejays and rappers discuss their latest projects. ShadE45 appeals to and promotes Eminem's three personas and allows Eminem to connect with his global audience without the censorship he has faced in other media platforms. The station also eliminates any unwanted fees his production company or publishing company might incur in the promotion of his music. To put it simply, ShadE45 allows Eminem to get the wrap on rap.

Eminem uses ShadE45 to market the artists signed to his own label Shady Records (@ShadyRecords) with manager Paul Rosenberg in 1999 after the success of his debut album *The Slim Shady LP.* Shady Records is under the umbrella of Universal Music Group and its products are distributed by Interscope Records and Aftermath Records. Artists on Shady's roster include 50 Cent, D12, Royce Da 5'9 (aka the other half of Bad Meets Evil), Joell Ortiz, Crooked I, Joe Budden (aka Slaughterhouse), and Yelawolf, who for Black Entertainment Television's Hip Hop Awards 2011, referred to themselves as Shady 2.0 and were voted the top cypher of the year. Shady 2.0 is Eminem's rebranded business upgrade that, by including rappers who identify as Native American and Latino, escapes the black-and-white box that has harnessed mainstream hip hop for far too long.

Shady 2.0 works hand in hand with Eight Mile Style LLC, Eminem's Detroit-based publishing company (as opposed to FBT productions, who signed him back in 1995). This company now owns and protects all of Eminem's copyrights (even though FBT is still entitled to a portion due to Eminem's early contracts and its successful legal case against Aftermath et al.). Eight Mile Style LLC has taken on the likes of Facebook, Apple and Audi in the process of making sure that Eminem is paid whenever his work is used commercially. Eminem and Eight Mile Style LLC sent shockwaves through the music industry when they entered into contract with global independent online music-publisher Kobalt Music Group and Los Angeles-based licensing and administration company Music Resources. This is big news according to *PR Newswire* because it shows the rapper's ability to maximize the richness of his music catalog and vast network of retail partners selling all other future products (like Shady Video Games and protégé's Shady Records music). Ever wondered why Eminem's music is heard in so many movies and commercials? It is because of this strategic deal and Kobalt's specialty in sample clearance.

Think about it. Eminem's Eight Mile Style catalog contains hits like the Oscar-winning song "Lose Yourself" (2002), "Guilty Conscience" (1999), "'97 Bonnie & Clyde" (1999), "Just Lose It" (2004), "My Name Is" (1999), "Without Me" (2002), "The Real Slim Shady" (2000), "Love the Way You Lie" (2010), and "Cleanin' Out My Closet" (2002) among other works written by Marshall Mathers III and The Bass Brothers, as well as frequent collaborators, Luis Resto and Steven King. Eminem's catalog also contains numerous songs recorded by multiplatinum artists, including 50 Cent, Tupac, Dr. Dre, Jay-Z, and Nas. With career sales estimated in excess of 70 million albums worldwide, Eminem is one of the best-selling music artists of the 21st century, and this deal is sure to keep him at the top of that list.[19]

And staying at the top of that list—reputation management—is what Eminem's transition from the courtroom to the boardroom is all about. In an interview I conducted with Craig E. Carroll, corporate communications professor and author of *Corporate Reputation and the News Media: Agenda-setting within Business News Coverage in Developed, Emerging, and Frontier Markets,* this perspective was confirmed. According to Carroll, "reputation management means four things: the battle for definition, the struggle to support your definition, the role of relationships, and an ability to manage multiple identities. Eminem appears to have mastered each of these through his music and business ventures."[20] In "The Way I Am" (2000), for example, Eminem set up the terms of the debate over his reputation by placing them in the context of media, corporate expectations, unimaginative racism, legal battles, marketing, and politics. In the song, he tells critics to take their battles with him from the press to the courtroom and eventually to the boardroom. He begins by outlining his plan for redefinition. Eminem is simply himself, deserves creative control over his music and money, and is an artist who deserves a degree of privacy despite his celebrity status. Attributes that people associate with him—that he is "mean," a "wigger," to be censored—are irrelevant. Eminem used the rest of the song to set up the new key terms, redefining the attributes associated with his personas, and setting the frame for his growing reputation. Rather than chasing after other people's terminology—"I am whatever you say I am"—he reminds us that he has the final say on his reputation—"If I wasn't, then why would I say I am?"

Next is the issue of matching the perception of Eminem's reputation with substance. If he is not a mean, idiotic, foul-mouthed wigger, then he has to prove it. Since the media and his record label censor him, he will use the law to vindicate his reputation and create evidence to separate the gossip from the truth. Read in this way, Eminem's many courtroom sagas actually create a public record and an evidence trail that others will be able to investigate. When we investigate, as we have in this chapter, we confirm that the reality Eminem has put forth is more accurate than the perceptions offered by his critics. This means that Eminem is actually who he says he is. He is savvy, entrepreneurial, generous, and he is polyethnic. Eminem made sure we would see him in this light by creating a public trail through legal cases and business ventures to refute the talk about him that did not match the talk he wanted to reflect. And his ever-increasing digital footprint on sites like Facebook, YouTube, Google+ and Twitter suggests that he understands how to use social media to give the impression of a candid and uncensored look at the man behind the personas. The only challenge that remains will be playing out the economic reality against his working-class personas. The facts of Marshall Mathers's and Eminem's class statuses have changed, and it remains to be seen how Slim Shady will maintain his working-class image.

Then there is the powerful connection between relationships and reputation. Relationships can lead to reputations and reputations can lead to relationships. We see this two-way street in action in Eminem's case because his association with Dr. Dre gave him a credible reputation as a rapper. Then, his credibility and power as a rapper created relationships with other artists that he can now produce and mentor. Here, relationships and reputations work together to create an artistic and a corporate reputation, and that is where the final issue of organizational identity, or how to manage multiple identities, comes into play. If nothing else, Eminem's career shows that it is possible, even if it is not easy, to create a reputation that represents multiple points of view. In addition, he gives us a peek into how it is done in the names of his enterprises and personas. It is all about being Shady and throwing shade. Eminem's shady enterprise, his reputation management plan, has been about doing those things he had to do to get to a place where he can be socially responsible. Slim Shady started by modeling murder and mayhem in order to get famous and rich. Once he got rich, Eminem created business ventures that allowed him to do something different. And now, because he can couch his change in the context of recovery from drug addiction, Marshall Mathers opens up a space to rebrand, to upgrade, to become Shady 2.0. But Shady 2.0 cannot change completely or else Eminem and Marshall Mathers will no longer be able to use the shade that made them famous. So, no matter what Eminem or Mathers do, Slim Shady will always have to come out to play. Shady will always wink at his audience, will always keep us wondering if the rapper is still going to do and say terrible things or if he will make a permanent turn. Shady will always make us question whether this kind of perceived transformation is what Eminem wanted to do all along in order to make sure Marshall Mathers became famous and rich or whether it is the rapper's way of silencing the critics and making personal and industry-wide reparations. One thing is certain: audiences are ready and willing to stay with him to find out.

The fact that one of the world's most successful rappers is at the forefront of large-scaled corporate, economic, and social change should not be surprising. Let's face it—that is what rap music and its artists have always done. They have created new ways of accessing power, prestige, privilege, and politics. They have always served a higher purpose, always done something for the larger community even as they do something for themselves. Eminem is no different. He entered the game as a phenomenon and excelled consistently at both the art and business of rap. The reality is dramatic: Given Eminem's infamy as an icon for "screwing up America,"[21] it is difficult to think of him as an activist who helped open the gates to digital reparations—compensation for contractual insult or injury—for all. But that does not mean it's not true. Before Eminem, musicians of all genres had to accept whatever crumbs record companies gave them by way of antiquated contracts. After Eminem, they do not. Game over. Battle won.

Coda: Shady 2.0

It's a cold Thursday morning in Queens, New York, in the winter of 2013 and I am sitting in my grandfather's old house searching for my final thoughts on The Real Slim Shady. These thoughts are not just about where Eminem is taking us next, but also about how we can all benefit from where he's been. How we can apply his social, spiritual, and economic acumens, in real ways, for the betterment of hip hop and society. The problem isn't so much knowing where to finish but knowing where to start.

Then, as if on cue, the brilliant engineers at Google sent the answer to my inbox in the form of a Google Alert for Eminem. The alert is made up of links featuring the rapper's exploits from the past several months. First, Slim Shady announces during a ShadE45 interview with DJ Whoo Kid that he's putting his latest movie project, *Southpaw,* on hold to compose his eighth solo album due out in 2013. Then, Marshall Mathers is featured prominently in Ice-T's documentary *The Art of Rap* as a lyrical scientist with a spiritual edge. Mathers is also featured on a new charity compilation *Rhythms Del Mundo: Africa,* which contains African remixes of well-known tracks in aid of Artists Project Earth (APE). As if that is not enough, Eminem also topped *Forbes*'s list of "Social Networking Superstars" by breaking social media records— again—when he became the first personality to amass over 60 million fans on Facebook and continues to expand his group of 13 million Twitter followers with promotional tweets.[1] In addition, beneath the announcements for tour dates in Europe, South Korea, and Japan, Eminem makes a guest appearance on Pink's single "Here Comes the Weekend" (2012), Skylar Grey's "C'Mon Let Me Ride" (2012), 50 Cent's "My Life" (2012), and appears as producer for Charles Hamilton's single "I Don't Care" (2012) and Slaughterhouse's album *Our House*. Then there are media appearances. Em's was the feature interview in the July 2012 issue of *Rolling Stone* as well as the November

2012 issue of *Vibe*. The rapper made fun of comedian Jon Stewart for poorly imitating his style from the film *8 Mile* in a routine on *The Daily Show* via Facebook. Em talked about playing a starring role in the prologue to Slaughterhouse's video "My Life" on MTV. In "My Life," Em depicts an obnoxious member of the 1 percent who flaunts his riches in the faces of the less fortunate. The message? Effects of social and economic problems cannot be reflected through so-called reality television or by politicians who run as people they really are not. Effects of social and economic problems are reflected in reality rap.

This news alone is an incredible validation of the perspective of Eminem—the polyethnic material man, the spiritual explorer, the socially conscious critic, and the altruistic entrepreneur—I offered in this book. Why? Because news of these new projects validated the lessons I learned through the first-ever extended evaluation of 200 of his songs over the course of nearly two decades. Lessons about personal resilience, about how the divine speaks to the disinherited, about how seeking reparations requires taking criticism and abuse, about the changing face of race in the new millennium, and about how the families we choose are often better than those into which we are born. And news of Eminem's new projects validated the fact that more than anything The Real Slim Shady is a powerful author who isn't done telling his story.

That said the next chapters of Eminem's story already involve a whole new cast of characters. Some are major players and some are minor. All owe him an incredible debt, as they fall in line with at least one of his three personas to increase their value in hip hop's cultural marketplace. Let me introduce them briefly and show you where they fit. The obvious place to begin is with Eminem's protégés who are signed to his label Shady Records. First up is D12 (aka Dirty Dozen), Eminem's boyhood hip hop group from Detroit. This group gave birth to Slim Shady and embodies every shady thing Slim represents—polyethnic identification, dysfunctional family values, outrageous speech acts, and the Detroit underclass. D12 is not very active lately because member Proof died, Eminem is now focusing on other projects, and Bizarre left the label to start his own group called The Weirdo Movement. Next up is 50 Cent, a hip hop mogul from Queens who is now outearning Eminem according to *Forbes Magazine's* 2012 list of richest rappers. Then there is Bad Meets Evil (aka Eminem plus Royce Da 5'9"), who explore many of Marshall Mathers's most provocative spiritual themes in their latest album *Hell: The Sequel* (2011).

The second generation of protégés, Shady 2.0, consists of Slaughterhouse (aka Joell Ortiz, Crooked I, Royce Da 5'9", and Joe Budden) and solo artist Yelawolf. These rappers joined their mentor for the 2011 BET Awards Shady 2.0 Cypher. The vision presented here gives us a look at how different races and ethnicities look, overlap, talk, and touch and, by consequence, how they bring unique cultures into contact over a break beat. They are continuing the polyethnic conversation Shady and Dre began with one another and their fans as Shady 2.0 artists address issues of identity in an increasingly diverse and networked society. Both Slaughterhouse and Yelawolf are taking cues from Slim Shady at the outset with songs that emphasize mixed race madness and mayhem like "Pop The Trunk" (2012), "Hard White" (2012), and "Hammerdance" (2012). Eminem "feel[s] like hip-hop needs"[2] Slaughterhouse. Why? To begin with they show us that just because a group or an artist is multiracial and polyethnic doesn't mean that the social problems about which it speaks will disappear. Translation: A polyethnic story doesn't always have to be a happy one. It can be shady. What's more, these artists are showing us that a full-color conversation about race and culture needs to stop thinking about hip hop in simple black-and-white terms. We need to think about how hip hop is impacted as much by history as it is by where rappers are now, by their class statuses and genders, by technology, by sociology, by their habits, and by their spiritual relationships.

But Shady's polyethnic influence isn't just felt among those he mentors directly. We must remember that Shady—along with Eminem and Marshall Mathers—has been in hip hop's consciousness since the 1990s so his impact is far reaching. For example, rappers like Nicki Minaj, Asher Roth, Mac Miller, and Angel Haze embrace many of Mathers's controversial spiritual themes in their music. Asher Roth questions the existence of Jesus and God in "G.R.I.N.D." (2010) and "Last Man Standing" (2011), Nicki Minaj undergoes an exorcism in "Roman's Revenge" (2010), Mac Miller tackles some of life's big questions in "Get Up" (2011), and Angel Haze describes her own sexual abuse and ultimate triumph in her powerful remake of "Cleaning Out My Closet" (2012).

And there's a little Slim Shady in most of today's burgeoning hip hop acts too. The shadiest of them all is Odd Future Wolf Gang Kill Them All (aka OFWGKTA), a group of rapping teenage vandals from Los Angeles, California. The *New York Times* refers to the collective as "gross, entrancing and thrilling." Sound familiar? Odd Future takes

Shady's imaginings to new heights by rapping about everything from taking drugs and stalking female neighbors to eating cockroaches, vomiting, and trying to hang themselves. But the crew seems to have been taking notes from Eminem's business insights too, as their four-year foray into hip hop landed them squarely in the digital age with an appropriately designed digital business model. Self-professed Tumblr and Twitter geeks, Odd Future used their Internet connections to their advantage. Since they didn't have a record deal, or notoriety among hip hop royalty like Eminem or Dr. Dre, Odd Future released several albums online and for free through the Odd Future Tumblr site. They also shot videos and released them through the Odd Future You-Tube channel. Soon they were picked up by National Public Radio, *Wired, Billboard,* and the *Los Angeles Times* and put in rotation on MTV. Eminem gave Odd Future his stamp of approval, particularly its troubled front men Earl Sweatshirt, who also raps about his mama issues, and Tyler, The Creator who will be appearing on tour with the real Slim Shady in the summer of 2013.

Like Eminem—and Slim Shady and Marshall Mathers for that matter—Odd Future isn't for everyone. For those with a more tradi-tional hip hop palate there is Machine Gun Kelly (MGK), the white rapper from East Cleveland whose flow can only be outpaced by the sound of an actual automatic weapon. MGK has taken Shady's poly-ethnic identification and multiracial family making to a new level by surrounding himself with a variety of black rappers, taking on a black girlfriend about whom he makes insensitive sexual statements, and fa-thering multiracial children. Shady 2.0 indeed. Shady's style has also influenced Bizzy Crook, a Latino rapper from Miami, Florida who says that *The Slim Shady LP* made him want to pursue a career in hip hop. In songs like "This Is Me" (2011), Bizzy's raps echo Slim's in so far as they talk about the failure of education, the nature of love relation-ships, emotions, and male neediness. However, Bizzy stops short of plotting to murder his female partners and get revenge on his former teachers. Taking a page from Eminem's social commentary in songs like "Sing for the Moment" (2003), Bizzy released a tribute to Trayvon Martin called "I Am Trayvon Martin" (2012) and a series of webi-sodes that comment on current events. Maryland-based rapper Logic, who many speculate could be the next act signed on Shady Records, is also throwing some serious shade. Although his flow is more like Em's on *Infinite,* his lyrical content and background are definitely Shady. Logic—who describes himself as half black, half white, and sometimes demonic—shares many of the real Slim Shady's life experiences with a broken family, a troubled academic career, a struggle with mental health, a disdain for record industry practices, and finding inspiration to overcome challenges through hip hop. Logic compares his uphill climb in the rap game to Shady's in "Young Sinatra III" (2012) when he raps, "I used to bus tables. Now I bust rhymes." Perhaps no young rapper has declared as much love for Eminem as Hopsin, who said, "he was my role model. That was the rapper that stood out more than any other rapper in the rap game. I didn't even like rap that much until he came in the scene."[3] Hopsin goes on to say that Eminem inspired him in the same way that LL Cool J inspired Eminem.

In spite of, or perhaps because of, hip hop's ongoing misogyny the ladies continue to make their mark in a way that would get Shady's attention. Some, like Oakland's White Girl Mob (aka WGM; Kreayshawn, V-Nasty, and Lil' Debbie) do it by repeating his mistakes. After gaining notoriety with the viral hit "Gucci, Gucci" (2010), the group came under fire for using the N-word in their lyrics. Kreayshawn has been known to tweet the word from time to time, but the real offender here is V-Nasty whose raps are laced with the epithet. While many have defended V-Nasty, the incident caused Kreayshawn to distance herself and the Mob is not recording together at this time. It seems that that WGM hasn't learned that an impoverished upbringing alone does not give a white rapper license to spit explicitly racialized rhymes.

Most of today's rappers—male and female alike—have learned from Eminem's experience and avoid using questionable racial terms. However, up and coming female rappers do face other challenges. Take Iggy Azalea and Azealia Banks. When white rapper Iggy Azalea was the first female rapper to be included in *XXL Magazine*'s esteemed freshman class issue in early 2012 black rapper Azealia Banks tweeted her discontent because some of Iggy's lyrics make light of African Americans' experiences with enslavement and lynching. The implication was that Iggy only got noticed because she is white and because she made fun of black people. And with both artists vying for the limelight with their first album releases things got even more complicated. Twitter beefs notwithstanding, Azealia Banks's lyrics in "Fuck Up The Fun" (2012) and "212" (2012) are reminiscent of Slim Shady's older dis tracks. And Iggy Azalea's "Pu$$y" (2012) and "Murda Bizness" (2012) do test the limits of free speech like much of Eminem's early work. Only time will tell which of these A-list female rappers will take the throne next to his and be crowned hip hop's queen.

From the King of hip hop to you, through the eyes and ears of a hip hop-loving professor from Queens, the essence of the Real Slim Shady is a polyethnic family man, a spiritual explorer, a fierce social commentator, and an altruistic entrepreneur. He's a complex and compelling artist whose failures and successes have given hip hop the update it needed to keep pace with an increasingly networked and diverse world. There you have it. Eminem's is an evolving story and a hopeful one—of material, social, and spiritual identity that is bound to keep growing, as he puts it, "just like the effing blob."[4]

Appendix: Chronology

1972   Marshall Bruce Mathers III is born in Saint Joseph, Missouri, to 15-year-old Debbie Nelson and Marshall Bruce Mathers II.

1973   Debbie and Marshall III escape the abuse of Marshal II.

1982   Eminem suffers at the hands of school bullies and nearly dies of a brain hemorrhage when D'Angelo Bailey, a schoolyard bully, attacks him and leaves him in a coma.

1986   Eminem first uses the stage name, M&M, which stands for Marshall Mathers, when he is 14.

1989   Eminem drops out of Lincoln High School before completing ninth grade.

1991   Eminem's uncle Ronald Nelson commits suicide. Eminem commemorates his uncle by getting a Ronnie RIP tattoo on his left arm.

1992   Eminem (as Soul Intent) records the controversial song "Fucking Backstabber/Biterphobia" on cassette.

1995   Eminem's daughter, Hailie Jade Scott, is born on December 25.

1996   Eminem releases first solo album on November 12, *Infinite,* which is not commercially successful.

1997   Eminem meets rapper/producer Dr. Dre and Interscope executive Jimmy Iovine after coming in second at the Rap Olympics in Los Angeles, California.

1997   Eminem releases *The Slim Shady EP* on December 6.

1999	Aftermath releases *Slim Shady LP* on February 23, the first major label and successful release of his career. This album is certified four-times platinum by RIAA.
1999	Debbie Nelson, Eminem's mother, sues him for $10 million for slandering her in his lyrics.
1999	Eminem marries Kimberly Scott, in Saint Joseph, Missouri, on June 14.
2000	*The Slim Shady LP* wins the 1999 Grammy Award for Best Rap Album.
2000	Eminem releases *The Marshall Mathers LP* on May 23, which becomes the fastest-selling solo album and fastest-selling hip hop album in U.S. history. The lead single "The Real Slim Shady" becomes Eminem's first song to enter in the top 10 of the Billboard Hot 100. "Stan" is the most successful single outside of the States, while it fails to reach the top 50 in the United States.
2000	Eminem is arrested twice in June—on a weapons charge after pulling a gun on a rival rapper and beating another man with his gun. He is sentenced to two years' probation for carrying a loaded weapon.
2000	Kim (Eminem's wife) sues him for $10 million, claiming the rapper defamed her in his lyrics, is an unfit parent to their child, and threatened to leave her broke.
2000	*The Up in Smoke Tour,* a concert film released on December 5, features live performances as well as backstage content from various rappers, including Dr. Dre, Snoop Dogg, Ice Cube, and Eminem.
2000	*E* is released on December 12. The video features seven director's cut versions of Eminem's music videos released up to 2000, as well as footage of the making of the "Stan" video. All songs are taken from his second and third studio albums *The Slim Shady LP* and *The Marshall Mathers LP.*
2001	FCC fines a Colorado radio station $7,000 for playing an edited version of Eminem's "The Real Slim Shady."
2001	*The Marshall Mathers LP* wins Best Rap Album at the 2000 Grammys. Eminem also performs "Stan" with Elton John.
2001	Eminem makes his acting debut in the film *The Wash.*
2001	Eminem and Kim divorce in October.
2002	*The Eminem Show* is released on May 26, debuting at No. 1 on the *Billboard* 200 and reaches the top spot on various charts internationally, as it goes on to sell over 19 million copies

worldwide. In the United States, *The Eminem Show* is the highest-selling album of the year.

2002   *8 Mile,* the film about a white rapper's rise from Detroit's darkest corners starring Eminem, is released on November 9. It earns $51 million during opening weekend, and $242 million in global sales.

2003   Eminem's "Lose Yourself," a guitar-powered anthem about working hard enough to shed old identities, overcome obstacles, and achieve dreams, wins an Oscar for Music (Original Song). The song also stays steady at No. 1 on the Billboard charts for 12 consecutive weeks.

2003   Eminem wins a Grammy for *The Eminem Show,* making him the first hip hop artist to win the Best Rap Album category at the Grammy Awards for three consecutive releases.

2003   Eminem sues Apple, forcing the company to pull an iPod ad featuring a young user rapping along to the lyrics of "Lose Yourself."

2003   *The Source* magazine attacks Eminem for lyrics written in the early 1990s that use racial and gender epithets against African Americans.

2004   Elton John describes Eminem as one of "The Immortals" (#82 Greatest Artists of All Time) for *Rolling Stone* magazine on April 15.

2004   *Encore* is released on November 16, which becomes the rapper's third consecutive studio album to reach No. 1 in the United States, Australia, Canada, New Zealand, and United Kingdom.

2005   *Eminem Presents: The Anger Management Tour* is released on June 28. The video highlights the 2002 concert in Detroit, part of the Anger Management Tour.

2005   Eminem checks himself into rehab in August.

2005   *Curtain Call* is released on December 6. It goes on to receive a double platinum certification from RIAA.

2006   Eminem and Kim remarry in Rochester Hills, Michigan, on January 14. Eminem files for divorce on April 5.

2006   Eminem's best friend DeShaun Dupree Holton, aka P, Big Proof, Proof, or Derty Harry [*sic*], dies at 4:30 A.M., on April 11 at the age of 32. The funeral, which Eminem attends, is on April 18. Eminem goes back to rehab shortly thereafter.

2006   Eminem founds his own charity, The Marshall Mathers Foundation, to help disadvantaged youth near his home in Detroit, Michigan.

2006   Eminem gets custody of daughter Hailie, adopts Lainie, Kim's sister's child, and Whitney, Kim's daughter from a previous relationship.

2007   Shady Records releases *Eminem Presents: The Re-Up,* a compilation album performed by Eminem along with various artists from the record label. The album receives a platinum certification from the RIAA in 2007 and sells slightly over a million copies in the United States.

2008   Eminem enters rehab again in April for his drug addiction.

2008   Eminem is named "The Best Rapper Alive" by *Vibe Magazine.*

2009   *Relapse* is released on May 15, becoming the rapper's fourth consecutive studio album to top the Australia, Canada, New Zealand, United Kingdom, and U.S. charts, with domestic sales of over 2 million copies.

2009   "Crack a Bottle" single marks Eminem's official comeback, placing the Shady trifecta—50 Cent, Eminem, and Dr. Dre—at the top of the Hot 100 for the first time together.

2009   Eminem teams up with *Family Guy*'s Stewie Griffin to present a series of special cartoons.

2010   Eminem stars in two self-referential Super Bowl commercials on February 7, Lipton's "Brisk Iced Tea" and Chrysler's "Imported from Detroit." The Chrysler commercial became one of the most viral SuperBowl ads of all time.

2010   Eminem's *Relapse* wins the 2009 Grammy for Best Rap Album. The album's "Crack a Bottle" single earns 50, Em, and Dre a Best Rap Performance by a Duo or Group Grammy.

2010   *Recovery* is released on June 18, which debuts at No. 1 on the Billboard 200 and becomes the world's highest-selling album that year. *Recovery*'s singles "Not Afraid" and "Love the Way You Lie," featuring Rihanna, become the rapper's third and fourth No. 1 songs on the Hot 100. "Love the Way You Lie" holds onto No. 1 on the Hot 100 for seven consecutive weeks and is Em's second No. 1 from *Recovery.*

2010   Eminem breaks the record for most successive U.S. No. 1 albums by a solo artist.

2010   In November Eminem becomes the first rapper to have four songs sell over 3 million downloads in the United States alone.

2011   *Recovery* wins the 2010 Grammy for Best Rap Album.

2011	Eminem becomes the first person to reach 60 million fans on Facebook in July.
2011	Eminem is named "The King of Hip Hop" by *Rolling Stone Magazine* in August.
2011	Eight Mile Style LLC, Eminem's publishing company, sues Audi on Eminem's behalf when they file a cease-and-desist order against the German carmaker in a Hamburg regional court for copyright infringement.
2012	Eminem puts plans for his second movie, *SouthPaw,* on hold in order to work on his eighth solo album.
2012	Eminem performs his sold-out tour of Japan in August.
2012	Eminem turns 40 years old on October 17.
2012	Tenth anniversary of the film *8 Mile* in November, marked by commemorative interview for *Vibe Magazine*.
2012	Eminem ranks third on *Forbes*'s list of the biggest social media celebrities, behind Rihanna and Lady Gaga. His official Vevo page on YouTube boasts over 2 billion views . . . and counting.
2012	*FBT v. Aftermath Records,* a case in which a team of Eminem's early producers sued a subsidiary of the Universal Music Group because they were not getting the royalties they were owed from downloads at iTunes and other digital stores, is settled for an undisclosed sum.
2013	Trailers for the children's film *Despicable Me 2* are scored to *Eminem*'s "Without Me" (2002).
2013	Eminem's song publisher sues Facebook and its ad agency, claiming they infringed the rapper's copyright. The complaint contends that a Facebook ad that was broadcast online April 4 copied music from Eminem's song "Under the Influence" (2000).
2013	In addition to releasing his next solo album (rumored for fall), featuring collaborations with 50 Cent and Dr. Dre, Eminem plans to tour the United States and Europe at the Reading Festival, Slane Castle, and other venues.
2013	Eminem reveals just how deep his prescription pill addiction was and how close he came to losing his life as a result in the documentary *How To Make Money Selling Drugs*.

Notes

PRELUDE

1. Lyle Owerko, *The Boombox Project: The Machines, The Music, and the Urban Underground* (New York: Abrams Image, 2012).

2. BBC News, "Eminem: The Real Slim Shady," July 11, 2000, *BBC News: Entertainment,* http://news.bbc.co.uk/2/hi/entertainment/828935.stm.

3. "Rakim Speaks on Eminem," YouTube video, 7:02, from a documentary broadcast by AbcDr Dudson on December 12, 2005, posted by "showbroadcaast," June 20, 2012, http://www.youtube.com/watch?v=I53vWm8dJGk.

4. William James, *The Principles of Psychology: Vol. 1* (New York: Henry Holt and Company, 1890).

CHAPTER 1

1. "Eminem Talks About His Mother," YouTube video, 0:44, from an interview televised by BET on May 27, 2009, posted by "eminemFanOfficial," August 2, 2011, http://www.youtube.com/watch?v=oVntOWXApug.

2. Lang Whitaker, "Interview: Eminem—Lang Whitaker," *Consumable Online 181,* July 2, 1999, http://www.westnet.com/consumable/1999/07.02/c990702.txt.

3. Lauren Bans, "Word to Your Mother: The 10 Gushiest Mother's Day Rap Songs," *GQ,* May 6, 2011, http://www.gq.com/entertainment/music/201105/mothers-day-rap-songs-playlist.

4. Michael Eric Dyson, *Holler If You Hear Me: Searching for TuPac Shakur* (New York: Basic Books, 2003), Kindle e-book, Chap. 1.

5. Anthony Bozza, *Whatever You Say I Am* (New York: Crown Publishers, 2003), 230–31.

6. Recording Industry Association of America, "Searchable Database: Eminem," June 1, 2012, http://www.riaa.com/goldandplatinumdata.php?content_selector=gold-platinum-searchable-database

7. David Stubbs, *Eminem: The Stories Behind Every Song* (New York: Thunder's Mouth Press, 2003), 173.

8. M. L. Elrick, "Eminem's Dirty Secrets," *Salon.Com,* July 25, 2000, http://www1.salon.com/ent/music/feature/2000/07/25/eminem_secrets/print.html.

9. Kenneth Partridge, "Hive Five: Great Songs With Mommy Issues," *MTV Hive,* May 6, 2011, http://read.mtvhive.com/2011/05/06/hive-five-great-songs-with-mommy-issues/.

10. Debbie Nelson, *My Son Marshall, My Son Eminem: Setting the Record Straight on My Life as Eminem's Mom* (London: John Blake Publishing, 2007), 101.

11. Ibid., 136.

12. Ibid., 171.

13. Ibid., 108.

14. Ibid., 165.

15. Nick Hasted, *The Dark Story of Eminem* (London: Omnibus Press, 2011), 6.

16. Seymour Spilerman, "The Causes of Racial Disturbances: A Comparison of Alternative Explanations," *American Sociological Review* 35, no. 4 (1970): 627–49.

17. Marshall Mathers and Sacha Jenkins, *The Way I Am* (New York: Penguin Group), 31.

18. Marcia Alesan Dawkins, *Clearly Invisible: Racial Passing and the Color of Cultural Identity* (Waco, TX: Baylor University Press, 2012).

19. Eric King Watts, "Border Patrolling and 'Passing' in Eminem's *8 Mile,"* *Critical Studies in Media Communication* 22, no. 3 (2005): 195.

20. Marcia Alesan Dawkins, "Is the Tanning of America Only Skin Deep?," *The Huffington Post,* May 17, 2012, http://www.huffingtonpost.com/marcia-alesan-dawkins/minority-http://www.huffingtonpost.com/marcia-alesan-dawkins/minority-births_b_1525238.html.

CHAPTER 2

1. Anthony Bozza, *Whatever You Say I Am* (New York: Crown Publishers, 2003), 230.

2. Isabelle Esling, "An Open Letter to Eminem," Slim Shady Online, August 26, 2001, http://rapgirrl-271.tripod.com/slimshadyonlinecom/id6.html.

3. "Eminem's Grandma Betty On His Childhood & Relationships—2001 Interview," YouTube video, 5:01, from a radio interview broadcast by Radio 1's Briggy Smale on February 9, 2001, posted by "2PointOBoy," June 20, 2012, http://www.youtube.com/watch?v=6bNXeZAGc38.

4. Barnaby Legg and Jim McCarthy, *Eminem: In My Skin* (London: Omnibus Press, 2004), 1.

5. Marshall Mathers and Sacha Jenkins, *The Way I Am* (New York: Penguin Group), 32.

6. Mathers and Jenkins, *The Way I Am,* 34.

7. Bang Showbiz, "Eminem Almost Quit Showbiz After He Was Booed," *The List,* August 5, 2012, http://www.list.co.uk/article/44005-eminem-almost-quit-after-he-was-booed/.

8. Jocelyn Venna, "Eminem Pays Tribute to Adam Yauch's 'Influence' Nas, Cee Lo, Jack Black, Green Day's Billie Joe Armstrong and More Remember the Beastie Boys' MCA," *MTV.Com News,* May 4, 2012, http://www.mtv.com/news/articles/1684539/adam-yauch-mca-beastie-boys-celebrity-reactions.jhtml.

9. Steve Stoute and Mim Eichler Rivas, *The Tanning of America: How Hip-Hop Created a Culture That Rewrote the Rules of the New Economy* (New York: Gotham Books, 2011), 276–77.

10. Nick Hasted, *The Dark Story of Eminem* (London: Omnibus Press, 2011), 37.

11. NME Online Magazine, "Ice-T: 'Eminem's Like a Scientist in the Studio,'" *NME Online Magazine,* June 19, 2012, http://www.nme.com/news/eminem/64401.

12. "Ice-T—Talking About His Acting Career, the History of West Coast Hip-Hop and Eminem," YouTube video, 9:11, from an interview on British television on 2004, posted by "therhymesyndicate," June 20, 2012, http://www.youtube.com/watch?v=QdJxn4cO6hw.

13. Mathers and Jenkins, *The Way I Am,* 34.

14. Stoute and Rivas, *The Tanning of America,* 71.

15. For a detailed discussion of exactly how Eminem (aka Slim Shady) pulled off this complex racial marketing strategy, please see Chapter 8.

16. Christopher John Farley, Melissa August, Lesle Everton Brice, Laird Harrison, and Todd Murphy, "Music: Hip-Hop Nation," *TIME Magazine U.S.*, February 8, 1999, http://www.time.com/time/magazine/article/0,9171,990164,00.html#ixzz1rdzMwylA.

17. VH1.Com, "Dr. Dre: Nuthin' But an 'M' Thing," *VH1.Com*, June 13, 2002, http://www.vh1.com/shows/series/ultimate_albums/marshall/interview_dre.jhtml.

18. Neil Strauss, "A New Look at Eminem," *New York Times*, December 26, 2001, http://www.nytimes.com/2001/12/26/arts/the-pop-life-a-new-look-at-eminem.html?pagewanted=all.

19. Ronin Ro, *Dr. Dre: The Biography* (New York: Thunder's Mouth Press, 2007), 160.

20. For a detailed discussion of these critiques from media and legal scholars, cultural commentators, and politicians, please see Chapters 7 and 8.

21. Mathers and Jenkins, *The Way I Am*, 35.

22. Ro, *Dr. Dre*, 161.

23. The music video received criticism for being less about hip hop or personal relationships and more about 360-degree publicity and promotion, as several products the rap duo endorses were featured prominently. Examples include: Ferrari, G-Shock, Hewlett-Packard, Gatorade, and Dre's signature headphones, Beats by Dr. Dre.

CHAPTER 3

1. Gail De Vos, Merle Harris, and Celia Barker Lottridge, *Telling Tales: Storytelling in the Family* (Alberta, Canada: University of Alberta Press, 2003), 102.

2. Steen Kaargaard Nielsen, "Wife Murder as Child's Game," *Danish Yearbook of Musicology* 34 (2006): 35–36.

3. David Stubbs, *Eminem: The Stories Behind Every Song* (New York: Thunder's Mouth Press, 2003), 195.

4. Ibid., 37.

5. Tom Gliatto, "Sugarless Eminem: With Two Arrests and His Wife Kim's Suicide Attempt, the Controversial Rap Star Faces a Rocky Road," *People Magazine*, July 24, 2000, 23.

6. Juju Chang, Lynn Redmond, and Gerry Wagschal, "Eminem's Ex: Love Turns to Hate," ABC News 20/20, February 2, 2007, http://abcnews.go.com/2020/story?id=2842070&page=1#.T-IxXr_gJFQ.

7. @Angry_Blonde. (2012, March 1). I am back to twitter!! The REAL Hailie Mathers I have NO myspace or facebook! only twitter. [Twitter profile]. Retrieved from https://twitter.com/Angry_Blonde1.

8. Sarah C. Nelson, "Eminem's Daughter . . . NOT! Twitter Hoaxer Returns," *Huffington Post UK,* January 5, 2012, http://www.huffingtonpost. co.uk/2012/05/01/eminems-daughternot-twitter-hoaxer-returns_n_1467719. html?just_reloaded=1.

9. Nelson, "Eminem's Daughter . . . NOT," http://www.huffingtonpost. co.uk/2012/05/01/eminems-daughternot-twitter-hoaxer-returns_n_1467719. html?just_reloaded=1.

10. @ClarkeMellichap. (2012, 4 August). @Angry_Blonde your dad is awesome and you must be for being his daughter. [Twitter post], https:// twitter.com/ClarkeMellichap/status/231931408321507328.

11. Jon Pareles, "Get Clean, Come Back: Eminem's Return," *New York Times,* May 21, 2009, http://www.nytimes.com/2009/05/24/arts/music/24 pare.html?pagewanted=all.

12. @Angry_Blonde1. (2012, 5 August). he's there for me no matter what and I will always be there for him:). [Twitter post], https://twitter.com/Angry_ Blonde1/status/232181011746783232.

CHAPTER 4

1. Rolling Stone, "Eminem, 'The Marshall Mathers LP,'" May 31, 2012, *Rolling Stone: Music,* http://www.rollingstone.com/music/lists/500-greatest-albums-of-all-time-19691231/the-marshall-mathers-lp-eminem-19691231.

2. The Cabletelevision Advertising Bureau.

3. Stephanie Raide, "Eminem—The Fast Rising Rapper," *Yahoo Voices,* June 8, 2011, http://voices.yahoo.com/eminem-fast-rising-rapper-8607941. html.

4. Anna Hickey-Moody, "Eminem's Lyrical Personae: The Everyman, The Needy Man, The Hegemon," *Culture, Society and Masculinity* 1, no. 2 (2009): 140–56. Moody borrows the following description of "Everyman," from *Encyclopedia Britannica Online:* "an English morality play of the 15th century . . . [which treats] allegorically the theme of death and the fate of the human soul—of Everyman's soul as he tries to justify his time on earth . . . " *Encyclopedia Britannica,* 11th ed., s.v. "Everyman."

5. Chuck Weiner, *Eminem: In His Own Words* (London: Omnibus Press, 2001), 44.

6. Mesfin Fekadu, "Eminem Thanks Fans for Their Help; Preps 'Recovery' Follow Up," August 10, 2012, *Billboard.Com,* http://www.billboard.com/#/column/the-juice/eminem-thanks-fans-for-their-help-preps-1007798352.story.

7. Jimmy Nsubuga, "From Lady Gaga to Rihanna: Top 5 Controversial Music Videos of 2011," December 24, 2011, *Metro.Co.Uk,* http://www.metro.co.uk/music/884253-from-lady-gaga-to-rihanna-top-5-controversial-music-videos-of-2011.

8. "Evol" is love spelled backwards. Mathers references this spelling in "Space Bound" (2010) as a way to symbolically represent the other, darker side of love.

9. Ebony A. Utley, *Rap and Religion: Understanding the Gangsta's God* (Santa Barbara, CA: Praeger, 2012), 81.

10. Stacy L. Smith, "From Dre to Dismissed: Assessing Violence, Sex, and Substance Use on MTV," *Critical Studies in Media Communication* 22, no. 1 (2005): 89–98.

11. Deanna Sellnow and Amanda Brown, "A Rhetorical Analysis of Oppositional Youth Music of the New Millennium," *North Dakota Journal of Speech and Theatre* 17 (2001): 34–36.

12. Smith, "From Dre to Dismissed," 90–91.

13. Richard L. Baxter, Dynthia De Reimer, Ann Landini, Larry Leslie, and Michael W. Singletary, "A Content Analysis of Music Videos," *Journal of Broadcasting and Electronic Media* 29, no. 3 (1985): 337.

14. Smith, "From Dre to Dismissed," 94.

15. Sellnow and Brown, "Oppositional Youth Music," 25.

16. Matthew K. Nock and Michael J. Prinstein, "Contextual Features and Behavioral Functions of Self- Mutilation among Adolescents," *Journal of Abnormal Psychology* 114 (2005): 140–46.

17. National Council on Alcoholism and Drug Dependence, "Youth, Alcohol, and Other Drugs," http://www.ncadd.org.

18. Sellnow and Brown, "Oppositional Youth Music," 19–36.

19. Pete Ward, *Gods Behaving Badly: Media Religions, and Celebrity Culture* (Waco, TX: Baylor University Press, 2011), 125.

CHAPTER 5

1. Diana Butler Bass, *Christianity After Religion: The End of Church and the Birth of a New Spiritual Awakening* (New York: Harper Collins Publishers, 2012).

2. Ebony A. Utley, *Rap and Religion: Understanding the Gangsta's God* (Santa Barbara, CA: Praeger, 2012), 81.

3. Jeffrey S. Victor, *Satanic Panic: The Creation of a Contemporary Legend* (Chicago: Open Court Publishing, 1996), 4.

4. Victor, *Satanic Panic,* 4.

5. Genesis 1:1 (The Message).

6. Galatians 6:2 (The Message).

7. Chuck Weiner, *Eminem in His Own Words* (London: Omnibus Press, 2001), 51.

8. 1 Corinthians 1: 19–21 (The Message).

9. Weiner, *Eminem in His Own Words,* 55.

10. Ezekiel 28:13 (KJV).

11. Luke 10:27 (The Message).

12. Albert L. Winsemann, "Eternal Destinations: Americans Believe in Heaven, Hell," *Gallup,* May 25, 2004, http://www.gallup.com/poll/11770/ Eternal-Destinations-Americans-Believe-Heaven-Hell.aspx.

13. Clayton Shorkey, Michael Uebel, and Liliane C. Windsor, "Measuring Dimensions of Spirituality in Chemical Dependence Treatment and recovery: Research and Practice," *International Journal of Mental Health and Addiction* 6 (2008): 289.

14. Ibid.

15. Ibid.

16. Ibid.

17. Domestic Violence Resource Center, "Domestic Violence Statistics: Domestic Violence and Children," February 1, 2012, http://www.dvrc-or.org/ domestic/violence/resources/C61/.

18. Chris Rojek, "Celebrity and Religion," in *The Celebrity Culture Reader,* ed. P. David Marshall (New York: Routledge, 2006), 393.

19. Peter Ward, *Gods Behaving Badly: Media Religion and Celebrity Culture* (Waco, TX: Baylor University Press, 2011), 107.

20. @Eminem. (2011, October 11). Music has the power to heal. Get a limited edition Eminem T-shirt at http://cityofhope.shop.livenation.com/Product.asp x?cp=49987_49992&pc=FXCTCOH52296 and help support @cityofhope. [Twitter post], https://twitter.com/#!/Eminem/status/123966120792301568.

21. Sailesh A, (10:32 a.m.), comment on Busted Halo, "Don't Do Drugs, Don't Have Unprotected Sex, Don't be Violent . . . Leave that to Me.—Eminem," *Busted Halo: An Online Magazine for Spiritual Seekers,* January 12, 2012, http://bustedhalo.com/dailyjolt/dont-do-drugs-dont-have-unprotected-sex-dont-be-violent-leave-that-to-me.

CHAPTER 6

1. Robert J. Sternberg and Karin Sternberg, *The Nature of Hate* (Cambridge, MA: Cambridge University Press, 2008), 110.

2. Chuck Weiner, Eminem: Talking (London: Omnibus Press, 2003), 48.

3. Rev. David Hino, e-mail message to author, February 14, 2012.

4. John K. Rempel and Christoper T. Burris, "Let Me Count the Ways: An Integrative Theory of Love and Hate," *Personal Relationships* 12 (2005): 303.

5. Ibid., 306.

6. Ibid., 308.

7. Sternberg and Sternberg, *The Nature of Hate,* 308.

8. Ibid., 73.

9. Kristen Lombardi, "Sexual Assault on Campus: A Frustrating Search for Justice," IWatchNews.Org, February 24, 2010, http://www.publicintegrity.org/investigations/campus_assault/.

10. Marshall B. Mathers III and Sacha Jenkins, *The Way I Am* (New York: Penguin Group), 20.

CHAPTER 7

1. Vincent Stephens, "Pop Goes the Rapper: A Close Reading of Eminem's Genderphobia," *Popular Music* 24, no. 1 (2005): 21–36. On page 22 Stephens writes, "Genderphobia is a more obscure term [than transphobia or homophobia], related to the terms effeminaphobia and sissyphobia, that refers to a more covert form of gender discrimination based primarily on behaviour rather than sexual object-choice or appearance."

2. Rachel Herz, *That's Disgusting: Unraveling the Mysteries of Repulsion* (New York: W. W. Norton & Company, 2012), 79.

3. Kim Kardashian, "My Response to Eminem's New Video," *KimKardashian.Com,* April 7, 2009, http://kimkardashian.celebuzz.com/2009/04/07/my_response_to_eminems_new_vid/.

4. Shaheem Reid, "Fox News Correspondent Calls Video's Dig at Sarah Palin 'Misogynist,'" *MTV News,* April 9, 2009, http://www.mtv.com/news/articles/1608906/eminems-we-made-video-slammed-by-bill-oreilly.jhtml.

5. Anna Hickey-Moody, "Eminem's Lyrical Personae: The Everyman, The Needy Man, The Hegemon," *Culture, Society and Masculinity* 1, no. 2 (2009): 218.

6. Lori Burns and Alyssa Woods, "Authenticity, Appropriation, Signification: Tori Amos on Gender, Race, and Violence in Covers of Billie Holiday and Eminem," *Music Theory Online: The Online Journal of the Society for Music Theory* 10, no. 2 (2004), http://www.mtosmt.org/issues/mto.04.10.2/mto.04.10.2.burns_woods.html.

7. Becca Frucht, "Will the Real Slim Shady Please Stand Up? Who Said It: Eminem or Rick Santorum!?!," *MTV ACT*, March 29, 2012, http://act.mtv.com/posts/eminem-rick-santorum/.

8. For a full discussion of these songs as they relate to issues of gender and parenting, please see Chapter 3, "The Shady Bunch."

9. Cathy Renna, "GLAAD Puts Hate Lyrics Debate Center Stage at the Grammys," *Common Dreams Progressive Newswire*, February 22, 2001, http://www.commondreams.org/news2001/0222-08.htm.

10. Marc A. Rutherford, "Mass Media Framing of Hip-Hop Artists and Culture" (M.A. thesis, West Virginia University, West Virginia, 2001), 35–37.

11. Rutherford, "Mass Media Framing," 35–37.

12. Zadie Smith, "The Zen of Eminem," *Vibe Magazine*, January 2005, http://www.thefreelibrary.com/Cover+Story%3A+The+Zen+of+Eminem-a01611417940.

13. Edna Gundersen, "Grammy Race Too Close to Call; Diverse Offerings Fill Jumbled Field," *USA Today*, January 4, 2001.

14. Howard Cohen, "Hard-Core Rap Acts Grab Grammy Slots," *Miami Herald*, January 4, 2001, sec a., p. 1.

15. Christina Saraceno, "Eminem and Elton to Duet at Grammys," *Rolling Stone Music*, February 12, 2001, http://www.rollingstone.com/music/news/eminem-and-elton-to-duet-at-grammys-20010212#ixzz1vdHYYqAU.

16. Sir Elton John, "The Immortals—The Greatest of All Time—Eminem #82," *Rolling Stone* Issue 946, April 15, 2004, http://web.archive.org/web/20080920224903/http://www.rollingstone.com/news/story/7249916/the_immortals__the_greatest_artists_of_all_time_82_eminem.

17. Anna Hickey-Moody, "Eminem's Lyrical Personae: The Everyman, The Needy Man, The Hegemon," *Culture, Society and Masculinity* 1, no. 2 (2009): 214.

18. Steve Stoute and Mim Eichler Rivas, *The Tanning of America: How Hip-Hop Created a Culture That Rewrote the Rules of the New Economy* (New York: Gotham Books, 2011), 282.

19. Deborah Solomon, "The Real Marshall Mathers," *New York Times*, June 16, 2010, http://www.nytimes.com/2010/06/20/magazine/20fob-q4-t.html.

20. Hickey-Moody, "Eminem's Lyrical Personae," 213–28.

CHAPTER 8

1. Baz Dreisinger, *Near Black: White-to-Black Passing in American Culture* (Amherst, MA: University of Massachusetts Press, 2008). Like other cultural critics Dreisinger suggests that Eminem is a white person passing as black. My research is the first to suggest that this is not entirely correct. In Chapters 1 and 2 I argued that Slim Shady is represented as black-and-white because Marshall Mathers is Native American and white. I extend that argument here, exploring how the idea that Eminem is passing as white redefines the many racial "beefs" in which Eminem has been involved over the years.

2. The U.S. Census Bureau did not allow people of mixed race the option to check "Two or More Races" on the Census until the year 2000.

3. The revelation of a white–Native American mixed race identity is indeed controversial in 2012, as Massachusetts's gubernatorial candidate Elizabeth Warren has learned. Massachusetts's voters have criticized the candidate for emphasizing her Native American identity as a way to take advantage of special race-based affirmative action policies in her education and career.

4. Anthony Bozza, *Whatever You Say I Am: The Life and Times of Eminem* (New York: Crown Publishers, 2003), 20.

5. Ibid., 157.

6. Ibid.

7. Kyle Anderson, "Eminem Beef With Insane Clown Posse Long Over," *MTV News,* September 20, 2010, http://www.mtv.com/news/articles/1647067/eminem-beef-with-insane-clown-posse-long-over.jhtml.

ICP saw success before Eminem did. So, Eminem approached them with a flyer to advertise the *Slim Shady EP* that said ICP might show up at one of his events. ICP did not take kindly to Eminem's unauthorized use of their name. In fact, they were downright insulted. And Eminem was insulted because ICP was insulted. Insults started flying in both directions as the artists played out their beef in interviews and song lyrics until 2005. When ICP released songs that parodied some of Eminem's biggest hits like "Slim Anus" (a parody of "My Name Is") and "Eminem's Mom" (a parody of "Cleanin' Out My Closet"), Eminem responded by simulating sexual acts against blow-up dolls whose faces were painted to look like the ICP onstage at concerts. ICP confirmed that the beef was over, thanks to Eminem's deceased best friend Proof, in a 2010 MTV interview. According to Violent J, "Proof squashed that beef before he passed away. . . . He contacted us and we had a bowling game—it was really cool. We're something different. They could have skipped over us and said forget them, but they included us and said let's squash it."

8. MV Remix, "Cage Interview Transcripts," *MVRemix.Com,* August 1, 2000, http://www.mvremix.com/urban/interviews/cage.shtml.

9. Roland G. Fryer Jr., Lisa Kahn, Steven D. Levitt, and Jörg L. Spenkuch, "The Plight of Mixed Race Adolescents," NBER Working Paper 14192 http://www.nber.org/papers/w14192.

10. Maria P. P. Root, "A Bill of Rights for Racially Mixed People," in Root, *The Multiracial Experience,* 3–14. Among other provisions, the Bill asserts the right of "mixed race" people to "identify . . . differently than strangers expect [them] to identify; to identify . . . differently than how . . . parents identify [them]; to identify . . . differently than . . . brothers and sisters; and to identify . . . differently in different situations."

11. William Bowers, "8 Mile," in *White Noise: The Eminem Collection,* ed. Hilton Als and Darryl A. Turner (New York: Thunder's Mouth Press, 2003), 21.

12. R. J. Smith, "Crossover Dream," in *White Noise: The Eminem Collection,* ed. Hilton Als and Darryl A. Turner (New York: Thunder's Mouth Press, 2003), 140.

13. Louis Chude-Sokel, *The Last Darky: Bert Williams, Black-On-Black Minstrelsy and the African Diaspora* (Durham, NC: Duke University Press, 2006). In this way Eminem can be likened to the great and controversial Vaudevillian black minstrel, Bert Williams, whose success allowed him to make changes to the minstrel form and take out some of the more offensive elements, like the multiple layers of blackface. As compelling as this example is, however, we must be careful not to equate the personal prejudice that Eminem may have faced during his early career with the ongoing institutional and structural racism faced by Bert Williams and all African American people whether they are involved in the entertainment industry or not.

14. Vibe Magazine, "Vibe Cover Story: Eminem and Yelawolf Were Born to Be Wild," *Vibe Magazine,* January 12, 2012, http://www.vibe.com/article/born-be-wild-eminem-yelawolf-pg2.

15. Ibid.

16. Nick Hasted, *The Dark Story of Eminem* (London: Omnibus Press, 2011), 205.

17. Nekesa Mumbi Moody, "Magazine Accuses Eminem of Racism for Old Song that Rapper Calls 'Foolish,'" *Associated Press,* November 20, 2003, http://web.lexis-nexis.com/universe/document.

18. "Ill Doctrine: The Last Word on That Word," Vimeo video, 2:55, from a blog for Animal New York.Com on June 7, 2012, posted by "JSmooth," June 8, 2012, http://vimeo.com/43636793.

19. S. Craig Watkins, *Hip-Hop Matters: Politics, Pop Culture, and the Struggle of the Soul of a Movement* (Boston: Beacon Press, 2005), 87.

20. Marcia Alesan Dawkins, "Close to the Edge: The Representational Tactics of Eminem," *The Journal of Popular Culture* 43 (2010): 463–85.

21. Rob Markman, "Benzino Apologizes to Eminem, Says I Was Wrong," *MTV.Com,* August 9, 2012, http://www.mtv.com/news/articles/1691538/eminem-benzino-feud.jhtml?utm_medium=referral&utm_source=pulsenews.

22. Sacha Jenkins, "Blow It Out," *XXL Magazine* (March 2004): 121–22.

CHAPTER 9

1. Rolling Stone Music News, "Introducing the King of Hip-Hop," *Rolling Stone,* August 15, 2011, http://www.rollingstone.com/music/news/introducing-the-king-of-hip-hop-20110815?link=mostpopular1&page=4.

2. *Bailey v. Mathers,* 2005 WL 857242 (Mich. App. 2005).

3. Nick Hasted, *The Dark Story of Eminem* (London: Omnibus Press, 2011), 1.

4. PR Newswire, "Shady Records Forced to Withdraw Lawsuit Against *The Source* to Avoid Public Embarrassment of Impending Trial," *PRNewswire. Com,* March 23, 2004, http://www.prnewswire.com/news-releases/shady-records-forced-to-withdraw-lawsuit-against-the-source-to-avoid-public-embarrassment-of-impending-trial-54355857.html.

5. *Harlene Stein v. Marshall B. Mathers III,* Andre Romell Young, Colgems EMI Music Publishing, Inc., Interscope Records, Eight Mile Style Music, Ain't Nothin' Goin On But Fuckin', Ensign Music Corporation, WB Music Corp, Famous Music Corporation. US District Court Central District of California, August 18, 2003, http://www.thesmokinggun.com/file/granny-socks-eminem-dre-sampling-suit?page=0; http://www.sfgate.com/cgi-bin/article.cgi?f=/g/a/2003/09/17/ddish.DTL&ao=all#ixzz1xiDEIiE7.

6. CBS News, "Eminem Sued By Aunt, Uncle," *CBS Entertainment News,* February 11, 2009, http://www.cbsnews.com/2100-207_162-786270.html.

7. IB Times San Francisco, "Eminem Sues Audi Over Ad's Use of 'Lose Yourself,'" *San Francisco International Business Times,* June 4, 2011, http://sanfrancisco.ibtimes.com/articles/157523/20110604/eminem-sues-audi-over-ad-s-use-of-lose-yourself.htm.

8. Steven J. Horowitz, "Eminem Settles Lawsuit Against Audi AG for Copying Chrysler Ad," *Hip Hop DX,* July 29, 2011, http://www.hiphopdx.com/index/news/id.15384/title.eminem-settles-lawsuit-against-audi-ag-for-copying-chrysler-ad.

9. Nolan Strong and Grandmaster Grouchy Greg, "Exclusive: Handwritten, $9 Million Lawsuit Filed Against Em Over Chrysler Ad," *AllHipHop.Com,* February 1, 2012, http://allhiphop.com/2012/02/01/exclusive-handwritten-9-million-lawsuit-filed-against-em-over-chrysler-ad/.

10. Steve Knopper, *Appetite for Self-Destruction: The Spectacular Crash of the Record Industry in the Digital Age* (New York: Free Press, 2009).

11. Ann Powers, "2010 Was a Very Bad Year for Trying to Sell Music," *NPR Music's The Record,* January 6, 2011, http://www.npr.org/blogs/thered cord/2011/01/06/132694660/2010-was-a-very-bad-year-for-trying-to-sell-music.

12. Eriq Gardner, "Leaked Audit in Eminem Royalty Suit Highlights Huge Stakes for Record Industry," The *Hollywood Reporter,* February 22, 2012, http://www.hollywoodreporter.com/thr-esq/eminem-royalty-lawsuit-aftermath-records-fbt-productions-293881.

13. Steve Jobs, "Thoughts on Music," *Apple.Com,* February 6, 2007, http://www.apple.com/fr/hotnews/thoughtsonmusic.

14. *F.B.T. Productions, LLC v. Aftermath Records,* 621 F.3d 958 (2010).

15. David Gomez, "Federal Ruing on Eminem Could Change Online Royalty System," *TG Daily,* September 6, 2010, http://www.tgdaily.com/games-and-entertainment-brief/51408-federal-ruling-on-eminem-could-change-online-royalty-system.

16. Edwin F. McPherson, "F.B.T. v. Aftermath: Eminem Raps the Record Industry," *Entertainment & Sports Lawyer* 29, no. 1 (2011).

17. Lauren K. Turner, "The Impact of Technology on Pre-Digital Recording Agreements: An Examination of FBT Productions, LLC. v. Aftermath Records," *West Virginia Law Review* 114 (2011): 369.

18. Jay-Z, *Decoded* (New York: Spiegel and Grau, 2010).

19. PR Newswire, "Eminem Publisher, Eight Mile Style Music, and Kobat Music Group Announce Groundbreaking Global Music Publishing and Technology Pact," *PR Newswire,* November 17, 2007, http://s.tt/1bFiF.

20. Craig E. Carroll, personal communication, June 19, 2012.

21. Bernard Goldberg, *100 People Who Are Screwing Up America (And Al Franken Is #37)* (New York: Harper Collins Publishers, 2005).

CODA: SHADY 2.0

1. *Forbes Magazine,* "Social Networking Superstars," *Forbes.Com,* August 10, 2012, http://www.forbes.com/pictures/mfl45lfhm/eminem-4/#gallerycontent.

2. Rob Markman, "Eminem Says 'Hip-Hop Needs Slaughterhouse,'" *MTV.Com,* August 9, 2012, http://www.mtv.com/news/articles/1691546/eminem-slaughterhouse-hip-hop.jhtml.

3. Chris Yuscavage, "40 Compliments That Rappers Have Given to Eminem Over the Years," *Vibe,* October 14, 2012, http://www.vibe.com/photo-gallery/40-compliments-rappers-have-given-eminem-over-years/?page=12.

4. Steve Stoute, *The Tanning of America: How Hip-Hop Created a Culture That Rewrote the Rules of the New Economy* (New York: Gotham Books, 2011), 284.

Index

Digital reparations, 7, 157, 160–61, 166

Dirty Dozen. *See* D12

Disgust, 107, 113–14, 116, 131–32

Dismemberment, depiction in song lyrics, 71

Dis rap, 15, 73

DJ Bazooka Joe, 2, 4, 24, 31, 32, 33, 74, 149, 171

DJ Whoo Kid, 167

Doe or Die (AZ), 2

Dort Elementary School, 18

Dozens, The, 10

Dramatistic perspective, 62–69

Dr. Dre, 3–4, 6, 12, 15–16, 27, 34–43, 57, 71, 74, 97, 139, 144, 149, 155, 163, 164, 165, 170, 173, 174, 176, 177, 182 n.23

D12 (Dirty Dozen), 7, 23, 136, 144, 148, 163, 168

Dyson, Michael Eric, 10, 147

Earl Sweatshirt, 55, 170

Eazy E, 38

Effeminaphobia, 186 ch.7 n.1

8 Mile (film, 2002), 23–25, 115, 133, 168, 175, 177

8 Mile Road, 21–22

Eight Mile Style LLC, 156, 163–64, 177

Elliot, Missy "Misdemeanor," 4, 33

Eminem (Marshall Mathers III, Slim Shady): 1999 *Rolling Stone* Interview, 11, 15, 18, 29; 2002 *Rolling Stone* Interview, 47, 127, 137; 2012 *Rolling Stone* interview, 167; accused of Devil-worship, 81; accused of plot to kill George W. Bush, 155; as producer, 167; as social critic, 7; as victim of child sexual assault, 109; bullying, victim of, 18, 40, 59, 74, 77, 154, 173; business ventures of, 162–65; children, adopted, 43, 51, 176; class identification in song lyrics, 143–44; creation of Eminem persona, 5, creation of Slim Shady persona as "material self," 3,5, 135–37; creation of Marshall Mathers persona as "spiritual" self, 5; disputes with record industry, 7, 157–61; dispute with GLAAD over hate lyrics, 121–127; dispute with Insane Clown Posse, 188 n.7; drug abuse by, 15–16, 18, 175, 176; evaluation of by Ice-T, 32–33; "father-son" relationship with Dr. Dre, 6, 34–41; first use of stage name M&M, 173; home auctioned on eBay, 14; importance of hip hop to, 31–32, 110; influence on next generation of hip hop, 7; lawsuit against Audi, 156–57, 177; lawsuits against Apple, 115, 156; legal problems, 153–57; marriage and divorce with Kimberly Ann Scott, 19–20, 43, 174, 175; musical confrontation with Tori Amos, 118–21; Native American ancestry of, 17, 19, 134–6, 143, 151, 163, 188 n.1; polyethnic identity of, via Slim Shady, 33–35, 37, 41, 150, 151, 168; promotion of polyethnic hip hop by, 141–42, 144, 145, 146, 150, 169; racial identity of, 23–24, 26, 133–35, 137, 140, 141, 142; "racial tutoring" for rap, 138–39; relationship with daughter Hailie, 13, 43,

About the Author

MARCIA ALESAN DAWKINS, PhD, is a Clinical Assistant Professor at the University of Southern California's Annenberg School for Communication and Journalism in Los Angeles, California. An award-winning writer, speaker, and scholar, Dawkins—known to "tweeps" as @drdawkins09—is the author of *Clearly Invisible: Racial Passing and the Color of Cultural Identity* (Baylor University Press, 2012). She writes frequently on diversity, technology, spirituality, communication, culture, and politics for several high-profile media outlets, including *The Huffington Post, Truthdig, The Root,* and *Cultural Weekly.* Her expert opinion has been sought out by NPR, WABC-TV Boston, *TIME Magazine,* The Leadership Alliance, The Mayo Clinic, The Nashville Public Library Foundation, and The Public Relations Society of America. Dawkins holds a master's degree and doctorate from the University of Southern California's Annenberg School for Communication and Journalism, a master's degree from New York University, and bachelor's degrees from Villanova. Contact: www.marciadawkins.com